PRISON DOC, THIRTY-FIVE YEARS

Memoirs of a Prison Physician Assistant

Bohdan Darnobid

ISBN: 1544617046
ISBN-13: 9781544617046

A society should be judged not by how it treats its outstanding citizens but by how it treats its criminals.
—Fyodor Dostoyevsky

CONTENTS

PREFACE

My intention in writing this book is not to second-guess, throw stones at, or condemn the New York State Department of Corrections or the New York State Department of Mental Hygiene. There are good reasons why things occur the way they do in corrections. Many decisions made about the care of the mentally ill in the prison system are based on the financial situation of the state. I do, however, question whether the state is doing enough to provide at least minimal care for the mentally ill. I cannot walk away and turn my back on my experiences working as a physician assistant for thirty-five years without writing about them in the form of this book. I hope that some changes will come about in how the mentally ill in the prison system are treated because of this book or that at least issues on the treatment of the mentally ill in prison will be brought to the nationwide forum for discussion.

My thirty-five years working as a physician assistant within the New York State Department of Corrections were challenging and fulfilling. Most of the people whom I worked with on a daily basis seemed to care about the individual inmates, treated most of them respectfully, and strived to do the right thing. Forgive me for my choice of words, but I can say that most employees of the Department of Corrections did "give a shit." There were only a handful of situations in the past thirty-five years where I felt inmates were being physically and psychologically abused or mistreated. I wish only to shed light on a way of life that many people on the street have no idea exists within the walls of a prison.

This book is about not just inmates in the New York State Department of Corrections but all the people inside the walls of the prison system. Correction officers, medical staff, and counselors all have direct contact with inmates on a daily basis.

I made it a point not to sit down and write after having a challenging or frustrating day at work or when I was upset or angry about something that occurred in the prison on that particular day. I wrote when I had time to think and to rethink my purpose in writing this book. I did not want to react with anger or frustration. After more than three decades of working as a physician assistant in the New York State Department of Correctional Services, it would be wrong for me not to put my experiences in writing for all to read. It would be wrong to take the memories of what I witnessed and was a part of firsthand to my grave and not share them with the world. It is also my purpose to shed light on the plight of mentally ill inmates—how they live and how they are treated within the walls of the prison. I feel a need to speak for the mentally ill inmates who have been removed from society and locked away and who cannot speak for themselves.

Some, if not many, people reading this book may not agree with my observations, and, granted, some of my observations may be wrong. People with different perspectives may see things and events totally differently from how I did. I called them as I saw them. I hope this book opens up discussions on the care and treatment of society's incarcerated. Some might consider my writings and comments just artistic license or overdramatic in order to promote book sales. I write about what I have witnessed. If I exaggerated or embellished situations, then I am wrong for doing it.

Again, my purpose is not to offend anyone but to enlighten society on the prison system in the state of New York.

As I discuss later in the book, I do not feel it is wrong to house the mentally ill in prisons after they have committed a crime. Their lives are more structured and organized within the walls of a prison than on the streets of New York. I am not saying, however, that mentally ill persons should be arrested and placed in prisons only because they are mentally ill. I think that it is a crime against society for a person to sleep on the streets in New York City, but not a crime against that person. The majority of the people you see sleeping on the streets of New York City are mentally ill and are not receiving proper psychiatric care. I am concerned about the underreporting and undertreatment of the mentally ill in the prison system and the lack of programming there for them. It is important that they are not merely warehoused in the prison system; some types of programs need to be developed to assist them in their daily activities and functioning.

In recent years there has been a movement in New York State to close the hospitals for the mentally ill, and more and more mentally ill people are finding themselves living on the streets. Anyone who has visited New York City will remember seeing the homeless living on the streets. Many of these mentally ill people who live on the streets self-medicate their mental illnesses with drugs or alcohol. It is just a matter of time before they find themselves in the prison system. We owe it to ourselves and to society as a whole to treat the mentally ill, not just to step over them as we walk by.

My second concern is the problem of prescription-painkiller addiction. In an attempt to relieve patients' suffering and pain, doctors have spawned an addiction epidemic. The use of oxycodone (OxyContin, Percocet, and Percodan) and hydrocodone (Vicodin and Lortab) is increasing throughout the country. At a recent addiction conference, I learned that an OxyContin 80 (eighty milligrams of oxycodone) costs up to eighty dollars on the street from drug dealers. At this conference, the speaker said that when people can no longer afford the high cost of OxyContin, they switch to the much cheaper heroin to satisfy their new addiction. Heroin is readily available on the street. Recently, a young fellow whom I had the displeasure of meeting in protective custody walked into a pharmacy in Long Island and killed innocent people to get his oxycodone. The people who were killed were beautiful people with families and dreams; they should not have died because of this person's addiction to oxycodone.

All addicted people find themselves in either a prison or an addiction-treatment facility eventually. Prisons that I have worked in do a much better job in treating addiction than addiction-treatment facilities outside prison do. People with addiction problems pass through treatment facilities for reasons decided by a judge or family member, many not by their own choice. I must mention that there are some prisons that hand out narcotic pain relievers like candy. Fortunately, I have not worked in them yet.

An article in the *Journal of the American Medical Association* in early 2012 reported an increase of babies addicted to prescription painkillers, an increase three times greater than in the past decade. Similar findings were presented at the annual meeting of the Pediatric Academic Society in Boston. In an article in *USA Today* in May of 2012, the Centers for Disease Control and Prevention (CDC) flagged prescription-painkiller abuse as a major health threat that now causes more overdose deaths than heroin and cocaine combined. This problem has been referred to by some as a national epidemic of prescription drug abuse.

I have always enjoyed going to work each day. The professional staff of nurses, physician assistants (PAs), nurse practitioners (NPs), medical doctors (MDs), X-ray techs, lab workers, and clerical staff are a pleasure to work with. Each and every one of the staff whom I have had the pleasure to work with respected all individuals, whether staff members or inmates. Recently, I spent a day in training for cultural diversity. I told the person sitting next to me during this training—a prison chaplain—that the training syllabus was old and outdated, probably written decades ago. I mentioned to the chaplain that at a recent medical staff meeting I was able to go around the room and see first generations of people from Vietnam, Nigeria, China, Haiti, Poland, India, and the Philippines. These people had many different beautiful accents and varied opinions that showed a different perspective and were very important. When they came to this country, they brought with them their own cultural experiences, which made working alongside them at the Downstate Correctional Facility a pleasure. This diversity is what made this country great in the past; something that I think has been forgotten.

On the other hand, on the same day, I cared for an inmate who had been in the United States for eighteen years. He had been in prison in New York State three times, not counting his parole violations, and claimed that he could not speak English. I was not sure if he *could* not speak English or *chose* not to speak English. I guess he came from a community where he did not need to speak English and was able to exist and survive without learning English. You can see this occurring often in New York City—large clusters of people who speak a different language and manage to get their needs met on a daily basis without the need to learn or understand English. When I was growing up in Haverstraw, New York, there was an Italian woman who lived upstairs in my building. She had never learned to speak English, even though both her husband and my father (both of whom were first-generation in this country) had for many years reiterated to her the importance of learning English. Because the area had a large Hispanic population, she instead learned to speak Spanish, which was easier to learn because of its similarities with the Italian language.

I would also like to mention that in all my years with the New York State Department of Corrections I have always been amazed at the level of professionalism and restraint demonstrated by the uniformed staff. Under the most difficult and demanding situations, the officers seem to keep it together and never lose their heads, even when dealing with the worst that society has to offer. Many of the correctional staff are directly responsible for the daily care and control of inmates who have committed the most horrific crimes against the young, the old, and women. On more than one occasion, I have read in the *Daily News* or the *New York Post* of a person convicted of, and sentenced for, a horrific crime in New York City or Long Island, and then I have come face-to-face with that person at Downstate.

There was a time when notorious inmates would be transferred out of city or county jails a day or two after being sentenced, just to shift the burden and cost of care to the state more quickly. The administrators of the city or county jails also wanted to get the accident-prone inmates out of their jails. Other inmates would remain in city or county jails for months before being transferred upstate. The Department of Corrections would ship some notorious inmates to Downstate from Rikers Island using the emergency services unit (ESU).

In the bullpens, large rooms where inmates are locked in together, mentally unstable inmates are currently mixed in with hardened criminals, pedophiles, and inmates doing short bids (short time in state prison) for offenses such as DWI. This all takes place in a very hot, loud room. Inmates wait in the bullpens for a long time to be processed into the facility.

As I hope I have made clear in this brief summary of the types of people I encountered inside the prison walls, the men and women come from a wide variety of backgrounds. Not surprisingly, many inmates and some staff members swear and use very coarse language. After reading a draft of my book, my wife questioned whether profanity could have been avoided. But profanity was a daily part of the prison life that I was a part of from my first day on the job. I did not want to sanitize my thirty-five years in the prison system. I hope the language used in the book does not offend anybody. Since I left the prison system, my language has returned to what it was in pre-prison days. In the year after ending my career, I have never once heard the word *motherfucker*.

If I use a person's name in my book it means the person had a positive influence on me and on society as a whole. This person should not be forgotten. Those who had a negative influence on me or whose actions I was critical of are not mentioned by name. I made all reasonable efforts to de-identify protected health information.

INTRODUCTION

My first impression of a prison was not a promising one; I really did not expect to spend my life working as a physician assistant in a prison at all, let alone working at Sing Sing. When I initially took the job, I felt that I would only last at Sing Sing for a year at most. But after working with a dedicated, highly professional group of correction officers—many young, only on the job for a few months, as well as many old-timers with years of experience—I began to think that prison was the place that I might be able to do something positive in some way and improve society. Many of my friends felt that prison was the place I belonged anyway.

I spent a year working at Sing Sing. Back in 1978 it was an easy job compared to working in the prison system today. In 1978 the population was much younger and much healthier than today's inmate population. There was no AIDS or hepatitis C, and tuberculosis (TB) seemed to be under control, with few reported cases. The number of drugs available to treat hypertension, chronic pain, and diabetes was very small compared to what is available today. Also, the mentally ill were treated in psychiatric hospitals for the most part.

In the past thirty-five years, things have changed dramatically. Today you have a very large number of physically and mentally ill inmates. Many have a very depressed immune system from HIV, which makes them susceptible to many life-threatening illnesses, some of which could be spread to other inmates or to staff. Many inmates within the walls of the prison today are bipolar or actively psychotic. There are a sizeable and growing number of elderly inmates, many with Alzheimer's disease. The number of drugs available to treat these sick inmates today is mind-boggling. Any practitioner prescribing medications now works very closely with the pharmacist because of drug-to-drug interactions. I find working as a PA in the prison system today much more demanding than it was when I began. On the other hand, it is much more rewarding and challenging. The need to stay current with medical trends and treatments is not only important but also vital.

When I first started with the New York State Department of Corrections as a health-care practitioner, I had no interest in working with inmates. However, I began to enjoy working days from 7:00 a.m. to 3:00 p.m., with weekends and holidays off. (Later on in my life when I had children, this schedule was invaluable, and I never missed a doctor's visit or sports event with my two sons.) Now I have to say that I did enjoy my work in the prison system and am glad that I stayed on in the Department of Corrections. It has been very rewarding. In the present economy, with both parents working or in households with only single parents, many people need to work from 7:00 a.m. to 3:00 p.m. on weekdays when the children are in school. This has made working in the Department of Corrections not only a sought-after position but also a position in demand by others looking for work in the health-care field. When an opening becomes available and is advertised, many physician assistants, nurse practitioners, and medical doctors always respond looking for work. The work is challenging, and there is always something new to learn and never a dull moment when you deal with convicted felons.

PART 1

My Early Years as a Physician Assistant

CHAPTER 1

IN A NEW PROFESSION

The physician assistant profession began in 1964 at Duke University. The program was created for army medics returning home from Vietnam. These highly trained medics, who had performed medicine and surgery on the battlefields in Vietnam, were specially trained to assist physicians in emergency rooms back home in the States. The profession grew slowly but steadily. In the early years, this midlevel practitioner was referred to as a physician associate. Today it's called physician assistant or just PA.

To become a PA I received a bachelor's degree in science; because of switching my major, it took me five years. The last two years are continuous studies, with classes continuing through the summers. At that time there were few PA programs. I was accepted to the program at Long Island University in Brooklyn. There were over one thousand applicants for about forty-two seats. I was very lucky. After completing the program I took and passed a national certification exam. To become a full physician one must graduate near the top of his high-school class and get accepted into a very competitive college or university. They must take a difficult major such as biology or chemistry and do well in it. After completing four years the next step is to take a qualifying exam call the MCAT, the Medical College Admission Test, and score highly on it. Upon graduation from medical school an additional three, four, or five years is spent in a residency program.

I spent my first few years as a PA correcting people who thought I was a doctor and asking them not to call me one. In the prison system, any male wearing a nice shirt and tie with a white lab coat is called Doc. One day, a dentist and friend who worked near me took me aside and told me to stop correcting people. He said, "Everybody knows that you are not an MD. They are not calling you *Doctor* but *Doc*, and you should learn to accept it." Today, there is a good chance that many of you or your family members have been cared for by a PA in one way or another. PAs work in just about every clinic, doctor's office, and hospital across the nation.

At the end of my second year at community college, after I had worked as an EMT for a handful of years, I was still not sure what I wanted to do with the rest of my life. I thought becoming a physician assistant would be a good next step for me. My grades were not too bad, so I thought I would have a chance. One day, after a morning class at Rockland Community College (RCC) in Suffern, New York, I was walking down a staircase in the student union building and then turned directly into the recruitment table for Long Island University (LIU). As it turned out, LIU did have a PA program, and with some luck, I was accepted into it.

It was very difficult to get accepted into a PA program at the few colleges or universities that had one. There were always many more applicants than available seats. I was not a great student in junior college, but my decent College Board scores, along with my community service as a volunteer fireman and volunteer ambulance member and some prayer, allowed me to get a seat in the Long Island University Physician Assistant Program at the Brooklyn campus.

While at Rockland Community College, I rode the local volunteer ambulance as an emergency medical technician and volunteered at a local hospital. During my volunteer work in the hospital emergency room, I met an unforgettable tall white doctor. He wore a heavily starched white shirt with a bow tie, not the typical scrub shirt that you see most doctors wearing in the emergency room. He had a strong southern accent and later admitted to me that he was from the great state of Georgia. I was sitting around waiting for my next job, and he noticed that I was reading a surgical textbook. We got friendly and had some time to talk because the ER was slow that particular night. When he saw that I was reading about appendectomies, he began to give me some pointers about the procedures. He told me that when he did an appendectomy on certain racial or ethnic groups, he would cut the vas deferens on male patients. The vas deferens carries sperm to the penis from the testicle; of course, only males have the vas deferens. This, he said, "would cut down the number of these types to reproduce." I was quite alarmed to hear this from a doctor and a person that I had never met before. To this day I still wonder if he was joking with me or really being truthful. It is funny how some things seem to stick in my mind. I would wonder how a highly educated person like an MD could be a racist or make a comment like that—to a stranger, no less.

I did not begin my lifelong trip in medicine because I enjoyed medicine, blood, and guts. I had no desire to become an ambulance driver or fireman. I had a great fear of blood and distrusted doctors. Then, one morning while I was watching Saturday morning cartoons, the woman who lived in the apartment above ours came running into our kitchen with a very young boy who could not breathe; he was blue and lifeless. The woman had let the child have one of those hard red candy balls, which he had attempted to swallow and was choking on. Without skipping a beat, my mother took the boy and placed him over the back of the kitchen chair, repeatedly hitting him between his shoulder blades. When the candy ball popped out of the child's mouth, he began to breathe normally, and his color returned to normal.

My mother was very angry that the woman had let the child have such a piece of hard candy, and boy, did she let this woman know it. Afterward, both the woman and my mother were very much shaken and upset. I was very impressed that my mother knew what to do and reacted quickly to save this child's life. The fear of not knowing what to do in this type of situation haunted me for years. I signed up for an EMT course, not because I wanted to be a fireman or drive an ambulance, but only to have some knowledge of what to do in a medical emergency.

One summer I worked in a bicycle shop on the main street in a small village. I was approached repeatedly by the village elders about joining the local fire department. Even my boss in the bike shop told me it would help the community and that he would continue to pay me if I had to leave work during my shift to respond to a fire. One day the local pharmacist who worked in the drugstore across the street from the bike shop came over to talk to me. In a way he was pressuring me to join the local fire company too. I told him I had no interest in polishing fire trucks, marching in parades, and drinking beer with the firemen in town. He became angry with me and told me that during the day, because we lived in a bedroom community, there was no one to get the fire truck to the fire because all the firemen worked outside of the village. It was a true bedroom community. He told me that the community was hard up for firemen who worked in the village and could respond to fires during the day. I am still not sure if I joined because I wanted to help the village or because the thought of driving a fire truck gave me a rush.

For one reason or another, joining the fire department was one of the better choices I made in life. I met a number of wonderful people who helped me a great deal. I will never forget them or what I learned the few years I was a fireman. By the way, this particular fire company did not drink beer. I was wrong to pre-judge all volunteer firemen. The group was very dedicated to help-ing one another and the community.

Once I started the physician assistant program, it was grueling. I had never worked so hard in my life. My prior two years in the community college were a breeze by comparison. About forty-eight students were accepted into the program, and about half went on to graduate and become PAs. Many who did not make it through the program were much better students then I was. They had much better study skills and a better educational foundation than I had upon entering the program. I had ranked in the middle of my high-school class and had gone to a community college prior to being accepted to the PA program at Long Island University. Many students in the PA program had bachelor's degrees from good schools. I had always had some difficulty getting things in my head. At times it took me longer to read and comprehend what I was studying, so I had to read and reread things more than once.

My wife reminds me frequently that I am dyslexic. *Wikipedia* claims that people with dyslexia have normal intelligence but have difficulty with learning to read fluently and with accurate compre-hension. It takes me a little longer to read and understand certain things, but once I understand what I am reading, it is in my mind forever. It has been a lifelong struggle. The reason I mention this is that people with dyslexia are commonly very poor spellers. I can-not spell for shit. Some of the transcription people at work com-ment about my handwriting and my spelling. I always tell them that if I could spell, I would write more legibly, and if I could spell, I would have been an English teacher. A few years back, a PA with much worse handwriting than mine started working alongside me at Downstate. He is a much better PA than I will ever be. He is also a better practitioner than many physicians I have worked with. I learned a lot from him and would not hesitate to go to him if a family member or I became sick. I always remind the transcription people that they have stopped complaining about my handwriting since he came on board at Downstate. I only mention my difficulties to let all the dyslexic people out there know that you are not forgotten.

While I am talking about myself, let me give you a bit of family history. Many people wonder about the origin of my first name, Bohdan. When I first met my wife, she questioned why my brother's name was Stephen, my sister's name was Irene, my father's name was John, and my mother's name was Helen. She wondered how I ended up with Bohdan. My friends call me Ben for short; I'm not sure where that came from. The name *Bohdan* is Ukrainian. It means "God-given" or "God's servant." My parents had been moved to Germany during the Great War to work on a farm. The regular farm workforce in Germany, mostly young people, had gone to fight in the war, and there was no one to work on the farms raising crops for the German war effort. My parents were very young when they were moved to Germany and had little choice in the matter, and Germany is where they met. My brother and sister were both born in Germany as well. In 1951 my family came to this great country as displaced persons, as many Ukrainians have. We owe many heartfelt thanks to Eleanor Roosevelt, who pressured the United Nations to allow displaced persons to immigrate to the United States. Joseph Stalin wanted all Ukrainians displaced by the war to return to the Soviet Union. They would have ended up in Siberia—I am sure of that. Stalin did not treat displaced persons kindly. He felt that they were traitors to the Soviet Union.

The physician assistant program was grueling—long hours and a lot of hard work. I did not think I had it in me to complete the program. I will never forget one of my professors, Dr. Benjamin Zamora. He was the head of the department of surgery, and I think he had been trained by the Jesuits in the Philippines. He was a stickler for fine details. More than that, he demanded that all his students know the fine details of medicine too. Dr. Zamora believed in the PA concept and was an important ally in the early stages of the PA profession. He helped train great PAs who could hold their own in any hospital or emergency room, in all circumstances. I mention Dr. Zamora by name because he was important to the new physician assistant movement. He truly believed in what PAs are capable of doing with the proper training. More importantly he was a truly compassionate person when dealing with the sick.

In the third year of the degree program, Dr. Zamora taught surgery. He was always on time and had the doors to the lecture hall locked at the precise time the lecture was to start. He could not, and would not, tolerate latecomers to his lecture.

His exams were very difficult, and after the exams were graded, he would hand them back to the class in grade order, the highest grade first and the lowest grade last. When the grades were posted, I would always make it a point to count the names on the list to make sure that I was in the middle. Those whose grades were in the bottom third did not make it. If you did not pass Dr. Zamora's course, you would have to sit out the rest of the year and retake the surgical course with him the following year. He always made it a point to welcome back the repeaters in front of the group.

After the exams were passed out, Dr. Zamora would review each question. God forbid that you were the only one in the class who got a particular question correct. He would have you stand and explain to the rest of the class your reasoning for the correct answer you had chosen on that particular question. If you were unable to explain the answer, he would request that you return the exam to him so he could deduct the credit. "You don't get credit for guessing," he would say to the group. After reviewing the exam, he would collect the exams to make sure that they would be not used in later years by other classes. He would not let the class leave until he had all the copies of the exams in hand.

Dr. Zamora was a very intimidating person. The entire class feared and avoided him. It was not uncommon for him to throw PAs and residents out of the operating room because they could not identify anatomical structures in the person on the operating table or could not close properly. When he taught basic suturing using pigs' feet (because they were close to the consistency of human skin), he would carry an eighteen-inch ruler to strike the hands of any student who was not holding the instruments properly. "He acted just like the nuns in Catholic school," someone in the class once commented. I was very fortunate that I was able to avoid him in my last two years of the program. It is important to say that he did do a great job in training residents and PAs; when they graduated from the program and did a surgical rotation with him, they could hold their own in any major teaching hospital. Dr. Zamora's office was on the fifth or sixth floor of Cumberland Hospital in Brooklyn, just across the hall from the elevator. One morning, everybody in the emergency room in the basement of the hospital, across from the elevator shaft, could hear him yelling at two second-year residents. His voice traveled all the way down the elevator shaft to the basement, where the emergency room was. As it turned out, a physician assistant had scored higher than the second-year residents did on a national PGY2 (postgraduate year-two) exam. From what I understand he fired the two second-year residents.

During one of my clinical rotations, a group of residents, medical students, and PAs were waiting for rounds to begin. One third-year, foreign-trained MD resident appeared very upset, pale, and ill. He was a friendly fellow who was well trained and had good command of the English language. More than one person questioned the resident: What was the matter with him? Did he see a ghost? At first he would not say, but after some prodding he said the person riding next to him in a packed subway car had wet leprosy—a very contagious type of leprosy, he said. I am not sure what he meant by *wet leprosy*—did it come from a tropical, wet climate, or did he mean the lesions were moist? Whatever he had seen on the subway, though, had upset him. Someone asked him if he was sure it was leprosy. I remember his response to this day: "You have to remember that I grew up and went to medical school in a country where leprosy is still seen. Seeing it on a crowded subway car during rush hour in New York City is alarming and unsettling." Keep in mind that this occurred in about 1977. It is my understanding that leprosy, or Hansen's disease, is not as contagious as one might think and is curable.

After completing my course work for the PA degree, I began my clinic rotations where I got hands-on experience in about eight different hospital settings. For my emergency rotation, I chose Cumberland Hospital, located in what was a dangerous section of Brooklyn near Fort Greene. Fort Greene is now a nice, desirable location in Brooklyn. Medical professionals who worked at the hospital would wear their scrubs or lab coats to and from the hospital, hoping that it would protect them from getting mugged.

I was fortunate to work with another PA student who was very smart and very skilled, and like Hawkeye Pierce in the sitcom *M*A*S*H*, had a great sense of dark humor. When drunks or people who had overdosed on drugs would be brought in by city ambulances, he would grab the unconscious person's arm, and I would grab the other, and we would race to see who could get the IV started first. He would look at me and say in a soft voice, "I'm in." It always had to be a large-bore, thick needle; butterfly needles would not be accepted in the ER at Cumberland. Then he or I would pull a very large syringe filled with a concentrated dextrose solution and inject it into the lifeless person. Most times, the person would come to and sit right up. It was like a miracle. Most of the time they were homeless drunks who had not eaten recently at the point that they passed out. If the person did not respond to the dextrose, we always had an amp of Narcan in our pockets to override an opiate drug overdose. If the person came to after the Narcan, which was given in the IV line, the PA would smile back at the other PA. We had a lot of drug and alcohol overdoses in the emergency room at Cumberland Hospital back in the day. I learned a great deal working with John and experienced a lot in the basement ER at Cumberland Hospital. It was a very busy place: a lot of trauma, a lot of illness, and a lot of suturing.

One day a uniformed police officer was standing in the hallway. He was very pale and appeared to be very upset about something. I took him aside in a quiet room and asked him if he was all right. After a few minutes, he told me that he had grabbed a twelve-year-old girl by her collar just as she had jumped from the roof of a seven-story building to commit suicide. He said that he had been barely able to save her. "What would drive a twelve-year-old girl to suicide?" he asked. He was quite upset and visibly shaken. Cumberland Hospital was a very busy place, it has since closed.

After exams at Brooklyn LIU, a group of us from the PA program would always meet in McSorley's Old Ale House on Seventh Street, in the Lower East Side of Manhattan. It was convenient for those of us who lived in Manhattan, near the Astor Place subway stop, an easy on-and-off stop from the subway on the way home from classes. We would meet in the back room to discuss the exam and vent about how depressed and anxious we all were. The cold beer helped. This was long before McSorley's became a popular place, especially before NYU students began frequenting it. Now McSorley's is a much different place from when a handful of Ukrainians would stop there for a cheap mug of beer.

One evening after our final exam, a small group of PA students from LIU met at McSorley's to rehash what we had all gone through in this PA program. I can clearly remember one of us questioning out loud what a physician assistant was: Would we get a job as a PA? Would we be accepted by the outside world as PAs? As it turned out, all of the graduating PA students had one or more good job offer before graduation day, many going on multiple job interviews and some with multiple offers. I was very fortunate to make it through the program without needing to repeat any courses. I had never worked that hard in high school or community college. I sure did make up for it at the university.

Upon graduation I went on a number of interviews in the Northeast. I had a number of good offers, but I was unsure which way to start my career as a PA. The Sunday after my interview at Sing Sing, I was in church; I needed to be there. I went with my father that Sunday and sat in the last row in the back of the church, as if I did not want anyone to see me. In life I have always believed that if you give difficult decisions a chance, an answer will appear. I was not sure if I should take a state job in the prison system or a more prestigious one in the private sector. The money in the private sector was much higher than in the state sector. In exchange, the hours were much longer in private practice, but the benefits with the state were better. At that time the pay the state was offering sucked. Sitting in the last pew in the church, I heard the Gospel according to Matthew, chapter 25:2 KJV. The priest read, "for I was hungry and you gave Me food; I was thirsty and you gave Me drink; I was a stranger and you took Me in; [36] I *was* naked and you clothed Me; I was sick and you visited Me; I was in prison and you came to Me." It was a strong factor in taking the job in the prison.

I have worked most of my life with crooks, rapists, and murderers. Maybe there is a hidden message in that I felt at home in dealing with the dregs of society. The only resistance I anticipated in working in this new uncharted profession was from older nurses. Many older nurses viewed PAs as a threat. I think the nurses did not want to take medical orders from this new, untested midlevel profession. This seemed to die down as years went on and these older nurses retired. I must also say that a few of the older nurses took me under their wing and helped me out a great deal when I was young and green. I will never forget them for their help. Back when I became a PA, there were only a few schools that had PA programs; Long Island University, SUNY at Stony Brook, Hudson Valley Community College, and Duke University were the pioneers in educating students in this new level of care.

After more than thirty-five years as a PA, I must say that I have enjoyed every day of being a physician assistant. The continual learning that always takes place in medicine keeps the job interesting and never boring. It is a job that I look forward to going to in the morning each day, and at the end of the day, I feel that I have accomplished something important by helping someone. I have worked through tuberculosis and resistant-TB outbreaks, and I treated HIV before it had a name and hepatitis C back when it was called non-A, non-B hepatitis. It's true that I was always scared of contracting some sort of contagious illness. I have had many sleepless nights worrying about bringing something home to my family. But would I have done it differently? Never—I would do it all over again in a heartbeat.

CHAPTER 2

A BRIEF HISTORY OF SING SING

The *Half Moon Press*, a New York City newspaper, wrote in its May 2000 edition that the first New York state prison was called Newgate and was built in Greenwich Village in 1796. It was named after the famous Newgate Prison in England. There was also a famous prison in Simsbury, Connecticut, called Newgate, built inside an old copper mine. What has been referred to as the first American penitentiary was the Walnut Street Jail, built in Philadelphia in 1790. According to W. David Lewis's book *From Newgate to Dannemora*, Newgate Prison, on the Lower East Side of Manhattan, was similar in construction to the Walnut Street Jail in Philadelphia. About twenty-five years after Newgate was built, in 1821 the second prison in New York was erected in Auburn. Auburn was far from New York City, and it was difficult to shuttle inmates there and back.

Sing Sing was built to replace Newgate Prison in New York City. In 1825 the state bought 130 acres from the Sint Sinck, or Sinck Sinck, tribe of Native American Indians. Inmates were transported from Auburn across the Erie Canal on barges to the

Hudson River, then down the Hudson on freighters to build Sing Sing. Sing Sing was constructed by inmate labor using granite that was available on-site. According to *Wikipedia,* the words *Sinck Sinck* translate to "stone upon stone." When it was completed, it was the world's largest cellblock at the time. The first prison built at the site was named Mount Pleasant. Shortly before the Civil War, the name was changed to Sing Sing after the town of Sing Sing. Once opened, it was a tough place, a tough prison. Sing Sing's inmates would walk in lockstep; they followed one another as closely as possible, their eyes downcast, and they were required to remain silent at all times. It was a rigid—and in a sense, seemingly mindless—discipline.

The lockstep was abolished in 1900. Today the inmates do what I refer to as the *Downstate Two-Step* or the *Downstate Shuffle.* This happens when inmates are prepared for transfer to another facility. Two inmates are shackled together with leg irons, both using the black box to hold their handcuffs at their waists. The black box is held closely to the body by a chain around each inmate's waist. Just before getting on the bus, they are lined up in the draft area. The inmates kind of shuffle together in step. While it appears that they have to walk in step, it's not because the guards make them but because it makes walking with someone chained to you a lot easier.

The inmates of Sing Sing wore striped uniforms until 1904; one stripe for first timers, two stripes for repeaters. Inmates with four stripes were considered incorrigibles. Inmates worked in the stone quarry or in various industrial shops. The items that inmates made were sold to the public, a practice that was later stopped because of opposition from the labor unions. Writer Guy Cheli writes in his book *Sing Sing Prison* that the Lincoln funeral train passed through Sing Sing in 1865 and that prison officials were permitted to board the train to view the casket of the late president when the train stopped there to have its water tank refilled.

From what I have read, Sing Sing Prison came to the area first, and the local village followed. The local village was first called Sing Sing and then later changed its name to Ossining in 1901 because it did not want to share the name associated with the famous prison. Years followed, and the name of the prison was changed again in 1970 to the Ossining Correctional Facility, named after the town of Ossining, to soften the prison's image. The local community was not at all happy with the name change and again did not want to be associated with the notorious prison. The prison's name went back to Sing Sing in 1983. In 1909 a new Sing Sing was to be built at Bear Mountain near Hessian Lake. The land at Bear Mountain was cleared by inmates, but the plan was eventually abandoned, and the area was later used for the Palisades Interstate Park system.

The term *up the river* came from a 1930 comedy movie of that name with Spencer Tracy and Humphrey Bogart, directed by John Ford. Spencer Tracy and Humphrey Bogart debuted in this classic film. In the movie, one actor who was used in a knife-throwing scene was named Dannemora Dan, referring to another great prison, the Clinton Correctional Facility, in Dannemora, New York. In the movie, the words *up the river* were never used, nor was Sing Sing ever referred to. The prison in the movie was not only modeled after Sing Sing but its scenes were also filmed there.

Five movies were filmed at Sing Sing by Warner Brothers: *Angels with Dirty Faces*, starring James Cagney and Humphrey Bogart; *Each Dawn I Die*, starring James Cagney and George Raft; and *Castle on the Hudson*, *20,000 Years in Sing Sing*, and *Invisible Stripes*. To thank Sing Sing for allowing the company to film on location, Warner Brothers built a gymnasium in 1934. It was located on the lower side of Sing Sing, across the railroad tracks near Tappan housing unit and across the courtyard from the "Death House." When I visited the Death House, I made it a point to walk over and read the metal plaque on the outside wall of the gym. I am sorry that I did not go inside to look around the gym. Both the New York Yankees and the New York Giants came up from the city to play games at Sing Sing for the inmates. I am not sure what years the games were played.

From July 7, 1891, to August 15, 1963, 614 people were put to death at Sing Sing. The most famous were Ethel and Julius Rosenberg, in 1953. For many years, the Rosenberg family claimed that their parents were innocent and were wrongfully put to death. As it turned out, Ethel and Julius were later proven to have been spies for the Soviet Union and had passed on important information to the Soviet Union.

According to *Wikipedia,* in his posthumously published memoirs, Nikita Khrushchev, leader of the Soviet Union from 1953 to 1964, said that he could not "specifically say what kind of help the Rosenbergs provided us," but that he learned from Joseph Stalin and Vyacheslav M. Molotov that they "had provided very significant help in accelerating the production of our atomic bomb." According to Andy Newman of the *New York Times,* the first death by the electric chair was in August of 1890 at the Auburn Correctional Facility in upstate New York. The electric chair was made at the Auburn prison. William Kemmler was put to death for the hatchet murder of his common-law wife. It was said to be the beginning of the modern era of capital punishment. Prior to that, hanging was the preferred method of execution.

On July 7, 1891, Harris Smiler was the first to be electrocuted at Sing Sing. After 1915, all of New York State's executions took place at Sing Sing. It should also be mentioned that there was a dispute between Thomas Edison and George Westinghouse as to what type of electricity would be better suited for the killing of a human being, AC current or DC current. AC current won out.

I do not believe in the death penalty, for both religious and moral reasons. I believe it reduces society to the same level as that of the criminal. The United States is one of the few countries that still has capital punishment.

In April of 2012, the National Research Council, whose mission is to improve government decision-making and public policy, questioned in a study whether executions have an effect on murder rates. The Committee on Law and Justice concluded that research on the effect of capital punishment on homicide rates is not useful in determining whether the death penalty increases, decreases, or has no effect on homicide rates. It has also been proven that the cost of putting a person to death is greater than the cost of keeping him or her in prison for the rest of his or her life. This is because of the attorney and courts costs involving appeals and motions.

I recently had the pleasure of visiting San Francisco for a vacation. One reason I chose to go to San Francisco was to visit Alcatraz. During the summer months, tours that visit the island fill up early. When you visit the website, you are advised to make reservations for a tour far in advance because Alcatraz has become a popular tourist destination for travelers from all over the world. My wife and I visited in October; the weather was great, with many sunny, warm days, which is unusual for San Francisco. I understand that San Francisco is frequently shrouded in fog.

The island of Alcatraz can be seen from just about any spot in the city. It looked grand from high atop Nob Hill and could be viewed from anywhere along the coastline, from the Ferry Building to Fisherman's Wharf. In some strange way, I found it to be breathtaking and beautiful sitting out in the middle of San Francisco Bay. It was once an army fortress and served as a military prison. Later it was turned into a federal prison and was closed in 1963.

Today Alcatraz is run by the National Park Service. It is described as one of America's most fascinating national parks. As a federal prison, it held a maximum of 325 inmates. The average number of inmates housed on "the Rock" was 260. The reason I mention this is that Sing Sing has housing blocks that are filled with about 500 inmates each. That is 500 inmates, including many who have serious mental illness or who are serious sociopaths. They interact on a daily basis with a large number of so-called normal inmates. Many of these borderline inmates, mentally and socially, are functioning just under the radar at Sing Sing, meaning they have yet to act out or hurt someone. Anyone who has ever worked at Sing Sing knows that at any given time, one of these inmates will flip out and cause harm to one or more inmates or prison staff.

Granted, the inmates at Alcatraz were the worst of the worst in the federal prison system and were moved there for that reason, but the guards knew what to expect from each inmate, and there were only about 260 to contend with on any given day. At Sing Sing, correction officers had many hundreds of inmates to contend with, many of whom could and would go off at any given moment and hurt someone—inmate or staff.

I have also visited Eastern State Penitentiary in Philadelphia, which is open to the general public for a fee. I suppose that it is a matter of time before Sing Sing is opened to the general public for tours. The state of New York would generate revenue running tours of Sing Sing, just as Philadelphia and the National Parks Service are already doing at Eastern State Penitentiary and Alcatraz. I understand that the city of Philadelphia did not know what to do with the very large fortress of the Eastern State Penitentiary. The process of tearing the prison down would have cost the taxpayers of Philadelphia millions of dollars. Someone suggested opening it up to the public for tours, and it became a cash cow for the city. As at Alcatraz, at certain times of the year, especially during Halloween, Eastern State Penitentiary is booked solid, and the price to tour the prison is not cheap.

CHAPTER 3
A NEW JOB

One evening during the summer of 1978, I was having dinner with a close friend of mine in Stony Point, New York. He had asked what I had been studying these past three years. When I told him I was a PA, he said he was not quite sure what that was but remembered that he had seen a job advertisement in the local paper for a PA at the Ossining Correctional Facility across the Hudson. Then he said, "What is a PA?" I had been on a few interviews already and had a few more planned. For reasons that were unclear to me, he tore the classified ad from the paper and gave it to me. The next morning I called and made an appointment for an interview.

It was a beautiful summer day when I went up to Ossining for the interview. I took the train from Grand Central up the east shore of the Hudson River to Ossining. Back in the late seventies, Grand Central Terminal was not the place that it is today, and the trains at that time were old and dirty. Metro-North was truly neglected back then.

When I went for my interview during the summer of '78, it was called Ossining Correctional Facility. It was all confusing to me—and I still don't understand the term *correctional facility.* It was, and still is, more of a warehouse for difficult people.

Getting off the train in Ossining on this summer morning, I walked about three-quarters of a mile to the prison. Then and now, the prison sat on a side of a hill facing the west shore of the Hudson River. Looking south, you could see the Tappan Zee Bridge. Across the river to the west was Hook Mountain just north of Nyack, New York. (Once I started working at Sing Sing, it was worth it just to be able to see the magnificent sunsets behind Hook Mountain from the large windows on the third floor of the hospital.) The Hudson River line of Metro-North and Amtrak passed right through the prison. I understand that a few escape attempts were made by inmates jumping onto the roof of a passing train. When I first saw the massive wall with the gun towers, I was awestruck. It reminded me of all the gangster movies I had watched on TV when I was a child. I must admit it was very intimidating to me. Even though I grew up north of Sing Sing, I can remember how the mother of a close friend who lived next door to my family would tell us that if we did not behave, we would be sent up the river for punishment, not realizing that Sing Sing was south of Haverstraw.

At the main gate of the administration building, I was met by a tough-looking guard who asked what my business was at Sing Sing. Before he let me in, he checked my ID through the iron-bar gate and then checked a clipboard to see if I had an appointment, and with whom. There were many prison guards with very large keys and barred gates in front of and behind them, preventing anyone from going in any one direction without their OK. Once I passed through the numerous gates, I began the climb up many stairs to the hospital area. It was more uphill walking than I had done in a long time, and I was winded and sweating. When I got to the hospital, another guard, wearing leather gloves at another iron-bar gate, directed me up to the third floor.

The third floor of the hospital building was where I had my first meeting with inmates, all dressed in green, as interested in me as I was in them. The first medical professional to greet me in the hospital was the nurse administrator, Ann Oakley. An older woman nearing retirement, she was a true nurse in every sense of the word. She was very proper and proud to be a nurse. Her lab coat was as white as snow and appeared to have been just pressed. She made it a point that the hospital should be clean and orderly. She said she was also very strict about the rule that all inmates on the hospital prison ward who were not medically required to remain in bed all day had to get up and make their beds after breakfast. They were not allowed to return to their beds or lie down on their beds until after the dinner meal. They had to spend the day in the common area at the end of the ward, either playing cards or watching television. I liked that. Now inmates spend the whole day just lying in bed, watching television all day.

After she took me around the facility to all of the departments to meet the staff, she then introduced me to the medical director. He reminded me of Idi Amin Dada—a short, pompous, overweight black man. During our interview he seemed rushed and in a hurry to be somewhere else. He gave me the impression that I was imposing on him. When the short conversation got to the point where he said they were looking for someone with more experience than I had, I figured the job was not mine and stood up from the chair to leave. Knowing I had other interviews pending, I was not upset or concerned. To my surprise, just as I stood up to leave the office, The medical director asked if I could start the following Thursday. I thought about working from eight to four with weekends off and twelve holidays a year, which was unheard of in the medical field at that time. I told the medcial director that I could start work in two weeks, which he agreed to.

After accepting the position, I moved back home again. I had grown up in the Hudson Valley and did not want to spend the rest of my life in the city; you could say I had had enough of the hustle and bustle of the greatest city in the world. The town I went back to was a small town north of the city on the west shore of the Hudson. It bordered the New York State Palisades Park. The drive to work each morning to Sing Sing from my home on the west shore of the Hudson was pleasant. I brought a Toyota Celica five-speed coupe for the daily commute to the "Big House." Driving north on Route 9W on a highway carved out of a mountain was not only breathtaking but also spectacular. Looking across to Anthony's Nose across from Bear Mountain, you saw Route 9D South, a road that laced up the mountain. Thank God not many people were on the road that early in the morning. I had the road to myself and my five-speed Celica. It is the most beautiful part of the majestic Hudson Valley from Manhattan north to Albany.

During a recent trip in Europe, I traveled with my wife down the Danube River to Vienna, Austria. Just before arriving in Vienna, we passed through the Wachau Valley, which was supposed to have breathtaking views of mountains on both sides of the Danube River. The tour guide on the cruise ship noticed that I was not totally impressed and asked why. My response was that the Hudson River Valley is much nicer.

Alexis de Tocqueville, a famous French political thinker and historian who was best known for his work *De la démocratie en Amérique* (*Democracy in America*) came to the United States in 1831 on a mission to examine prisons and penitentiaries in America. Any time you read about the prisons in early America, one name that frequently comes up is that of Alexis de Tocqueville. He was famous for his theory of crime and punishment and traveled to the United States to study the American penitentiary system to help form his theories of punishment. He and a colleague, Gustave de Beaumont, wrote a book on the penitentiary system in the United States and compared it to the penitentiary system in France. Basically, he believed strongly that criminal offenders could be rehabilitated and did not need to be harshly punished. De Tocqueville strongly opposed the death penalty. He loved the Hudson Valley, as seen in his writings. He wrote, "Except for the view of the Bay of Naples... the world has not such scenery," referring to the Hudson Valley. De Tocqueville's visit to the Hudson Valley occurred about six years after Sing Sing was opened. In the winter months, when the sun shone on Anthony's Nose across from Bear Mountain, or when it was covered in snow, I felt sure that there was a God and he created all this for us to love and appreciate. Later on in my career, I transferred to Downstate Correctional in Fishkill, New York, about thirty miles north of Sing Sing. In the winter I would travel down to the area below the Bear Mountain Bridge to see the eagles that would come to this area of Hudson to hunt for fish in the Hudson River. The eagles would come down from as far away as Nova Scotia, looking for food during the very cold months of the winter. The rivers and lakes in Canada would freeze over, and the eagles were not able to get fish to eat. So much of the Hudson was frozen in the north that eagles came to the river south of Bear Mountain Bridge. I was told that because of the violent current just below Iona Island the fish would be near the top of the water. The eagles would ride the ice floes, waiting to pluck the fish out of the Hudson. I also was told by a local that because the water near the power plant at Indian Point was warmer there were more fish near the surface of the water for the eagles to catch. When I would travel to New York City for court or for medical conferences during the winter months, I always made it a point to sit on the river side of the train heading south to look out and see the beautiful, large eagles sitting on the ice floes. I think the commute to Sing Sing played an important role in my job satisfaction. It was always a great way to unwind from the stress of working with demanding convicts at the Big House.

When I worked evenings doing extra service (overtime) at Sing Sing, I would sit looking out the large windows in my office on the third floor facing the Hudson. I always loved to watch the giant ships carrying new cars from Europe and Asia up the Hudson River to be unloaded in Albany. Datsun (which is now Nissan) and Volkswagen had oversized ships that looked like giant ferries that came up the Hudson on a regular basis. I must admit, I felt like a young boy again watching these ships make their way up the beautiful Hudson River. At the time of day when I would watch from a very large window on the third floor of the hospital, the floor was empty, inmates had returned to their cellblocks, and the sun was setting behind Hook Mountain in Nyack. What a way to spend a summer evening on the Hudson and get paid at the same time.

On my first day on the job at Sing Sing, I was handed about thirty patient charts by a PA who already worked there. He pointed in the direction of my new office and said, "Good luck." He told me if I had any problems, he would be next door. Because the inmates had to return to their cells for the noon count, I had to be finished by 11:30 a.m. I learned quickly that in the prison system everything revolved around "the count," which was when all inmates would return to their cells to be counted. The count occurred many times throughout the day and night to make sure that no one had escaped from the prison. The inmates would not be released from their cells to report to their workstations or school until the count was cleared. A common question heard frequently in the prison system of New York was "Did the count clear yet?" This meant that all inmates were accounted for and would be released from their cells to report to their assigned locations.

Sing Sing was dark, dank, and dirty—a tough place to be and to work. Some of the housing blocks were five tiers high with more than five hundred inmates per block, more than twice as many as the total number housed at the famous Alcatraz. Even the "honor block" was a very intimidating place. The building consisted of four floors with three catwalks allowing access to cells on both sides of the cellblock. I heard that inmates would be thrown off the upper tiers by other inmates just for changing the station on the television. The buildings were all connected by a network of tunnels that were worse than any subway tunnel in New York City. At the time I was there, they were very poorly lit, with all kinds of murderers and rapists passing you in the dark hallway.

To make matters worse, Sing Sing housed the worst of the worst, inmates who had been convicted of horrific crimes. There was one convict who had sprayed acid on a woman's young, beautiful face to try to get her not to testify against him in court. He had mixed acid, molasses, and soda water in a bottle, walked up to her, and sprayed it on her face. The soda was used as a propellant, the acid to disfigure and burn, and the molasses to stick to the skin. Who could ever have thought of doing something so horrendous? Inmates like this would cut your throat on a dare from another inmate. Many had serious mental illnesses or were serious sociopaths. As mentioned before, many of these borderline inmates were just functioning under the radar, meaning they had yet to act out or hurt someone in prison. Any person who has ever worked at Sing Sing knows that at any given time, one of these inmates might flip out and cause harm to one or more inmates or prison staff. And at Sing Sing, correction officers already had many hundreds of inmates to contend with who could, and would, go off and hurt someone at any given moment. As I mentioned earlier, I have visited Alcatraz in San Francisco and Eastern State Penitentiary in Philadelphia and have worked in Sing Sing, but Sing Sing is a much more intimidating prison. Just the sheer number of inmates compared to the number of correction officers made watching them frightening. Many mornings I would see drops of blood on the floor leading up to the prison emergency room. After the porters, who cleaned the hallways, were locked in after dinner, it was difficult to get them out of their cells on an "out count" (inmates to be counted on someone else's roster at a different location in the prison) to clean up the blood. The blood would stay put until the morning. My interest was in whether the blood was fresh or not. If it was fresh, then I knew I had suturing to do, which would push back my busy morning schedule. If the blood appeared dry, I would assume that the injury had occurred hours ago and that the inmate had probably been sent out to the local community hospital or the PA on call had come into the facility after hours to suture the inmate.

One spring afternoon, an inmate was brought up on a stretcher badly beaten—bloody and bruised with abrasions on his face and body. He had been beaten repeatedly with a rock in a sock. It was the common weapon of choice back in those days because it was easy to lose the rock in the outside yard after you had struck some-one with it. The nurses cleaned the inmate up as best they could. He refused to go out to the local emergency room for X-rays and refused to be admitted to the facility hospital for observation. He just wanted to get back to his cellblock. There were many "white shirts" (sergeants and lieutenants) in the room while we were car-ing for and cleaning up the inmate. They all questioned him re-peatedly about what had caused these injuries, but all he said was that he "fell in the shower."

"I fell in the shower" is a common explanation I have heard for years for when one inmate is beaten up by another inmate. We found out later that day that two other inmates had used a rock in a sock to beat this inmate nearly to death so that he would change his testimony in an upcoming court appearance. Lou Morrison, the day-shift nurse, laughed at the inmate's story that he had fallen in the shower. He winked at me and said, "Wait until tomorrow."

After the injured inmate was cleaned up and returned to his cell, he spent the night sharpening a piece of metal into a point by rubbing it on the cement-block cell wall. This made a weapon known as a "shiv" or a "shank." The next day, his attackers from the day before approached him again. When the time was right, and his attacker had his arm raised in the air to strike him, the injured inmate took his freshly made shank and shoved it into his attacker's chest as deeply as he could, just below his armpit. Not knowing what had happened, I was called to rush up to the ER as quickly as possible because an inmate was in very bad shape from a stabbing. On the way up to the fourth floor, I happened to bump into my supervising MD in the hallway, and told him that I would need his help in the ER. Sternly, he asked what the inmate's vital signs were. I told him that I hadn't gotten that far yet and that I was on my way up to check. In a loud voice, he said, "Well, when you get the vital signs, call me right away."

The ER looked like the front line of a war zone; anyone could see that the inmate was seriously injured. Fresh blood covered the emergency room and had dripped down the hall and stairs, all the way back to the staircase where he was found. The shiv had been thrust into his chest wall below his armpit in the direction of his heart. I told Lou to call the doctor with the vital signs and then to call an ambulance. Lou hung up the phone and began to laugh at me. He'd been told that the doctor had just left. "Like a bat out of hell," the person on the other end of the phone line said. "You're on your own, Darnobid." Having trained in a city hospital emergency room, I was not afraid, or maybe I was too naïve to be afraid. We were able to get two large-bore IV lines started, one in each arm, and kept him alive until the ambulance showed up. Still, I could have used the help.

The inmate with the shiv shoved deeply into his chest survived, much to my surprise. Weeks later, he thanked me for saving his life. He pulled his shirt up to his chin and his pants down to his pubic area to show me the scar running from the bottom of his neck, down his chest and abdomen, to just above his pubic bone. It was the longest surgical scar that I have ever seen. Since that episode, I have learned not to ask how an injury occurred to inmates in prison. I have gotten tired of hearing "I fell in the shower" from the inmate.

Another morning at Sing Sing, an inmate was stabbed just after the first count, when the cell gates opened for the first time in the day. Correction officers told me the inmate had been transferred down to Sing Sing from a prison in the northern part of the state. He was "getting short" (hoping to go home soon) and was transferred to Sing Sing to be closer to the city and to his family. It is a common practice to use cells nearer to the city as a reward for good behavior in prisons upstate. These inmates get preference over sick inmates who need to be held in cells nearer to the city to continue ongoing medical treatment. Yes, this annoys me to no end. This new inmate had gotten to his new cell on the upper tier late because of the long bus ride down from upstate, and all the other inmates were already locked in. The tier was dark, and it was difficult to see without a flashlight. Within a very short time, the new arrival struck up a conversation with the old-timer in the cell next to him. First only small talk, then about how each had ended up in prison, and eventually the conversation went on to where each man was from in the city. As it turned out, both came from the same neighborhood in the city, but because of their ages they did not know each other. As the night went on, the old-timer asked the new inmate if he knew of a woman in a certain building in a certain housing project in a certain area in the city. The new convict on the tier told me that he not only knew her but also had been intimate with her on a regular basis. Prodded on by the old-timer, the new con went on long into the night talking about what the two had done together while they were alone in her apartment.

According to what other inmates said the next morning during the investigation, the last question the old-timer asked was "Where was this woman's husband during all of this?" The new convict's response was "That fool is in some prison upstate." As it turned out, the old-timer was the husband and had had to listen all night long to how the young fellow had been having sex with who he thought was his faithful wife—a woman whom, up until that point, he was still very much in love with. In the morning when the cell gates opened for the first time of the day, the old-timer reached across and sent a shiv up into the new man's epigastric area, toward his heart. I don't remember if the inmate lived or died.

In the facility infirmary, there was an older, obese inmate who looked European. He kept to himself for the most part, never said much to the nurses or correction officers, and did not spend much time with the other inmates in the hospital. He was in the hospital for a very long time. Although he didn't appear to be very sick, he was never transferred to a regular cellblock. One day I asked the other PA why he was not transferred upstate or moved into the regular population like all the other inmates. The PA told me this inmate was a snitch, and as part of a plea agreement with the state, he was to be housed in a hospital at a facility near New York City, closer to his family. Years later I learned that the day after the inmate was released back to the street, the state police came to Sing Sing looking for his dental records. It seems that two bodies had been found in a Cadillac in Staten Island. Both bodies were shot, and the car was burned. The bodies were so badly burned, identification was next to impossible, which was why the dental records were needed. As it turned out, the Cadillac was registered to the inmate's brother.

Sing Sing had a small psych department on the second floor of the hospital; I had little to do with the staff—just passed them in the elevator or stairwell. It was unclear what their function was at Sing Sing. One should remember that this was in the late 1970s, just before the state psychiatric hospitals began to reduce the number of beds they had, dumping mentally ill people back in the community. Many mentally ill patients ended up in the prison system. It was proven that it was, and still is, much cheaper to place a person with mental-health needs in a prison than in a psychiatric hospital.

I would spend time talking to inmates when my workload was light. An inmate once told me that the level of care in the prison system was much better than in the state mental hospitals. It was not so much that the direct care was better, he said, but that other inmates would look out for the mentally ill. He explained that mentally ill patients were moved frequently in and out of different psychiatric facilities on the street, which was not the case in the prison system. This inmate went on to tell me that he would go from a psychiatric hospital to "single-room occupancies" (SROs), which were old hotels that were converted into housing. The SROs were located in the most difficult and unsafe parts of the city. Some had bathrooms down the hall shared by many, and the rooms were small and filthy. What would happen, the inmate said, is that most psychiatric patients would stop taking their psych medications once placed in the SRO. In time, they found themselves back on the street decompensating without their psych medication, and they would end up in the local city hospital emergency rooms. Outside of the hospital, the mentally ill would switch to street drugs or alcohol to control their symptoms of mental illness. From the local ERs, they were sent back to the hospital, and the cycle would start over again. This particular inmate said that the reason he was in prison was that the SRO that he was in had no heat. During the cold winter, he started a fire to keep warm in a large coffee cup next to his bed in the center of the floor. The bedding caught fire, which destroyed much of his room and then later the old building. He said no one was hurt, but the building was destroyed. This mentally ill patient found himself in front of a judge who sent him up the river to Sing Sing, saying that he was an arsonist. The inmate said he did not intend to burn the place down; he just was very cold and wanted to get warm. He told me prison wasn't bad. "The nurses make sure that I take my medicine, the COs make sure I eat and come out for recreation with the other inmates, and the other inmates look out for me, making sure no one picks on me," he said. "The prison is somewhat clean, and I have my own room. I am treated with more respect here than on the street."

Later in my career, I saw the percentage of mentally ill inmates climb in the state prison system as state mental hospitals closed down. Later on in this book, I will review how the mentally ill were cared for at the Matteawan Correctional Facility in Fishkill and what led the court system to remove the care of the mentally ill from the New York State Department of Corrections and place it in the care of the New York State Office of Mental Hygiene.

On Friday afternoons early on in my career, Rikers Island would clear out its psych unit, sending many of the mentally ill inmates to Sing Sing to make room for the incoming weekend arrests. The Rikers bus would arrive at Sing Sing between one and two o'clock in the afternoon. By this time the staff from Sing Sing's small psych department had usually left to get a head start on the weekend. One Friday afternoon, I watched as a Rikers Island correction officer walked down the long hall of the third floor of the Sing Sing hospital building. He asked me who I was, asked me to spell my last name, and then handed me a folder with a list of inmate names. The names on the list were inmates who had recently been on suicide watch at Rikers Island and had just gotten off the bus at Sing Sing. The Rikers Island correction officer had not been able to find anyone on the psych-unit floor. I went looking myself for someone to pass this information to. Just as the officer said, there was no one to be found on the psych floor; it was just about all locked up, and most of the lights were off.

I went back upstairs to my third-floor clinic and typed a letter to the facility watch commander, informing him what I had just been handed. "There were five inmates on suicide watch at Rikers Island who were just transferred by bus to our care at Sing Sing," I wrote. He responded in person, and I can remember the look on his face, and his anger, like it was yesterday. "Do you expect me to place these inmates on one-to-one suicide watch through the weekend?" he shouted at me. Suicide watch consists of one correction officer watching only one inmate, at great expense to the state. Putting the five Rikers inmates on suicide watch would require five additional correction officers every shift through the weekend until the psych department could reevaluate the need for one-to-one watch on Monday. Being young and stupid and not expecting a long life in corrections, I responded that I did not care what he did with the information in my memo and walked out of his office. As it turned out, he called the superintendent, who told him we had no choice but to place these inmates on suicide watch.

On Monday the shit hit the fan, and I was the bad guy. My responses were very clear. First, I asked, did all of the psych-department staff put time-off slips in to indicate that no one would be available Friday afternoon (I doubt that), and was this common practice at Sing Sing? Second, did Rikers Island call beforehand to indicate that they would dump their suicidal patients on Sing Sing on Friday afternoon? Finally, I told them, if they were not impressed with my response, they shouldn't drop the bombshell on me at two o'clock on Friday afternoon the next time the bus arrived from Rikers full of mentally ill inmates that needed immediate attention. The head of the psych department was most unhappy with me. He assured the group that my actions were overstated and that I had overreacted (which was bullshit). I was not happy with the response of the executive team or the psych department. At that point I realized that they were more interested in the cost of keeping an inmate on a one-to-one suicide watch than the inmate's life. I also realized the psych department had no interest in working Friday afternoons—what a great job to have. I suggested that the transfer of serious mentally ill inmates should take place on Thursday and not on Friday afternoon. I must mention that this incident occurred very early on in my carrier, during the late 1970's.

The following Friday, the same thing happened. On this occasion I made photocopies of the list of inmates who should have been on suicide watch and placed it in my files. I was quick to grab a psychologist from the psych department (a clinician is a nonphysician physiologist who may or may not have a PhD in the field) who was on his way out the door for an early start on the weekend. I am being kind not to mention his name, because I still remember it to this day. The clinician felt that this was not an urgent matter that needed to be taken care of at that moment and decided the evaluation could wait until Monday morning. I looked the clinician in the eye and said, "I hope you're right." His response was bullshit.

Over that weekend, one inmate made an honest attempt to take his own life. This occurred during the correction officers' strike during in 1979. Because of the strike, I was in the facility. On Saturday, I received a call in the hospital reporting an attempted hanging. The nurse said CPR was started. With the help of National Guardsmen who were assigned to Sing Sing during the strike, the inmate was placed in a National Guard ambulance and was rushed out of Sing Sing. While receiving CPR, the inmate was taken to Phillips Memorial Hospital, a few miles south of the prison in North Tarrytown. This all happened in a matter of minutes. It was the quickest ambulance ride and the bumpiest ride of my life, and I have taken many ambulances rides in the past. The driver did not miss any potholes in the road on the way to the hospital. I told the National Guardsmen that the bumpy ride is what brought the inmate back to life again.

While I was at the Phillips Memorial Hospital emergency room, the watch commander from the prison called and admonished me for taking an inmate out of the facility without any correction officers. I told him that he had known the inmate was in very bad shape, near death, and that we were doing CPR on him. I said that I could not understand why he chose not to send any correction officers with me to the hospital. He was not amused at my attempt at humor and told me not to lose sight of the inmate until nonstriking correction officers came to Philips Hospital with leg irons and cuffs. I responded, "This guy ain't going anywhere for a while."

When I returned to the prison, the first thing I did was check my saved list for all the names of inmates who were dumped on us from Rikers Island that prior Friday afternoon. His name was one of the names on the list of inmates taken off the suicide unit at Rikers and sent to Sing Sing the Friday before. I was angry at the system and how it had failed. Thinking that I would not be working long at Sing Sing, I let the feeling go and did not complain to anyone.

Some of the medical staff were just as unmotivated as those in the psych department at that time. Often, when there was a medical crisis at Sing Sing, no doctor could be found or contacted by phone. When we had a difficult patient, I would look for the medical director or his second-in-command. Sometimes the inmate was truly sick, or he was just a demanding person. The medical director or the assistant medical director would ask me to write the inmate's name and DIN number (department identification number) on a piece of paper and give it to him. The very next morning that inmate would be on the bus headed upstate to Clinton Correctional Facility in Dannemora, New York. Clinton Correctional Facility was up the Northway at the northernmost point of New York State. Moving inmates with complicated medical needs to other facilities was referred to by many staff members as "bus therapy." The inmate's medical problems supposedly were resolved because the inmate was on the morning bus. The medical director would stop at the head clerk's office on the way out the door to give her the name of the inmate who was to be moved. The medical director only worked half days, if that, so he was able to get the names down to the person responsible for making facility moves happen early enough to get the inmate placed on the morning bus to Clinton.

Clinton was the only prison in the state and probably the nation—if not the world—that had a ski jump within the walls of the prison. Once I asked an inmate how he had acquired such a deformity of his leg. He laughed and said I would never believe him. "Of course," I said, "try me," and he went on to tell me that he had broken his leg in many places while ski jumping at Dannemora. I told him that I had never met a Hispanic ski jumper before, and we both laughed. As I asked many old-timers about the ski jump, they all laughed and told me more stories about inmates breaking their bones on the jump. Because Clinton Correctional Facility was so far from New York City—I would guess about seven hours by car and even longer by Amtrak—you never had trouble from New York City lawyers up at Clinton. What lawyer in his right mind would drive up to Dannemora to see an inmate who probably would not pay him?

On one occasion, an inmate was assigned to me to renew his Talwin order for chronic back pain. The other PA who worked at Sing Sing with me did not want to have anything to do with this convict. It was clear he was addicted to this potent opiate pain reliever. After meeting the inmate for the first time, I could understand why. He had been on Talwin for years, and I felt, as did the other PA, that he was addicted to this controlled pain reliever. He always asked for the dose to be increased. After reviewing his chart and X-rays, I thought it might be a good time to try something else, something different. I did not want this guy to go into withdrawal because he had been on a hefty dose for a long time. The convict was the most intimidating inmate and person I was ever to meet. His arms were bigger than my thighs were. If it were not for the tattoos on most of his body, he could have been on the front cover of any bodybuilding magazine.

After seeing this inmate for many months, I was able to taper him off the Talwin and put him on a medication that did not have such a highly addictive profile. It was not easy. I offered physical therapy, which was a joke to this bodybuilder, and he declined. I was proud of myself for getting this guy off addicting medication. This inmate could not be moved to Clinton because he had been placed at Sing Sing, closer to his family, because of good behavior.

Shortly after successfully switching the former Talwin addict to a new medication, I went on vacation, and my cases were covered by the assistant medical director. I didn't ever warm up to this guy much because he always seemed annoyed when I asked him a question and was always too busy to talk to me about anything. He did not want to work or be in the prison—it was clear that he hated the place. When I returned to work, a nurse I passed in the hallway smirked at me and said, "Guess who is back on Talwin again?" After all my hard work to detox the inmate, the assistant medical director had renewed his Talwin prescription. I became very angry; from that point on, I refused to see the inmate any longer. I told the nurse administrator that the assistant medical director had to renew the Talwin from then on, since he did not care if any inmate was addicted to anything.

One day I spotted this same inmate coming toward me at the end of the hall. It was months after I tried switching him off Talwin. The officer for the floor was nowhere to be found. As I previously mentioned, this guy was one of the scariest, most intimidating inmates that I have ever met in my thirty-plus years as a PA in corrections. He was big and all muscle. His head was shaved bald. As I came down the hall, he walked toward me and said, "We have to talk." I almost shit my pants.

"Of course," I said, "Come into my office."

He asked if he could close the door. He looked worried about something. He confessed that he had developed a strange rash on the shaft of his penis and thought he might have contracted some sexually transmitted disease. When I asked, he told me that he was not sexually active, nor had he been in many years while in prison. He was adamant that he was not homosexual and was angry when I asked. When I told him he had nothing to worry about because he had not had sex with anyone for the past many years, he became noticeably more anxious. He asked me to look at the rash, which I did, and I reassured him that it did not look like any sexually transmitted disease I had seen in the city clinics and hospitals where I did my training. I was still unable to reassure him that I did not think that his rash was caused by a sexually transmitted disease. He then admitted to me that he was having anal sex with a young male back in the cellblock on a regular basis, but he again reassured me that he was not a gay or homosexual man. He went on to explain to me that when a man was doing a long prison sentence, he needed to vent his sexual frustrations in one manner or another. He said that the sex was consensual and no one was hurt, but in no way did this make him a homosexual. "I ain't no fucking faggot," he said in a convincing, loud voice. With the help of a topical cream, his rash did clear.

Later on in my career, when HIV had become prevalent, I was at a medical conference in New York City. During a roundtable discussion, I informed the group of experts that a large number of patients were not being counted in the databases—namely, men who had sex with men but didn't consider themselves homosexual. This large group of men was not represented in any data collection. Since that time, history forms and data collection sheets now include men who have sex with men (but do not consider themselves homosexuals).

Back in my early days with corrections, inmates played a vital role in the functioning of the jail, fulfilling many duties that are now done by paid security and civilian staff members. Not only did they work as facility custodians (porters) and in grounds maintenance, but an inmate also compiled the count at Sing Sing. Yes, an inmate added all the numbers together for the total number of inmates at Sing Sing at a given time in the day. This number changed many times during the day, with inmates going in and out of the jail for court trips, hospital trips, and transfers in and out from county jails like Rikers. I still ask old-timers how this could have been possible.

At the time, the inmate who kept track of the count was a tall, handsome white male who always kept his clothing neatly ironed and his hair slicked back. For some reason he didn't look stupid and did act somewhat well educated. Whenever I entered the room where the count was being done, he always seemed busy doing paperwork of some type. One day I stopped a regular daytime nurse in the hallway and asked her what the story was with this inmate. I can still remember her response. The guy had been a straight-A student at Columbia Graduate School. He was not happy when a professor had given him a B when the inmate thought he deserved an A in the course. After the grad student, now an inmate, could not convince the professor to change the grade to an A, he had pulled out a gun and shot the professor to death. That was thirty years ago. I wonder what the inmate is doing now.

Inmates also ran many offices in the prison. For example, an inmate dental clerk scheduled dental appointments. It would cost two packs of cigarettes for an early appointment. When I first saw an inmate placing two packs of cigarettes on the dental clerk's counter, I thought that was very nice of him. Later in the day, after thinking about what I had seen take place earlier, I felt like a jerk for not realizing what I had witnessed. For an inmate to get anything done in Sing Sing, it would normally take two packs of cigarettes. The common phrase heard by inmates at Sing Sing was "It'll cost ya two packs." If you wanted to see a certain dentist or wanted an appointment in a hurry, you needed to tip the inmate dental clerk two packs of cigarettes. They always seemed to be Marlboros.

The biggest surprise to me was seeing inmates handling medical records. The medical records department had four or five inmate clerks pulling medical charts and filing consults and lab reports in the charts, and there were inmate health assistants who checked vital signs of medical patients. The woman in charge of medical records was bright and did a great job. She was tough as nails. Remember that she was working with four or five convicted felons and in an office down the hall from the guard. She would never put up with any nonsense from these hard-core inmates, some of whom were doing time for murder. I once made the mistake of asking an inmate health assistant what another inmate was doing time for. The inmate was very quiet and kept to himself most of the day, not speaking to anyone. The inmate health assistant looked at me, laughed, and said, "Five bodies." I thought he was joking until I asked someone down front.

The woman ran a tight ship. She kept the inmates who worked for her in line and made sure that they were on time and did what they were supposed to do in a timely manner.

Early on in my career at Sing Sing, Albany Central Office was not happy when a group of PAs told them that having convicted felons handle medical records was not only unacceptable but against the law. Shortly thereafter, inmate medical record clerks were replaced with civilians. In time, all of the inmate clerks in medical records, the infirmary, and the dental office were removed and replaced with civilian staff.

Another interesting job that an inmate could have was taking care of cats. There were cats everywhere at Sing Sing; I was told that inmates were allowed to care for the cats to keep the rat population in check. Down across the railroad track in the Tappan housing area, many inmates would tell about four-legged rats that would come up out of the Hudson River at night to feed; they said that they were as large as dogs. Prisons are full of two-legged rats.

Years later, while I was working extra service at Sing Sing late one evening, I saw something that I will never forget. I was called to the fourth floor of the hospital to see an inmate who had become severely ill and needed my attention. Getting off the elevator in the hospital, I turned left in the hall and passed a number of single rooms on the right. A kitchen and pantry were on the left side of the hallway. These rooms were used as isolation rooms or held sick inmates who were problem inmates and could not be mixed in the ward with others. These rooms had a terrific view of the Hudson River. While I was walking past one of these rooms, much to my surprise I noticed an inmate with the largest raccoon that I have ever seen in my life; it must have weighed thirty pounds. The inmate was sitting on the edge of his bed, hand-feeding the raccoon his dinner. The raccoon was sitting up on its hind legs as a dog would, begging for more food. His hospital door was wide open, as was the very large window.

As it turned out, the raccoon would climb up the four-story building using the gutter drainpipe. He would then walk along the ledge just outside the windows of the single rooms. Sing Sing was very old, and the drainpipes were built to be very strong; a large man could have climbed up the drainpipes. The ledge was about a foot wide and spanned across the entire front of the building.

I was standing in the hallway about four feet from the raccoon. I said to the inmate porter working on the floor that I was very concerned for the inmate because I thought the raccoon might have rabies. The inmate porter said that he was more concerned for the raccoon because he knew the inmate had AIDS. This occurred early on in the AIDS crisis, when no one wanted to work around inmates or with inmates who had anything that resembled AIDS. It was a scary and sad time for me as well as for all of the people who worked in medicine in general. There was an evening correction officer who worked on the fourth floor and knew this raccoon was coming up the side of the building on a regular basis. I know he was scared, not only of the raccoon but also of the inmate who was infected with the AIDS virus.

Later on during the 1980s, Sing Sing's infirmary held a number of HIV-infected inmates. Early on, many of these inmates were very sick and near death. On Christmas Eve in 1985, Mother

Teresa visited the AIDS unit in the infirmary at Sing Sing. During her tour of the facility, one of the very sick inmates asked Mother Teresa not to let him die in prison. Mother Teresa told the inmate that he would go with her that afternoon, out of Sing Sing, to Saint Clare's Hospital in New York City. I learned that a high-ranking security staff member, part of the entourage escorting Mother Teresa, turned to another security staff member and whispered, "Nothing in New York State happens that fast. What is the matter with this woman, telling an inmate he is going to be transferred this afternoon, on Christmas Eve, no less?"

Mother Teresa turned away from the sick inmate and told a high-ranking staff member to get the governor (who was Mario Cuomo at the time) on the phone. The phone was down the hall in the nursing station. From what I understand the governor took her call, and she spoke with him and asked him to furlough the inmate to her care. Because of this Christmas Eve request from Mother Teresa to Governor Mario Cuomo, three inmates suffering with AIDS were released from prison on that day. Joyce Purnick of the *New York Times* quoted Ed Koch, mayor of New York City: "When Mother Teresa calls and says she wants something done, it happens." At Mother Teresa's request, more prisoners with AIDS were later released to her care.

From the third floor of the hospital, I was able to look out the window to the Hudson River. Across the Metro-North railroad tracks was an oddly shaped building next to the water, at the south end of the prison. A large housing area called Tappan was just north of it, also along the Hudson. I asked an inmate what that building was, and he responded with a laugh at my stupid question. He said that was the Death House that had made this prison famous. He also pointed out the boat landing where inmates got off the boat from New York City to start their sentence, or their state "bid." The word *bid* is a very common term within the New York state prison system. You will see it mentioned in this book frequently. After an inmate is convicted of a crime in New York State, he is sentenced to do time, which is referred to as a *bid*. I'm not sure where the term originated. Every time an inmate is sentenced for a new crime, he gets another bid. If he comes upstate four times on different crimes or convictions, then he has four bids. This is not to be confused with coming back into the state system because of parole violations, which could bring an inmate back many times after being released on parole. Then the inmate is a parole violator or is referred to as a *PV*. Years ago, some inmates would refuse to be released on parole because the inmates did not want to deal with parole officers on the street and the strict requirements placed on them by parole officers. They would rather do their full time within the walls and *max out*, meaning serving all the time in prison without being responsible for reporting to the parole department. It is my understanding that inmates are no longer able to refuse to be paroled to the street. Another very common term in the prison system is *CR date*, or *conditional-release date*. The CR date is when an inmate can and will be released to the street under the control of what used to be the parole system in New York State.

One other term that used to be heard and is not anymore is *drop a dime*. In the old days when someone would squeal or report someone else for doing something wrong, a blue shirt or green shirt (officer or inmate) would say, "Someone dropped a dime on him." (Back in the day, there was no her.) This meant someone had placed a dime into the pay telephone to make the call squealing on someone.

There are other terms only used in the prison system that are important to mention here:

On the count: In the prison system, everything revolves around the inmates being counted. Many times a day the inmates have to be accounted for, and officers go around and count each inmate. Frequently I would hear the officers yell out, "On the count." The most frequently asked question in prison is "Did the count clear?" This means, did the numbers add up to the total number of inmates that were supposed to be in the prison? I was always amazed that the count cleared. At Downstate, which is a central transportation hub for the New York State Department of Corrections, more than twenty-five thousand inmates pass through the draft area every year. Each and every one of these inmates is accounted for multiple times a day, every day of the year. It is astounding that the count clears—that is, that the count is correct.

On the rec: I am not sure where this term originated, but all announced commands in the New York state prison world began with "on the," as in *on the rec* (recreation), meaning it was time to go outside or to the gym. Similarly, *on the count* means each inmate must stand up to be counted, and *on the sick call* means sick call is starting. The term is still being used in all New York state prisons.

On the morning boat: An expression used frequently by inmates when I first started working with convicts was that someone was *on the boat in the morning* or *on the morning boat*, meaning that he was on the transfer list to another prison in the state system. The term was left over from the days when inmates were brought up the river from New York City on a boat and transferred farther up the river on other boats. Today the term that is used is that an inmate is *on the draft in the morning, on tomorrow's draft*, or is being *drafted out*, meaning that he or she is going to another facility.

Keep lock: Whenever inmates misbehave, they are punished. For minor offenses, they are restricted to their cells, or *keep* *locked.* For more serious offenses, they are moved to "the Box," or what is called the special housing unit (SHU).

On one beautiful afternoon when I had a light sick call, I took a walk down to see the place where many inmates were put to their death. When I arrived at a locked door, an old-time correction officer let me enter to look around. He was friendly, knew who I was, knew I was coming, and was happy to answer any of my questions. Even though Sing Sing was a very large prison, everybody knew everyone else. The guard did not ask why I was there; he seemed to know. He was eager to show me around the Death House. At each room or location, he gave me a short explanation of what went on in that particular area.

The correction officer explained that each inmate on death row was assigned one correction officer to watch over him until his death. I guess the state did not want the inmate to commit suicide before the big day, spoiling the expected event. The inmates were kept in regular-type cells in the Death House, and days prior to the execution, the condemned man or woman was moved just down the hall to a padded cell. The walls of the padded cell were about twelve inches thick, covered with very thick leather, the kind of leather found on a horse's saddle. The leather was very old and cracked but not dry rotted. The thickness had to be made up of cotton or something similar, because foam rubber had yet to be invented when those cells were constructed. I am not sure what was used behind the thick leather to make the wall so spongy. This was done so the inmate would not bang his head against the walls, according to the correction officer. We had to keep the inmate alive so we could execute him.

This reminds me of an inmate I knew at Downstate, years later, who was a head banger. He would start at a far end of the dayroom, a windowed observation room in the infirmary, and make gestures like a bull in a bullfight, shuffling his feet on the floor and then running headfirst into the concrete wall across the room. I can remember that all the people who were watching would turn their heads and close their eyes when he hit the wall head-on. Later in the day, he would complain to the nurse that he had a headache. Everyone watching this guy had a headache. I could never understand why some sort of padded cells are not used today, considering the hesitancy of psychiatrists to order chemical or physical restraints to keep inmates from hurting themselves. We need to find a way to stop inmates from hurting themselves.

The officer in the Death House then showed me what he referred to as the "longest mile"—the distance from the door of the condemned man's cell to the electric chair. When I visited the Death House, the chair had already been moved and was being stored at Green Haven Correctional Facility. I am not sure where the chair is now. Many of the old-time correction officers referred to the chair as "Sparkie." When the chair was in use, it was in the center of a large room with a giant exhaust fan over it. The fan was used to quickly remove the smell of burning flesh from the room. Off to the right of the inmate was the viewing area; the electrician was off to the inmate's left in a small room that housed the electric panel and switches. Actually, according to the officer, most executions were on Thursday nights at eleven o'clock. (I know many readers of this book will check to see if this is true.) He claimed that the lights in the village of Ossining would flicker, and the locals would say that another inmate had bit the dust at Sing Sing. I learned later that this was not true because Sing Sing used its own electric power from its powerhouse just up the hill from the Death House.

I had a few quiet summer afternoons at Sing Sing when I had nobody on the schedule to see and nothing to do. On one of these afternoons, I went through the *PP and G Manual*: that is, the *Policies, Procedures, and Guideline Manual*. It was a kind of cookbook on how Albany wanted things to be done within the prisons. In the back of this very large black binder, I came across an application for reimbursement to attend professional conferences. It was an old-looking form that I doubted anyone had ever used. Thinking I had nothing to lose, I filled out the form and requested money to attend the annual physician assistant conference in New Orleans and mailed it off to the central office in Albany.

A few weeks later, I received a phone call from a person with an attitude who asked me in a harsh tone why I thought the state of New York should send me to this conference and not someone else. Thinking quickly, I asked if anyone else had applied for this conference. To that question, the answer was no. Then I responded, "Would you send someone who did not ask to attend this conference?" Then I asked if anyone else had applied to go to New Orleans. Not only did I make my point, but I also did get the money to go to New Orleans. It was a great conference, and it was my first opportunity to attend a national-level conference.

CHAPTER 4

THE STRIKE OF '79

Even though Sing Sing was a difficult place to work, the schedule allowed me to be available for my family in the evenings and on weekends. The only time a supervising MD ever called me at home back then was when the correction officers walked off the job in 1979. It was about 5:00 a.m. when the phone rang. The MD told me that the correction officers had walked out of the facility, leaving a few remaining guards, security supervisors, and civilian staff running the prison. As all of the inmates remained locked in, food had to be cooked and delivered to each of the cells. He wanted me to come in right away. I did not know what to expect and did not think that the strike would go on for a long period of time. Boy, was I wrong.

When I arrived at the prison, the sun was just coming up over the walls. New York State trooper cars, filled with four young officers in each car, flew by me on the road leading up to the main gate at the prison. Each police trooper car stopped quickly, the four doors of the car popped open, and out jumped four intimidating young troopers with their very short haircuts and their Stetson hats. I must admit I was impressed and somewhat scared. As the cars stopped, the trunks opened automatically so the troopers could grab their large black gear bags and shotguns. A ranking trooper was beginning roll call and yelling out what towers each trooper would be assigned to. Troopers were not placed inside the walls of the prison but manned each of the watchtowers. I remember them looking down from the towers with their binoculars held up to their eyes in their left hands and shotguns in their right, with the butt end of the guns on their hips. You were able to see in an instant that these guys meant business. Holy shit, I thought, this was the real thing. The front parking lot was full of trooper patrol cars.

Someone told me that because of the riot at Attica Correctional Facility a few years before, New York State troopers were not allowed inside the walls of the prison. At the end of the first day of not doing very much other than sitting around the medical department and taking care of the few emergencies that did come up, I was somewhat tired of the underlying stress. The inmates at Sing Sing seemed to be on their best behavior during the strike, and not much occurred in the way of medical emergencies or inmate fights. After twenty-four hours of not being able to leave, I began making rounds, looking for a place to sleep. I first attempted to sleep in the hospital ward. There were about sixteen beds on the unit, with nothing between each of them but a nightstand. Looking around, I saw the hospital ward was full of many sleeping correction officers, lieutenants, and sergeants. There were not many inmates on the unit, and they were at the other end of the ward. There was one open, made-up bed with new sheets near the front door, which I quickly lay down in. I told the night nurse which bed I would be using in case an emergency came up. Even though I was tired, with all the loud snoring that was going on I was unable to fall asleep. You could hear from the snoring of all the white shirts (security-ranked officers) that they were all exhausted.

After a short time I began looking for another place to sleep that was not as noisy. Opening the gate at the elevator on the second floor, where the psych department had offices, I found a quiet room. Looking further, I also found a number of aluminum cots. After placing a cot near a desk, I called the emergency-room nurse to inform her of my phone extension. This was very early in the morning, and I was tired. I took off my shoes and socks and shirt and quickly fell asleep. At some point the phone on the desk rang, and when I answered it a voice shouted, "Hang up." It took me a moment to realize that the person on the other end of the phone was the ER nurse, and he was telling me that someone has hanged himself. Putting on my shoes in a hurry, I forgot to put on my socks. The inmate who had hanged himself had no pulse, and the nurse was doing CPR. I was able to start two large-bore IVs, one in each arm, and had the inmate transported to the local community hospital. I was very surprised that the inmate lived and had no brain damage.

One day during the strike, I had to see an inmate who was allegedly sick in HBC, Housing Block C, which was the special housing unit (i.e., SHU or the box). I took along with me two New York State National Guardsmen who were assigned to me and were to escort me to the box. The three of us had to pass through Seven Block, the honor block at Sing Sing. Seven Block was a very intimidating place. The block had four floors with three catwalks, allowing access to the cells on both sides of the cellblock. You see this sort of setup repeatedly in old prison movies. There was a large television at one end of the block just over the door to the tunnel to Housing Block C.

While we were passing through Seven Building, the inmates, all of whom were locked in their cells, began yelling and catcalling at the National Guardsmen. They were yelling obscenities, some quite colorful and some humorous. After we passed through Seven Building and got to the tunnel on the other side, the two National Guardsmen were shaking, sweating, and visibly upset. I told the two that this was an honor block and that the inmates were just fucking with them. Actually I could see the expressions on the faces of the inmates locked in their cells on the lower tiers; they were only joking. These inmates had little contact with the outside world and were looking to amuse themselves. Many of these inmates worked in the hospital area, and I had had direct daily contact with them in the past. Sad to say, I kind of enjoyed their hazing. The inmates and I laughed about it when the strike was over.

During the strike, I spent a lot of time doing absolutely nothing. I was surprised how smoothly things went; the convicts were on their best behavior. We all expected the worst. I heard from the others that inmates at Clinton Correctional Facility were busy cleaning and polishing up the facility during the strike because they were afraid there would be retribution if the returning guards found the prison dirty or messy. One officer told me that he saw an inmate using a toothbrush to polish up the brass bolts that held the toilets to the floor to make them shine for the returning guards.

When I got bored during the strike, I would walk out the main gate, and through a spotting telescope I would watch striking correction officers watch me through their spotting telescopes. Some waved; some did not. After about the third day, I began to smell funky and asked a ranking officer at the command post if I could go home for a shower and some new clothing. Of course he had to check with the command post in Albany to see if it was OK to let me go home. Reluctantly I was allowed to go home, but only for a short time. Upon returning I was instructed to call the command post in the prison to request a pickup point somewhere in the local community. It seems that there had been some vandalism to cars of the people who remained or who were called back into the facility to work.

When I returned to the Ossining area, I called Sing Sing and was told to meet a man in a brown polyester suit at a local strip mall. After a few minutes of waiting on the sidewalk, I was approached by this person wearing a suit. The suit was one from a large stock that inmates were given when they finished their state bid and were returning to society. Of course that practice stopped long ago, and now inmates are only given a sweatshirt and cheap blue jeans. The man who approached me asked me my name and then called someone on a radio. I could hear him say on the two-way radio it was me. Within two minutes, a "deuce and a half" (a two-and-a-half-ton army truck)—owned by the National Guard—came around the corner to pick me up. In the back of the truck was a well-dressed older man whom I did not recognize at first. Not until we pulled up to the picket line with its shouting striking officers did I realize the person sitting with me was the superintendent of the prison. Neither of us said a word to each other; each of us could see that we both had things on our mind at that time.

The strike lasted about seventeen days. About two thousand prison guards walked off the job, leaving the inmates locked in and to be watched over by a few nonstriking guards, civilian staff, and later the National Guard and the state troopers. There was a great deal of anger and discontent among correction officers, both before the strike and for decades after. I did not realize or understand much of the hostility until after the strike. The Taylor Law made the conditions worse after the strike. The striking correction officers had to give back two days' pay for each day that they were out on strike. It took many years for the officers to pay back what they lost. All in all, having never belonged to a union or having a family member who belonged to one, this experience was an eye-opener for me. I saw friendships and families torn apart, and I witnessed a great deal of pain and anger, which lasted for decades after the correction officers went back to work. I never thought of the word *union* in the same light after what I witnessed and was a part of.

Many weeks after the strike, when I was on my way out the front door, an officer whom I did not know and had never met refused to open the main gate to let me leave the facility. At first I was caught off guard, not expecting this to occur, let alone to me. I had thought that I did not mean much to the correction officers, in the big scheme of things. The guy looked me in the eye, and in a loud voice that everyone could hear, said that I was "one of them." At that point I reached for the telephone next to the front gate to call the superintendent, not because we were friends, but because it was the easiest phone number to remember in the prison. Before I had a chance to dial the phone, another correction officer intervened and told the guy that I was not a bad guy and he should let me out, which he did.

CHAPTER 5
THE RIOT AT SING SING

Actually, the prison was called Ossining at that time, not Sing Sing, but "the riot at Sing Sing" sounds so much better. On a beautiful Sunday morning in January of 1983, about four years after I had transferred to another prison, I was still in bed when I got a call from Department of Correctional Services (DOCS) Central Office. The caller told me that the inmates had taken over B Block at Sing Sing and that I needed to go there and stand by for any medical emergencies that might arise. He said that things might get ugly down at Sing Sing, and he did not know what to expect. It is important to mention that Sing Sing had the worst of the worst inmates. As mentioned before, these guys would cut your throat on a dare from another inmate. To join a gang, an inmate had to randomly slice the face of another unsuspecting inmate. These were deep cuts, from chin to ear. I have seen a few in my career. Many cuts were so deep that these inmates had to be sent out to have their wounds closed by plastic surgeons in local community hospitals.

In the end, nineteen guards (some said seventeen guards) were held hostage for more than fifty hours. I told the person in Central Office to make sure that he called the superintendent at Downstate to tell him where I was going be. I had left Sing Sing about four years earlier and transferred to Downstate Correctional Facility.

The takeover had begun the previous night in B Block, a very large cellblock holding more than five hundred inmates. B Block cells are organized into two galleries, or rows, of cells on each of five tiers. The bottom tiers, with cell doors opening directly on the ground level, were referred to as "the flats." Cells on the flats were most sought after by inmates who claimed they could not climb the stairs to the upper tiers, or maybe they were afraid of being thrown off the upper tiers by fellow inmates. To access B Block from the main floor of the hospital, you had to pass through a locked gate, with access monitored by a guard. It was dark and dirty and very intimidating, like a scene from the early movies about the Big House.

To get to B Block, you had to pass through Seven Building, which was an honor block when I first started there in 1978. Honor blocks were populated by the better-behaved inmates in the prison. After passing through Seven Building, you would enter a tunnel to take you to A Block. Back in the day, the tunnel was not a bright place but dark, dirty, and musty. You would turn right at A Block, go through the kitchen, and arrive at the B Block gate. B Block had a tunnel that led to the back of the chapel.

The state had plans to close the maximum security prison at Ossining, but because of overcrowding in the other prisons this plan was shelved, and the state was forced to reopen the once-abandoned B Block. Today, Sing Sing is used to place inmates closer to their homes in New York City if they behaved while upstate. There was also talk of turning Sing Sing into a tourist site, as was the Eastern State Penitentiary in Philadelphia. The Eastern State Penitentiary is a big moneymaker for the city of Philadelphia.

The problem underlying the riot seemed to be inmates who had nothing to do all day long. The inmates involved were referred to as transient inmates, because they were waiting for transfer to their permanent facilities upstate. Because of this, they were not eligible for what the Department of Corrections refers to as *programming*, meaning education, arts and crafts, working on their General Education Development (GED) tests, or work duties. The inmates on B Block could be held there for as long as eight months with no programming. To make matters worse, the transient inmates were allowed fewer visitors than other prisoners. DOCS officials did not believe that the takeover was planned, and according to Louis Ganim, a DOCS spokesman, it was assumed that many of the inmates in B Block at the time of the takeover wanted no part of the confrontation. Twelve inmates left the cellblock, either for medical reasons or by jumping over a fence, according to an article written at the time by James Feron of the *New York Times*.

Transient inmates in B Block were held, or I should say *warehoused*, there as they waited for the six-hour bus trip to the reception center for the Department of Corrections at the Clinton Correctional Facility in Dannemora in upstate New York. During the riot, the first negotiations were held by telephone from the mess hall between A Block and B Block; then later they were held face-to-face through the gates that separated the mess-hall tunnel from B Block.

After hours of sitting around and doing nothing during the early hours of the riot, I began to walk around the jail. My first trip was to the mess hall and to the gate separating the rioting inmates from the rest of the facility. Later on I walked outside to the chapel and down to the tunnel where a barricade had been set up by the Orange Crush. The Orange Crush, officially referred to as the Corrections Emergency Response Team (CERT), consisted of a large group of officers trained to respond to this type of difficulty. They had been called in to suppress the riot. The Orange Crush got its nickname from the officers' orange jumpsuits. The correction officers were sitting on the floor of the tunnel with their backs up against the wall. All had helmets, and many had shotguns. It was a very quiet and somber area just this side of the barricade. Through the barricade at the gate at the end of the tunnel, I was able to see the inmates running back and forth in B Block. Many of them were carrying sticks and makeshift weapons. There was quite a bit of shouting going on in the distant B Block. I did not know what to expect.

When the hostages were released, it was through the chapel tunnel, two hostages at a time. They were wearing inmate clothing at the time of their release. I later learned that it was common practice to remove correction officers' uniforms and make them wear inmate clothing. The inmates did this so that if there was a forced takeover by the prison guards, the incoming guards would not know who the hostages were. The first thing the hostages did was quickly remove the green inmate uniforms and put on new corrections uniforms that were waiting for them in the chapel. The last hostages were released just after midnight Monday. All of the hostages appeared shaken up and tired. I know they had emotional scars that they would carry with them for the rest of their lives. A few of the hostages returned to work in the prison system, and I learned that one has returned to Sing Sing.

After the hostages were released, the inmates locked themselves back in their cells. The takeover of B Block began just before 8:00 p.m. on Saturday, January 8, 1983, and ended just after midnight on Monday, January 10, and lasted about fifty-three hours. It had been twelve years since the riot that resulted in the deaths of forty-three inmates and correction officers at the state prison at Attica. When the last of the correction officers came out of the chapel, I received a phone call from Central Office thanking me for my help and informing me that I was no longer needed at the facility. The person from Central Office told me that a fresh team of physician assistants were on their way down from Green Haven to help with the mop-up of B Block. Later in the week, I spoke with one of the PAs, who said not much happened during the cleanup.

Each inmate was locked in his cell, and the Orange Crush went cell to cell, dumping all the belongings and mattresses down from the tiers onto the flats. It created one giant garbage heap in the center of the cellblock.

Public legislative hearings later revealed that prison officials had seen the riot coming. The *New York Times* reported that the superintendent, Wilson E. J. Walters, had reported to his superiors two months before the January uprising, "We have all the ingredients for a major riot." The *New York Times* said that a senior official in the Department of Correctional Services, Francis Sheridan, had told the commissioner that "the potential for a riot at Ossining is imminent." Weekly early warning–system reports showed an increase in assaults and a rise in the number of serious grievances at Ossining. In a report presented to the then governor of New York State, Mario Cuomo, the state's director of criminal justice said that Ossining Correctional Facility was known to be a troubled institution long before the eruption of this riot.

In later years the jumpsuits the CERT team wore were changed to dark navy blue, with the extraction teams wearing black padded jumpsuits. Extraction teams consisted of specially trained correction officers used to remove inmates from their cells when they did not want to come out freely. I have read that in some states— including Texas, I think—instead of using a number of correction officers in hockey gear, correction officers would just place a very large, very mean-looking dog out in front of the inmate's cell. Just before the dog began to growl, the inmate would be informed that if he did not come out of his cell, the dog would go in. No one was ever hurt using the dog to extricate the inmates from their cells, and I understand that the dog never had to go into the cell.

CHAPTER 6
HOUSING BLOCK C—THE BOX

I was on the job for about a week at Sing Sing when I was told it was my turn to make rounds in the special housing unit (SHU), which was called "the box" by inmates and staff. At Rikers Island, the special housing unit was called the segregation unit, or referred to as "the bing" by inmates and staff. I am not sure how they came up with the word *bing* at Rikers. I recently toured the Eastern State Penitentiary in Philadelphia, which was closed in 1971, and learned the segregation unit there was called "the hole" because it was down in a cellar, with a ceiling about five feet high and no windows.

The SHU at Sing Sing was also a very dark and damp place, especially the lower tier. The box was also called HBC, or Housing Block C. The box was located away from the main prison and was off limits to regular staff and inmates. It was where they housed problem inmates and inmates in protective custody—that is, inmates who needed protection from other inmates. Severely mentally ill inmates, some of whom were on suicide watch, were kept on the bottom tier.

There was an inmate who was being treated for tuberculosis with ethambutol and was housed in the lower tier at Sing Sing for many months in a dark cell. One of the possible side effects of ethambutol is loss of vision. The inmate did not realize that he had lost his vision until he was released from the box and everything remained dark after he was moved from the box. A Snellen exam, an easy eye-chart exam, had not been done when it was required, and the inmate's vision was permanently lost. The inmate did well in court from what I was told, but I think that no amount of money is worth losing one's eyesight.

Back in the days of the Eastern State Penitentiary, when an inmate was moved to the box, a black cloth bag was placed over his head so he could not have eye contact with the other inmates on the tier. Today at Downstate, when an inmate is moved to and from the SHU, all inmates in the hallways have to turn and face the wall. This prevents eye contact with regular inmates and SHU inmates.

To get into the SHU at Sing Sing as a medical staff member, you had to call and see if you were able to make your rounds. If the officers were in the middle of something on the unit, they would ask you to call back later. The SHU had a large, very thick metal door with a small window with a slide over it; the window was opened when you rang the bell. It was the same type of sliding door seen in speakeasies during Prohibition during the 1920s and early 1930s. After the correction officer checked you out through the small window, the large door was opened. After the large metal door came a large gate. All gates were locked within the unit. To go up and down a tier, you had to wait for the correction officer to come down to open the gate. Those staff members who did not have a good rapport with the officers or were disliked by a particular officer often had to wait. There were no female correction officers working in the box at that time. I must say that it was very intimidating to me. When you first entered the unit, you passed the office where the correction officers were; then down a long hall on the left, there was a set of tiers back-to-back on the same floor. Each tier had about ten cells. On the floor below, there was another set of tiers, again back-to-back. Between the cells was a narrow walkway to allow correction officers to walk behind the cells.

Inmates with behavior problems, protective-custody inmates, and severely mentally ill inmates were all housed in SHU. They were not housed together on the same tier but were clustered on one of the four tiers. The psych patients were on the bottom floor nearest the courtyard where the inmates would have their hour of daily recreation. Many days, I remember seeing a correction officer sitting on a picnic table in the hall outside a certain cell making sure that the inmate in the cell did not hurt himself or commit suicide. This was referred to as *special watch*. Many inmates on special watch were stripped down to their underwear or stripped completely naked and had no mattress or anything else in the cell so as to prevent them from hanging themselves. Some inmates on special watch were obviously psychotic—yelling, screaming, and not making any sense at all. There were those severely mentally ill inmates whom the guards referred to as *finger painters*. They would take their feces and write on the walls, or even eat their own excrement. One question always came up: Did the inmate do this because he was truly psychotic, or did he do it to make himself appear mentally ill? As far as I am concerned, anyone who would eat his or her own feces had to be mentally ill and not in his or her right mind. I would give the person the benefit of the doubt and say he or she was crazy.

There were also inmates who threw their excrement on others, either on staff or other inmates. Old-time correction officers would tell me that in the past they would get the two-and-a-half-inch fire hose off the wall and wash down the cell walls, with the inmate in the cell, when he attempted to throw excrement. I was told that this would cure the inmates of their bad habits. It might have been tolerable in the summer months, but if an inmate chose to throw feces in January, he would be soaked with very cold water.

After the inmate and cell were hosed down, the inmate would be then moved to a new, dry cell on the tier. All of the soaked contents that were in his cell were thrown away—all of his legal paperwork, clothing, and any personal belongings he might have had in the cell. The state shop (where inmates got their clothing) was then called to get the inmate new clothes. If he were smart, he would have done the throwing when he was in a strip cell, when all of his belongings were packed up in storage. I have never seen an inmate being hosed down firsthand but did see the mop-up afterward. This cleansing would usually cure the person of this type of behavior. It did not matter if the inmate was mentally ill or not; this behavior was never repeated again by the inmate.

One morning, while I was having my morning coffee with the SHU officers, waiting for the correction officer to allow me to make my rounds, I heard a very loud banging noise from downstairs in the lower cell tiers. The noise was disconcerting to me. It was customary to have to wait until the correction officers had their breakfast before I was allowed to make my rounds. This did not upset me, as it gave me a chance to sit for a short time and take a break. At first I did not think much of the banging going on down the hall. It sounded as if someone were hitting the hull of a metal ship with a sledgehammer. The banging was constant and persisted for a long time.

I finally asked the correction officer if the plumber was on the unit making all that noise. Without getting upset or emotional, he responded that it was an inmate in the lower tier on the psychiatric side, banging his head against the wall. The cell walls were made of a solid sheet of about one-quarter-inch-thick steel. Behind the rear wall of the cell was a narrow walkway for access to the plumbing and electric service to each cell. The loud noise echoed off the steel walls. When I learned that it was a person banging his head against the wall, I began to get a headache. I was a bit upset with the officers that nothing was being done to protect this inmate from himself. When questioned, the correction officers reported that the psych department had been called, and they were waiting for a response. At this time in corrections, the medical staff were unable to physically restrain any inmate, and the psych people were very reluctant to chemically restrain an inmate. I left the unit upset and angry, but not sure at whom.

When a new person came on the tier in SHU and the inmates heard his voice for the first time, the inmates would all stick small mirrors out of their cell gate so they could look down the hall to see the new person on the block. Many, if not most, of the inmates in SHU were angry, hostile, demanding, and verbally abusive to everybody they came in contact with. Even the inmates in protective custody were demanding and had this sense of entitlement. This would annoy the shit out of me, especially if the inmate was a child molester. I did find it somewhat amusing that an inmate in protective custody would have a demanding attitude.

On my first day in SHU, an inmate let me have it: verbally abusing me, attacking everything about me—the color of my skin, sexuality, name, and education. I did not stop at his cell to talk with him but just walked past the cell down the tier. This made him more upset—that I did not engage him and chose to ignore him. This behavior went on for about three days, becoming less loud and less abusive each day. Finally he asked me in a proper tone why I did not speak with him. I smiled and laughed and said that he never gave me a chance. He tried to claim that his behavior was because he was in renal failure and it was affecting his mood and behavior. In time the two of us learned to accept each other to some extent, and he became a less hostile person and more of a person in need of help. The COs watched how I handled this difficult inmate. I guess it was some type of test for the new PA on the unit. I think they wanted to see me get cranked up.

After my first encounter with this inmate, who I will call Bill , I returned to the clinic everyone asked with a laugh if I had met him. Laughing in return, I responded by saying what a nice guy he was. I was too young, too new in the system, and too stupid to get angry. I think this made him angrier toward me. I never minded making box rounds. It never upset me or stressed me out. It was a good place to hide out away from others. Maybe I was not troubled by the box because I thought in the back of my mind that I would not be doing this for long and would be moving on to another job. Others who made box rounds would come back noticeably upset and stressed out.

The COs who ran the box kept it neat, clean, and orderly. After a while, I became friendly with the COs who ran the unit. They were always happy to see me and always asked me if I wanted a cup of coffee before making my rounds. They were a pleasant group of guys who always acted in a highly professional manner in the most difficult area of the prison.

There were a number of other prisons in the Hudson Valley that had a direct effect on me and my career, both as a person and as a professional. After my short stay at Sing Sing, about one year, I transferred to a recently built prison in Fishkill, New York, called Downstate Correctional Facility. Directly across Route 84, just south of Downstate, is an old fortress that housed Matteawan State Hospital, later known as Matteawan Correctional Facility and finally as Fishkill Correctional Facility. I did extra-service work (overtime) at Sing Sing for many years after I left. I also did extra service at the Fishkill Correctional Facility. Downstate was not built as a regular prison but as a facility to get inmates ready to return to the street—a reentry prison to get the inmates the things they would need to survive once released. That concept did not last long, and Downstate was made a reception center for the state.

CHAPTER 7
MATTEAWAN STATE HOSPITAL

The Utica Lunatic Asylum, opened in 1843, was the first state institution in New York for the insane. Of course it was in Utica, New York. Most of the patients were civil commitments, but psychiatric patients from local jails and state prisons were also mixed together. Civil patients, many of whom admitted themselves voluntarily, were looking for a tranquil environment for treatment of their mental conditions. They were housed with violent, depraved cutthroat criminals. These criminals exposed the civil patients to physical, moral, and emotional harm.

To correct the problem of mixing civil mentally ill patients with criminal mentally ill patients, New York State opened the State Lunatic Asylum for Insane Convicts in 1859. This was opened on the prison grounds in Auburn, New York, in the center of the state. The only problem with the new lunatic asylum was that it would only take in convicted persons, persons who became mentally ill while in state prisons. Inmates who were not yet convicted and were too insane to stand trial and people who were acquitted by reasons of insanity were still the Utica Lunatic Asylum's problem. This was an important early principle back in the late 1850s and early 1860s. The concept that convicted insane and unconvicted insane people should be held separately in different facilities and not mixed in the same hospital became an important building block in the treatment of the mentally ill.

Thirty-three years later, New York State opened a new facility in the village of Matteawan to accommodate 550 patients. Matteawan was about halfway between New York City and the city of Albany on the Hudson River. It was built between the Hudson River and Mount Beacon in what is today Beacon, New York. The city of Beacon was the combination of two villages in New York: Fishkill Landing and the village of Matteawan. Many different types of facilities were on the large, vast area of Matteawan. In April of 1892, the Asylum for Insane Criminals was opened. The next year, the name was changed to the Matteawan State Hospital. In 1899 the state opened another prison hospital in Dannemora, New York, on the grounds of Clinton Correctional Facility. It would hold only male convicts who had become insane while serving their sentences.

Matteawan would hold both convicted and unconvicted males and females. The Beacon Institution for Defective Delinquents, which was later renamed the Beacon State Institution, was opened on the grounds of Matteawan in 1966. Also on the grounds of Matteawan was the Glenham Correctional Facility, where inmates who were considered as having borderline normal intelligence, who had IQs of 70–85, were placed. Fishkill Correctional Facility (no relation to today's Fishkill Correctional Facility) was opened in 1972 for women considered uncontrollable. At the end of the 1970s, what is known today as the Fishkill Correctional Facility emerged. Because of the abysmal care given to the mentally ill by the New York State Department of Corrections, in a 1977 settlement of a lawsuit the state agreed that the Department of Mental Hygiene should assume the responsibility for all mentally ill inmates in the New York state prison system. This was a landmark decision, stipulating that the Department of Corrections would no longer care for psychiatric patients but the Department of Mental Hygiene would step in.

I learned a lot about the old Matteawan from old-timers who had worked there and then transferred across the highway to Downstate when Downstate first opened. When I first began at Downstate Correctional Facility, the physicians and physician assistants would make rounds three times a week as a group in the infirmary. This was done so the staff could review the weekend admissions and the PA who was going on call for the next week could familiarize himself or herself with the patients in the infirmary. Central Office wanted it to be referred to as the inpatient component or as the IPC, but the old-timers referred to it as the prison hospital.

During these rounds I became friendly with an officer named George, not his true name . George was the regular hospital officer who would be with us on rounds, locking and unlocking the large doors and making sure the inmates behaved themselves. He was old-school and did things by the book. He treated the sick inmates with respect and was always in a pleasant mood. George was around for decades; he had worked at Matteawan for a long time before coming to Downstate. George would often talk about the old days at Matteawan when he worked the psych ward. He would talk about "shit cans" and straitjackets (referred to as *camisoles* by professionals), and he referred to psychiatric medication as "bug juice," "rocket fuel," or even "jet fuel." He referred to the psychiatric inmates as "bugs" or "space cadets."

I heard that in its early days Thorazine was referred to as "jet fuel" by correction officers. I heard this name repeated by older, seasoned correctional staff. I also heard many times that an inmate was "shot," meaning severely mentally ill and in need of treatment. I didn't think much about George's stories at first, thinking that most seemed exaggerated and far-fetched. It wasn't until I became friendly with other correction officers who had worked on the psych ward at Matteawan and heard the same stories that I realized that there was some truth to these stories that George told me. For instance, George was right about the shit cans in the psych ward. Inmates were not kept in cells on the psych ward at Matteawan but in small rooms with a large solid-metal door with a small window-type opening covered with a grid. These rooms were not cells because proper cells had toilet facilities; these rooms had none. The mentally ill inmates confined to these rooms had no bathrooms to use. Instead they had what was referred to as a shit can, a number-ten can (like a very large coffee can) once used to store vegetables and sent up from the kitchen. They had no toilet paper. Inmates locked in isolation cells would be let out once a day to empty their shit cans.

The use of shit cans was brought out in a case heard by the US District Court in 1974. Valentine A. Negron et al. sued the commissioner of the New York State Department of Corrections, who was Peter Preiser at that time. The opinion of the court was given by Robert J. Ward. It is important because Robert J. Ward would come up in a later case against the Department of Corrections, *Milburn v. Coughlin*. My impressions from my readings were that Judge Ward was not a fan of the Department of Corrections or the state of New York. Robert J. Ward should not be mistaken for Benjamin Ward, who became the commissioner of corrections after Peter Preiser and who would later appear in an appeal in the case. Someone directly involved in the case once told me that Judge Ward did not believe what he heard in his courtroom about the conditions at Matteawan. He summoned his car to drive up to Fishkill to get a firsthand look. Importantly, the jury found in favor of the plaintiffs and awarded compensatory damages. (This gets better.)

Occasionally a correction officer (I think they were called prison guards at that time) would bring drinking water down the tier to each window and offer the inmate water through a straw inserted through the grid on the door.

When an inmate was on suicide watch, he was in a "stripped cell," a term I was recently told by my superiors not to use anymore. In a stripped cell, the inmate was bare-ass naked—no clothing, not even underwear. The only thing the inmate might have had was a roll of toilet paper, if he was lucky. One day when I was making box rounds in the bowels of Sing Sing's Housing Block C unit, an inmate was in a stripped cell on a cold winter morning. Because of the smell, the officer on suicide watch had all the windows open on the unit, and he sat in his state-issued winter parka on a picnic table in the corridor outside the inmate's cell, watching this inmate. To keep himself warm, the inmate had made a blanket using the toilet paper. It was a sad sight to see. I complained to the psych department, but the staff did not seem to care. It was not until a lawsuit in 2007 that prisons were prohibited from placing inmates in stripped cells bare-ass naked. The state was required to have some type of smock made up. Today the the staff refers the smock as a Barney Rubble suit, as seen in the famous cartoon series *The Flintstones.*

When I was speaking with many correction officers who worked on the ward at Matteawan, the use of straitjackets always came up. The unwritten rule was that if the correction officer on duty put an inmate in a straitjacket, it was that officer's responsibility to take him out of it. This was a problem on days the officers had off. If a correction officer placed an inmate in a straitjacket on one day and had the next two days off, the inmate would remain in the straitjacket until the officer returned from his or her days off. If the inmate had no clothing on when he was placed in a straitjacket, he would only have the straightjacket on with no underwear and would walk freely on the ward, with other inmates taking advantage of him. I hope you get the picture. I heard this story repeated on more than one occasion by old-timers and the sons of correction officers who are now correction officers.

One important development in the treatment of the mentally ill occurred in 1954: the introduction of Thorazine, a sedative. It was described as the single biggest advance in psychiatric treatment and would dramatically improve the prognosis of patients in psychiatric hospitals worldwide. Chlorpromazine, referred to by its trade name, Thorazine, was utilized at Matteawan. Thorazine did not simply sedate patients; it also led to the improvement of their thinking and their emotional behavior. Thorazine was being used in this country to treat schizophrenia, mania, and other psychotic disorders. T. Turner wrote in the *British Journal of Medicine* in 2007 that "the effect of this drug in emptying psychiatric hospitals has been compared to that of penicillin and infectious diseases." It was responsible for the deinstitutionalization of severely mentally ill patients from psychiatric hospitals.

In 1956 the numbers of inmates in psychiatric asylums began to fall dramatically. Before the use of antipsychotics, schizophrenics were considered untreatable and were housed in mental hospitals for long periods, many for years. With the advent of antipsychotics, there was now an alternative treatment that could place patients back into the community. The inventor of the new drug referred to it as a pharmacological lobotomy or chemical lobotomy. I also heard it referred to as a "chemical straitjacket" by old-timers who worked in the early wards of Matteawan. The patients were awake but sedated with no anxiety or pain.

Thorazine replaced the use of electroconvulsive therapy (ECT) and insulin shock therapy. But Thorazine had many side effects. The side effects were referred to as extrapyramidal side effects; the extrapyramidal system is the part of the nervous system that regulates posture and muscle tone. These side effects included *akathisia,* which is the inability to sit still; *dystonia,* which is a condition involving repetitive movements and abnormal postures; and

71

twisting, tremors, and rigidity. *Tardive dyskinesia,* which results in involuntary uncontrollable movements, especially of the tongue, trunk, and limbs, was another side effect related to the long-term use of Thorazine. The term "Thorazine shuffle" was used by the correction officers to describe the way inmates walked after being on Thorazine for a long time. The use of Thorazine fell from the late 1960s. Today we use what many in the prison system refer to as "Vitamin H": Haldol (haloperidol), a major antipsychotic intra-muscular injection.

Early on at Matteawan, the prison guards (today called correction officers) gave out the psychiatric medications I was told if there was a football game or baseball game on the television and the guards did not want to be interrupted, they would pour out a little more medication to sedate the inmates later in the day. In later years, nurses were hired to dispense medication on the psychiatric ward.

Because of all the inadequacies in the delivery of mental health-care needs of inmates in Department of Corrections (DOCS), the state legislature amended Article 16 and transferred care of mentally ill inmates to the Department of Mental Hygiene in 1976. Since I started as a physician assistant in the prison system in August of 1978, I missed this transition. As a result of the litigation, standards were established for the operation of special housing units, formerly called isolation cells, the box, or solitary confinement cells. One of the standards set was that a qualified medical practitioner was required to visit special housing once in every twenty-four-hour period to examine the status of the health of the inmates confined in such units. Inmates held in segregation must now be eyeballed and given the opportunity to voice medical complaints on a daily basis to a PA, doctor, or nurse. It is important to mention that this settlement did not include the psychiatric isolation cells.

These changes all took place before the state and county psychiatric hospitals began dumping sick individuals back into the community years later. It was, and still is, felt that mentally ill patients could be controlled as outpatients, treated with oral medications and loose monitoring. Many of these psychiatrically sick individuals found themselves in New York state prisons. It has been proven that housing the mentally ill in prisons is much less of a tax burden than keeping them in mental hospitals.

It has been my experience that psychiatrically ill individuals do receive decent care in the prisons. While in prison, mentally ill inmates have programs to attend at some facilities, and the other inmates and correction officers look out for these individuals, making sure that their daily needs are being met. For example, I have witnessed correction officers or inmates reporting that an inmate is not showering or not reporting for meals and acting strangely. In prison there is no rush to return the person back to the community, as can be the case in state-run psychiatric hospitals, because many prison inmates have a lengthy state bid.

CHAPTER 8

DOWNSTATE CORRECTIONAL FACILITY

One day the nurse administrator from a new prison about thirty miles north of Sing Sing called me to see if I was interested in working at a new, clean prison farther up the Hudson. The new prison was named Downstate Correctional Facility. It was built on the north side of Route 84, across from a much older prison that was once called the Matteawan Correctional Facility and is now called Fishkill Correctional Facility. Downstate Correctional Facility is frequently mistaken for Downstate Medical Center in Brooklyn, New York. Downstate was created to be a separation center for inmates who were almost finished with their state bids and in the process of being returned back to the civilian world. The nurse administrator informed me that the MD who was there was going on a long vacation back to his home country somewhere in Asia. Downstate needed someone to cover the facility. She had worked with a PA in the past and was impressed by the work that PAs did. Because the MD was going on vacation in August, the prison needed somebody soon.

After meeting her and the nursing staff in person and taking a tour of the facility, I decided I liked the place and staff. How could anyone not like a prison? I don't remember meeting the facility health-services director the day I came for the job interview; I think he might have been away already. It did not seem to matter to the nurse administrator, because I got the impression that she ran the department and was in charge of all major decisions. Both of us hit it off, and I was impressed with her and the nursing staff at the new Downstate Correctional Facility. The nurses appeared to be interested in keeping Downstate clean and in order. I got the impression that they all cared about doing the right thing. Patient care seemed to be important to all of the nurses I met. After my interview and tour of the facility, I said to myself, "I can do this for the next few years." I took the job and told the nurse administrator I would start in two weeks. I was the second PA to work in the Hudson Valley at that time. The other PA worked in the Northern Dutchess Hospital in Rhinebeck and had been well received by the community.

When the superintendent at Sing Sing got word that I was transferring to Downstate, I was called down to his office. The first thing the superintendent tried to do was to talk me out of transferring to Downstate. When I told him that I had made up my mind, he picked up the phone in front of me and called Central Office in Albany to block my transfer. Fortunately, Central Office did not respond to his demands. I think Albany Central Office was hard up for someone to cover at Downstate. I started in two weeks; the doctor was still away on a long vacation. The nursing staff did most of the work at Downstate at that time. The older nurses who had never worked with a physician assistant before were very supportive of me. They did not know what to expect of me and what I was capable of doing. They all had a great knowledge of medicine and were just a pleasure to be around. We formed somewhat of a bond.

Occasionally they spoke about the doctor, implying that he was not the easiest person to get along with and very hard to understand because of his broken English.

Downstate became a reception center instead of a prerelease facility. It took over the reception processing from Clinton Correctional Facility, six hours north of NYC. To this day it processes almost all inmates from the eastern half of the state, including New York City. A small number of minimum-security and medium-security inmates are processed at Ulster Correctional Facility in Napanoch, New York, just on the other side of the Shawangunk Mountains. The inmates processed at Ulster Correctional Facility have to be free from any mental illness, because those services are not available there, and free from hearing or visual problems. Downstate processes everybody else: maximum A felons (the worst of the worst convicted felons), the deaf and blind, and the inmates who are mentally and physically ill. During processing, each inmate is screened by the psych department and has an extensive medical history and physical done, including blood work, chest X-ray, and EKG. The inmates are tested academically and are screened for placement at a facility somewhere upstate. When it is determined that the inmate needs additional testing or special placement, he is moved to the extended classification unit, Building 1. A deputy superintendent once said that the selection process for a specific prison is as stringent as student selection for colleges. I doubt that.

I believe the average annual cost of attending a private college is about the same as the cost for keeping an inmate in a prison cell in New York State, however. I remember reading in the *Poughkeepsie Journal* that the cost to incarcerate an inmate in New York State is about $53,000 a year. I must also add that you will often read in the print media that it is cheaper to keep an inmate in prison for life than it is to execute the person because of all the legal fees, court costs, and appeals. That may not be true in Texas, however, which leads the country in executions.

Downstate is surrounded by a very tall fence covered with razor wire. A raised patrol road known as the berm runs around the outside gate of the facility with a number of posts. The prison buildings sit in a valley inside the berm. The facility itself is made up of five main buildings: four housing buildings and the central core building, which houses administrative services and is known as Building 5. Buildings 2 and 3 house general-reception inmates who receive standard classification procedures. Building 1 is dedicated to extended classification. The building with the extended classification unit also houses the special housing unit (SHU), also called the box, as well as protective custody (PC) and a gallery where the mentally ill are clustered together. The gallery for the mentally ill is referred to as the "forensic diagnostic unit" (FDU).

Building 4 houses the cadre inmates who cook, clean, cut the grass, and work in the libraries. The cadre population is more stable, composed of inmates who keep the facility running. Cadre inmates work in the draft area, lawn and grounds, the maintenance shop, and the kitchen. Some have referred to the cadre inmates as civilian inmates, because they tried to disassociate themselves from the reception inmates. At one time the cadre inmates were specially selected for Downstate; they were healthy, with no psychiatric issues, and eager to work. Today's placement of inmates in Building 4 is a lot more lax.

Upward of thirty-three thousand inmates (yes, I said thirty-three thousand) passed through the draft area in a year during Downstate's busier time in the 1980s. Today the number is about twenty-five thousand. Fewer than ten thousand are new reception inmates, and a few thousand are parole violators. Both of these groups require extensive medical workups.

Downstate is also a transportation hub. Thousands of inmates pass through Downstate each year. Any inmates in the state who need to go to New York City for court pass through Downstate and are held there until the Rikers Island bus takes them back down to the city. The Rikers buses drop off a load of inmates in the morning; the Rikers correction officers have lunch at a local eatery, pick up a new load of different inmates at Downstate, and then return to Rikers. For an inmate to be transferred from one facility to another, the inmate also has to pass through Downstate. I have seen inmates who are coming from Attica, on the western side of the state, and going to Clinton, on the north end of the state, pass through Downstate.

One morning the draft nurse approached me and said an inmate from the Suffolk County Jail had incomplete medical records. I called the jail, and a wise guy of a correction officer said he would not fax me the proper medical records without a signed medical release from the inmate. I told the correction officer the inmate was still in Suffolk County custody in the bullpen. He nastily responded, "You don't understand; I will not fax you any medical records without the inmate signing a release form." I told the officer to hold on and shouted out not to release the Suffolk bus, because we needed to send an inmate back to Suffolk for incomplete medical information. Hearing this, the wise guy changed his tune.

Many of these inmates do not find out where they are going until they get to Downstate, and once there, they will do anything to stay at Downstate. Faking illnesses, swallowing foreign objects, and attempting to hang themselves are all common occurrences with transient inmates. This is all labor-intensive and time-consuming for the medical staff. When many inmates find out that they are going to a SHU 200 facility upstate, where they will be locked in a cell 24-7 with another inmate, they get what is called the Downstate flu, or the Upstate flu, an illness they claim makes them too sick to get on a bus.

Many inmates put things into their rectums to make the "boss chair" go off. A boss chair can sense if a foreign metal object is in a person's rectum. Before the boss chair was available, an inmate was stripped naked and placed on a "shit watch," and his stool was checked by a correction officer after each bowel movement. More than one inmate has told me that he inserted some metal into his rectum so he would not be transferred to a facility like Upstate or Five Points Correctional Facility. Some facilities don't care if the boss chair goes off; they just isolate the inmate from other inmates and inform the next facility that he has something in his rectum.

The draft area is a large secure holding area where inmates come into Downstate from other jails and prisons, and it is where they leave from. It is a very busy place with controlled confusion, requiring the meticulous processing of the worst society has to offer. At the end of the day, the count must be correct. The number of inmates who come in must equal the number of inmates who go out. Inmates are shaved, showered, and interviewed by the psychiatrist and a medical nurse. The officers do not tolerate nonsense from the inmates in this area. There is not enough time, and there are too many people, to put up with inmate bullshit. Problem children (inmates) are quickly removed from large holding areas, called bullpens, and placed in small, isolated rooms. Inmates who have funky rashes or appear to be very sick are also quickly isolated. The draft area smells like the worst locker room one could imagine. With many inmates moving in and out of the draft area, showers going, and staff processing inmates, it is not a nice place to spend eight hours of the day.

My days at Downstate have always been split between initial medical assessment of new inmates and sick-call services to inmates who have already been processed. If I get to sick call early, see everybody, take care of my outside consults (inmates who need care we are unable to provide in-house), and get my prescriptions turned in to the pharmacy and they are legible, I show up in the square area for an afternoon of inmate physicals. The square is the center core building at Downstate where much, but not all, of the processing is done for the medical, psych, and dental departments. Every new reception and parole-violator inmate has a battery of medical testing done. At noontime, the mental-hygiene department screens all incoming inmates. Every inmate is interviewed by a clinician, who may be a psychologist or a social worker. This is the second time in a short period of time that someone from the mental-hygiene department interviews the inmate. All inmates are interviewed twice: once in the draft area within hours of arriving at Downstate, and again the next morning by a nurse doing a complete history.

Often, when inmates got into trouble at other facilities involving altercations with other inmates or with correction officers, they would be snatched up and brought directly to Downstate—often to the box. This was done to get them out of harm's way of future attacks by others. Many times these inmates would show up in the SHU with noticeable injuries, without any medical records, and requiring (and in most cases demanding) care and follow-up. The inmates were taken out of the facility so quickly—snatched up, as we say in the prison system—that there was no time or staff available to pack up their medical records or to do anything about their injuries. It seems to me, in my many years of experience, that the worse the inmate looked with the obvious signs of physical trauma, the less he complained to me about being involved in an altercation. The more vocal he was and the more complaining he did, the less noticeable his injuries were. Either case required lengthy examination, documentation, and possibly X-rays, and many times pictures had to be taken by security to document what did or did not occur. I always liked pictures to prove or disprove alleged injuries. This was done to protect everyone involved.

For the most part, Downstate had few inmate-on-inmate or inmate-on-staff altercations in my early years. In places like Green Haven or Shawangunk, inmates were always going off. Again, this was time-consuming and would tie up the emergency room and take me away from the reception process, which some people did not understand. It always appeared that managment was more interested in the processing of inmates and transferring them to their appropriate facilities upstate than in treating alleged injuries. This always changed when someone in the front-office staff had to go to Foley Square to testify on the stand in federal district court.

At 1:00 p.m., whichever PA, NP, or MD is not busy finishing up his or her sick call or dealing with someone in the emergency room will show up in the square to start doing physical examinations on the new draft. We usually do anywhere from forty to sixty physical exams a day. The work is spread out among the staff, which, on a good day, includes four physician assistants, one nurse practitioner, and one doctor. On a bad day, it could be only one or two practitioners trying to do as many as sixty physical exams. We start at 1:00 p.m. sharp, and the rooms are last filled up with inmates at 2:30 p.m. The inmates are stripped down to their boxers and socks and are waiting to be examined. The history is reviewed, the inmate is asked a few questions about his past health, and then we do a quick physical exam.

What slows us down are frequent interruptions, either from the ER, pharmacy, infirmary, or the draft nurse. I often find that I become distracted in my thoughts and writing when charting. Many times on the way home from work, I wonder if I entered important medical information on the inmate's chart when I was interrupted. Sometimes I would get angry and tell the person to stop talking until I finish my writing and look up to them. Everyone is very interested in finishing his or her work and getting out on time. Many days we do not finish, and the work backs up and has to be done on another day. The physical is a quick snapshot of the physical condition of the inmate. It is not very long and not very comprehensive.

When Downstate was first opened, the cellblocks were called *pods*. I guess it was to bring the prison culture into the twenty-first century. I bet *Star Trek* had something to do with that. When an old-timer correction officer became the deputy superintendent for security, he made it a point to change the names back to *cellblocks* and *galleries*. He would correct anyone at meetings or in the hallway who used the term *pod*.

There was a time when corrections ran their version of Con Air (convict airways). A few times a year, the state would bring all the illegal aliens in the Department of Corrections to Downstate. It was all kind of secret stuff. On a given Sunday night, in the wee hours of the morning, the illegal-immigrant inmates would be bused over to Stewart International Airport in Newburgh for a chartered plane flight back to their home countries in South or Central America. The nurse working the weekend and the PA on call would be told ahead of time that in no way, shape, or form would these inmates remain at Downstate. If they were near death, threw themselves down a flight of stairs, or did anything not to get on the plane, we were not to get involved; security would handle it. Con Air did not go on for long, for reasons unknown to me.

Older prisons such as Attica, Dannemora, and Sing Sing were built like castles, made to last forever. You can see that castle appearance when passing through Sing Sing on a Metro-North train. You can look up at the large, thick walls of the old prison—very intimidating, very impressive. Downstate was just slapped together in a hurry, and it didn't stay looking new for long. The company that built Downstate went belly-up and declared bankruptcy before, or shortly after, Downstate was completed. The buildings began falling apart even before the place was inhabited by inmates. Two of the four core buildings were even condemned before the prison was opened. The foundation was not poured correctly, which caused the floors to sink. The roofs in Building 1 and Building 3 began to cave in on themselves. Giant beams had to be installed across the roofs of the core buildings to pull up the sinking roofs, and the floors had to be repoured with concrete to raise the level of the sunken floor.

Temperature regulation was also a problem in the beginning. While the old prisons were overbuilt with electric plants and steam plants to produce much more power than the facility would need, Downstate gets its steam to heat the entire prison from Fishkill Correctional Facility. The heat is piped under Route 84. The officers' workstations in each gallery, commonly referred to as "the bubble," were very hot in the summer and impossible for anyone to stay inside for long because of the heat. Air conditioners were later installed in each bubble, which made the conditions somewhat bearable.

Downstate was a new, clean prison farther up the Hudson in beautiful Fishkill, New York. When it was first built, Downstate was full of many seasoned officers who were high on the state seniority list and who wanted a fresh start in a new prison. Because of the state seniority ranking on work assignments, referred to as *work bids*, a correction officer needed to be on the job for more than fifteen years to get a weekend-off work assignment. To accept a promotion as a sergeant or lieutenant, a correction officer would have to accept an assignment at a prison much farther away, usually working the most undesirable shift at that prison. He would then begin transferring to facilities closer to Downstate when positions became available. Working with seasoned officers made my life a lot easier. Officers with many years of experience did not take crap from the inmates; they kept the facility clean and spotless. Having worked within the walls of other prisons, the correction officers knew how to handle potentially serious situations and defuse inmate hostilities.

In the early years, the correction officers did not warm up to me or the medical staff. Our role in the prison had not yet been defined. Many felt that we were there only to help the inmates and that security took a back seat to medical. This opinion later changed, and a close working environment developed between the medical and security staff. Many of the nurses were married to officers or were related in some other fashion. This was very common in the prisons that were way upstate. The joke was that in the old days, everybody was related to one another in prisons such as Clinton Correctional Facility. If you got into an altercation with one guard in the morning, his father or brother would be the guard on the same tier in the afternoon. If during the altercation you needed to go to the medical department, the nurse taking care of you could be the guard's wife or sister. I heard a story, and maybe it is not true, of an inmate who claimed he was thrown down a flight of stairs by correction officers at Clinton. When he got to the local community hospital emergency room, he reported to the doctor that he was thrown down a flight of stairs. The ER sheet, however, reported that he tripped and fell down the stairs. The ER doctor was directly related to the correction officer involved in the incident. These relationships with the locals were not seen as much at facilities in the southern part of the state.

Early on, when Downstate was not yet fully operational as a reception center, the then deputy superintendent for security drove his own car up onto the berm in the hope of catching a correction officer sleeping on his post. When he approached the first post, he was greeted with a revolver pointed at his temple. It was a warm summer evening after a rainstorm, and his window was down. He identified himself as the deputy superintendent for security at the prison. He was then asked in an unkindly fashion to get out of his car and lie facedown on the ground. He explained to the officer that his ID was in his back pocket, and that would clear things up. He then was told a second time to get out of his car and lie facedown on the wet, muddy ground. When backup arrived, the officer did find the superintendent's ID in his back pocket. The officers helped him up and brushed the mud off.

On a good day at Downstate, if we are fully staffed, with no PAs, MDs, or NPs out sick, on vacation, or in training, I am able to start sick call early. I am fortunate that the X-ray technician pulls my sick-call charts very early in the morning. She does not have to do this, but it is a great help to me and to the staff. I try to get in to work about 6:30 a.m.

Many times I am greeted by the night hospital correction officer or the night nurse with a request to clear an inmate for the draft—in other words, to clear him medically for the bus ride to his next facility. Out front, near the bus sally port, buses and state vans line up as they do at the Port Authority bus terminal on Forty-Second Street in New York City. Buses going upstate leave early in the morning, many before seven o'clock. Some inmates are held in the infirmary overnight because they were not able to make the long walk back into the facility housing areas. Often inmates just don't want to be transferred to their next facility and will fake some illness. When they learn that they are being transferred to a facility that has double bunking, they will do whatever it takes to remain at Downstate. They will fake a seizure, complain of chest pain or shortness of breath, or just claim they are unable to walk to the draft area to get on the bus. After going to the trouble of locating their medical records and determining that this is a common occurrence with this particular inmate, we then place him on the bus. Years ago, if an inmate refused to get on the bus, he was carried and placed in the front seat of the bus. Today, in kinder and gentler corrections, if the inmate makes a big fuss, the bus leaves without him. At some point in the near future, he is either placed on the next bus out of Downstate, or if he turns out to be a bigger problem, he is transported upstate by state van.

Getting out to sick call on time is sometimes difficult. Last week as I was getting ready to leave, a nurse stopped me in the hall and, with a grin on her face, announced to me that we had a slight problem. An inmate was standing at the end of the hallway by himself away from everybody, covered from head to toe with chicken pox. It was one of the worst cases I have seen. The bullpen was over-crowded; I said to the nurse that I hoped that he had not been mixed in with the inmates in the bullpen. She was a great nurse and had picked up on the fact that he was contagious. She had had him stand down the hall, away from the other inmates. Then she smiled again and said, "We have another problem. The hospital is full, and we do not have a place to hold him." As I was working to find an isolation room for this inmate, the ER nurse came up to me with a smile and said, "We have another problem." A transient inmate from Upstate Correctional Facility, who was just passing through Downstate for a medical visit at Coxsackie Correctional Facility, had swallowed a large number of Benadryl tablets.

When I walked into the ER, I could see by the look on the in-mate's face that he had overdosed on something. When I questioned him, he admitted that he had taken twenty Benadryl tablets, but he was not sure of the strength. When I asked him where he got the Benadryl tablets, everyone in the ER chuckled or laughed. I knew that I had not written any Benadryl prescriptions for anyone in the SHU recently and that inmates in the SHU were limited to how many pills they were allowed to have in their cells. The inmate announced in a loud voice that he had brought the Benadryl in from the facility he was transferred from. I turned to the correction officer and asked why the pills did not turn up when the inmate was strip-frisked. The correction officer laughed and told me to ask the inmate. I turned and looked at the inmate, who said the pills had been up his rectum. I responded back to the inmate, "I hope the pills were wrapped in plastic."

Jokingly, the correction officer said, "We do not check the trunk on incoming inmates." One of the other PAs who was on duty took over this case and sent the inmate to the local hospital while I took care of the chicken-pox patient.

As it later turned out, while at the outside hospital, the inmate who had overdosed complained of stomach pain, and an X-ray indicated that the inmate had also placed a long nail, which had been inserted in a pen sleeve, into his rectum. Days later when I saw the inmate again, he told me in front of the psychiatric team that he would do whatever it took—swallow anything, place anything in his rectum—to keep from being returned to Upstate Correctional Facility. I suggested to the team that he be kept in a stripped cell under close observation until he was transferred out of Downstate. I did not take the time to inquire why he did not want to return to Upstate Correctional Facility. Not uncommonly, when an inmate knows that he is going to Upstate, he will do something stupid that will keep him at Downstate. I think that this has to do with the fact that inmates do not want to be double bunked in a SHU cell.

After cleaning the morning transfer messes, I review and organize my charts and then head over to the box for SHU rounds. At 7:00 a.m. most inmates are fast asleep, so stupid requests by the inmates are limited. Demands for shower slippers, shampoo, and body lotion are not heard. My presence on the unit is now announced on the loudspeaker. I make it a point to see the inmates who submitted sick-call slips the night before. Most are for medication renewals. Inmates in the box are only allowed to have one week's supply of medication to prevent overdosing. Years ago when I was doing box rounds at Fishkill and Sing Sing, inmates would demand sleeping pills, especially Dalmane. The psych department refused to order sleeping pills, which was a smart thing.

When I get finished with the problem children (inmates) in SHU, I then go on to check my mailbox for abnormal labs or consults that need to be addressed, and then I check the computer for e-mails or consults that have been pending. All outside medical consults and requests for special procedures are reviewed by a third party. If additional information is needed, this individual will send it back to the person who requested it for further comments. If the person reviewing the consults deems the consult not appropriate or not indicated, he or she will deny the request, which sends it to a higher-up authority in the Department of Corrections for review. The system works very well, as far as I am concerned.

In the early days of Downstate when it was just opened, during a building inspection an inspector asked why there were no emergency battery-operated lights in the hallways and stairs. The man in charge of buildings and maintenance responded that because we had two generators, there was no need for backup lights in the facility. After that comment, the inspector asked that the backup generator be started. Both generators would not start, so the inspector requested that backup battery-operated lights be installed throughout the prison. Since that inspection every week at Downstate we have a generator test done.

PART 2

Formative Years

CHAPTER 9
EXTRA SERVICE

Now I have to say in retrospect that I did enjoy my work and am glad that I stayed on with the Department of Corrections. The work is challenging, there is always something new to learn, and there is never a dull moment when you deal with convicted felons. The most important lesson I have learned is to treat those who need to be treated, not those who demand to be. Many, if not most, sick-call slips, pieces of paper requesting to be seen by a PA or MD, start out with the inmate stating that he wants something: "I want my hernia fixed," "I want Accutane for my acne," "I want my ACL repaired."

More importantly, as I recently explained to a new PA who was starting his career with corrections, the first and most important thing is to assess the level of intelligence of the inmate you are trying to help. You must look him or her in the eye and see if he or she comprehends the questions you are asking. The inmate may be academically or emotionally challenged, there is a good chance he or she may be mentally ill, or he or she could be attempting to manipulate me or the system to get something he or she doesn't require. I told the new PA that you do not get any points for cranking up stupid or mentally ill inmates. It's the demanding, slick, manipulating convicts that you get credit for cranking up. A perfect example was when a returning parole violator began to get angry with me on his first day back in the system. He wanted me to submit an orthopedic consult to get his knee ACL repaired. When I told him it would be considered at his permanent facility, he became angrier with me. I clearly explained to the inmate that Downstate was a reception center and what could be done for him during his short stay at Downstate. In a loud voice he said, "You told me that bullshit last time, and it didn't happen."

I then asked him how long he was out on the street this time; his response was about three years. "What did your doctor on the street suggest?" I asked him. Of course, his response was that he had been too busy to see a doctor on the street, and he did not have insurance. Then I began to walk out of the office, and he became louder, and others in the waiting area could hear him. He complained that he was unable to walk, especially up and down stairs, because of severe knee pain.

At that point I began filling out a physical restriction form. The inmate asked what I was doing, and I informed him that he would no longer need to walk up and down stairs because his meals would be delivered to his cell. He then asked, "What about the yard and the gym?"

My response was that going to the gym and yard required climbing stairs, and I didn't feel comfortable with him in the gym playing basketball or yard playing softball with his unstable knee.

"How long will this last?" the inmate asked, and I responded, "Until you see the orthopedic doctor at your permanent facility."

In the past, many practitioners did not want to work with demanding, hostile, and violent inmates. The state had to rely on foreign-trained doctors who had difficulty with the English language, or on unlicensed doctors. The practice of hiring unlicensed doctors ended when physician assistants became more common and less expensive then physicians.

Because of the shortage of medical workers, there has always been overtime available, also called "extra service," which is working in other prisons where they could not hire PAs. There are always hiring problems in the prisons where the inmates are the nastiest and the most demanding. The neediest and most labor-intensive convicts are housed in the special housing unit or in protective custody. Inmates in protective custody seem to think they did nothing wrong and that the state owes them. After working awhile in protective custody, you can get the sense of what the inmate is there for—who are the snitches and who are the molesters.

Early on in my career, a small group of medical personnel from Downstate would travel down to Sing Sing a few evenings a week to do physicals and cover the emergency room. Two registered nurses, another PA, and I would go down a couple of nights a week. This would cut down on the number of outside medical emergency trips. This was during the "slice and dice" period in corrections. As I mentioned before, for a convict to get into a gang, he had to slice the face of another inmate at random. To do this the inmate would place half a razor blade lengthwise between the second and third finger of his right hand. Looking at the hand with the fingers tightly together, it was hard to see the razor between the fingers. Walking by some other inmate sitting in a chair or on a bench, he would move his hand up the side of the inmate's face. In one clean sweep, the inmate would place a large, gaping slit in the side of the victim and then let the razor go flying down the hall, dayroom, or courtyard, many times never to be found. This was done so quickly that the inmate sitting in the chair usually reported he did not feel the cut; only when he saw the blood dripping down his shirt did he realize he was hurt.

The cutting left many young and old inmates with very large facial scars that can still be seen in all prisons today. When they came to the prison emergency rooms, they were a bloody mess. Many lacerations took hours to close. Remember that this cutting was done at random. Some lacerations were so deep and long that the inmates had to be sent out to the local community emergency rooms. I can remember one night when the local emergency-room doctor wanted nothing to do with an inmate with a very large, very deep cut up the right side of his face. The doctor insisted that I close the wound up at the facility and not send him to the ER. I explained at length that it was obvious that the salivary duct was cut and that it needed a proper repair that I was incapable of doing. Not suturing the salivary duct properly would let saliva flow down the outside of the person's cheek every time he smelled food. I sent the inmate to the hospital; I am not sure what the outcome was.

I can remember one busy evening on the third floor at Sing Sing when the other PA I was working with was just about to start a physical on an older inmate. I heard the inmate announce to the PA in a loud and pompous voice that he was a physician. In a louder, more pompous voice, the PA responded, "You ain't no physician; you're a piece of shit. You were convicted of murdering your wife, and then you tried to leave the country with your nurse and a black bag full of money." (The convicted MD had been stopped while boarding an international fight out of the country with his nurse and his doctor's bag full of cash.) The nurses working outside in the hallway and I heard all of this, looked at one another, and just laughed. He was well known in the prison system for his crime and for providing second opinions to other inmates on the gallery. Sometimes inmates would come to sick call with notes from this guy telling the PA or the MD what needs to be done.

On more than one occasion, the group of us four medical professionals was turned around and told to return home. This would frequently happen at the last minute; we were informed that we were unable to work at Sing Sing that particular evening because of a security issue. Either the count did not clear (all the inmates were not accounted for in the prison), the facility was locked down because of some sort of gang violence, there was a missing key ring, or there was just a shortage of correction officers, resulting in nobody being there to work with us.

When the extra service at Sing Sing dried up, Fishkill Correctional Facility called asking for someone to make box rounds five days a week. Again, box rounds required an MD or PA to visit all inmates in protective custody (PC) and in the special housing unit (SHU). The inmates were held in special housing because of their behavior; protective custody is self-explanatory. As I said before, inmates in PC and SHU tend to be demanding and nasty, and some are verbally abusive. No one wanted to work with or treat this group of inmates.

I worked at Fishkill for a long time doing extra service. I made rounds on the SHU and PC for many years, and much later in my career when the new SHU 200 opened, I made rounds on that unit. SHU 200 was a specially constructed prison for problem inmates. Early on, while making my visits at Fishkill, I noticed that a lieutenant was following me around and paying attention to what I was doing. When I walked on the unit, I would announce that I was making sick-call rounds by yelling "On the sick call!" down the very long corridor.

Walking down the hall, I would look into the small window on each cell door. Most of the inmates were young and demanding. Many demanded shampoo, dry-skin lotion, shower slippers, special custom-fitted boots, or sleep medication. For the most part, I went up and down the long hallway denying most of their requests, referring them to the commissary. Occasionally I would have an inmate take off his shoes or his shirt for a quick examination, but for the most part, very few had legitimate medical concerns. Those who needed their medications renewed were taken care of on the unit; some needed to be placed on a medical callout to be seen at a later date in the clinic by an MD or PA.

After I was finished making my rounds, the lieutenant informed me that because of inmate complaints, he was asked by the front office to observe me on my rounds. Inmates were complaining that I was not giving them what they demanded. With a smile on his face, the lieutenant told me "Nice job" when I was finished, and he also told me that he would include in his report that I was doing what was required in a highly professional and proper manner.

I continued to work at Fishkill at the new SHU 200 when it opened. In the SHU 200, inmates were locked in a cell with another convict for an entire day, with limited contact with people other than their bunkies (cellmates). When it was time for the inmate to have his mandatory hour of outside recreation, the console correction officer would announce on the cell speaker that in five minutes, the door to the recreation pen would be open, so inmates should get ready. The officer who opened the doors and turned on the showers was away in a distant location, watching everything on a closed-circuit television. The pen was a small cage that was attached to the back of the cell. Inmates in cells next to each other would not rec together, so there was little in the way of communication between two inmates. When the rec hour was up, the door was reopened for the inmate to return to his cell. Food was passed through a small opening in the door.

The inmates had very little contact with others. A nurse would make daily rounds, eyeballing each inmate. If the inmate had to come out of the cell, a sergeant had to be present, along with an officer, at all times. Having a sergeant present whenever an inmate was taken out of a SHU cell was a must; an inmate might fake an illness and then jump the officer if he was alone. All contacts were recorded on video cameras that were everywhere. This type of segregation had an important direct effect on violent attacks on staff and on other inmates. After the SHU 200 opened, the instances of inmates slashing one another's faces dropped dramatically, and the occurrence of inmates throwing food or bodily waste on staff also went way down. SHU 200 seemed to work.

Inmates were afraid not only of the isolation but also of being locked in a cell with some sociopath, a psychotic person, an inmate who was racist, or a transgender inmate. A nurse once told me that word got out that a mentally ill inmate had killed his bunkie by beating his head into the floor by holding his ears in each of his hands. Because the sergeant on duty was at the other end of the building (mind you, these building are very large, very long), all the correction officer could do was watch through the window while one inmate beat the head of another inmate into the floor until he died. Word has it that it was a bloody mess. Imagine being in a cell with a very big and ugly murderer who did not like your snoring. Bunkies frequently fought each other when SHU 200 first opened up. I am not sure what the incidence of inmate-on-inmate violence is now.

Because of the isolation in the new SHU 200, suicides have increased, but I must say the state has taken many steps to minimize the suicide risk of these inmates. They are evaluated before they go into a SHU 200, and rounds are regularly made by the mental-hygiene staff.

The second most important deterrent tool that was instituted for inmates who would throw human waste or food at staff was the loaf diet. Most everyone has heard that the worst of the worst inmates in prison were fed bread and water. To this day, inmates who assault staff or throw feces or urine at staff are fed what is popularly called a loaf diet but formally known as a deprivation-ordered diet. This is a tool used by the Department of Corrections infrequently. While working in the new SHU 200 a few times, I was asked to review the medical charts of inmates who were going to be placed on the loaf diet. The loaf diet was another method to punish an inmate when all other forms of punishment failed. I was told a PA or MD needed to check the inmate's medical records but did not get to approve or disapprove the diet. Because the majority of the inmates who would be getting the loaf diet were young, healthy men, there were few reasons why they could not be on the diet. The loaf diet consisted of a loaf of bread with many different vegetables, such as cabbage, baked right into it. It was baked on-site at Fishkill Correctional Facility. From what I was told, it had all the daily requirements for calories, proteins, carbohydrates, and vitamins all baked into one loaf of bread. The loaf was given to the inmate first thing in the morning and was meant to be his breakfast, lunch, and dinner. No juice or milk was given to inmates on this diet; they only had the water out of their sink to drink. I don't remember inmates being on it for a long period of time. Staff who tried the loaf said it did not taste too bad. Some people said it even tasted good after you toasted it and put butter on it. I tried many times to get a loaf to take home to my sons for them to experience, but I was not allowed to. To this day, someone in the New York state prison system is feasting on the "loaf."

While I was doing box rounds at Fishkill early in my career, I received one of those Central Office phone calls that I hated. Because of staff shortages, a PA needed to make rounds on Cellblock 1A at Green Haven protective custody. At the time I could use the extra money, so I said sure, but it would have to be done at 6:00 a.m. each morning because in the afternoon I was making box rounds and PC rounds at Fishkill. The regional medical officer from Central Office said that all the inmates would be sleeping at that hour; could I come after making rounds at Fishkill? I really did not want to drive out to Green Haven late in the evening, so first I told him that the *PP and G Manual* (*Policies, Procedures and Guidelines Manual*) did not stipulate when, meaning what time of the day, box rounds had to be made; it just said that they had to be made once in a twenty-four-hour period. I told him I would make it work at 6:30 a.m. He agreed because he was hard up for staff.

Inmates on A1 were informed the night before that if they needed to be seen, they should leave a note on their cell door and I would make sure to wake them up on my rounds. Most problems that I handled were medication renewals. Inmates would leave their empty medication bottles on the cell door, and I would renew the medications for them. If they needed to be seen, I would place them on a medical callout later that day. The system worked well because most of the inmates in protective custody at Green Haven were older, more seasoned convicts, unlike the young punk inmates on Cellblock O+P and Housing Unit 4-2 at Fishkill.

Very early one morning when I was getting to the end of the gallery of the cellblock on A1, in the last cell on the left, a young inmate was standing butt-ass naked, apparently waiting for me to come by. Not only did this inmate have a penis that he appeared to be proud of, but he also had a set of very large, perfect breasts that he was also very proud of. I must admit I did not expect to see that, early that morning. The inmate was very eager to see my reaction to him standing there butt-ass naked. My lack of response angered him. He shouted out, "People pay a lot of money to see this in New York, you know!" I guess people in New York pay to see a man with large breasts.

Staffing in corrections was difficult early in my career when the pool of PAs was limited. It was hard to find health-care providers to work in the Department of Corrections, especially at Green Haven. One program that was tried was offering PA students money to pay for their college tuition if they would sign on to work for the Department of Corrections. I was involved early on in the program, interviewing the students. The interviews were done at the newly built Downstate Correctional Facility, where there was a happy group of PAs and MDs. The MDs enjoyed teaching and working with PAs. Downstate was a great environment to work and to learn in, with a lot of support from a great team of doctors, nurses, and other PAs. As it turned out, the Department of Corrections took all students who applied; none were refused employment. There was an interview process to be accepted into this new program. DOCS needed and wanted warm bodies. The students were led to believe that they were specially selected after a review of their applications and an interview. As I later learned, anyone who applied was accepted, regardless of their application or interview.

What I began to see was that upon graduation, these students were placed at Green Haven Correctional Facility, one of the most notorious prisons in the nation. To me it was clearly a bait and switch. Interview these new, young students at a beautiful new facility with supportive staff, and then assign them to Green Haven, which was a dingy, very intimidating prison. It was a very dangerous place to work. The people who worked there did not want to be there, let alone watch over and be responsible for a new, insecure PA. When I figured this out, I did not want to have anything to do with this program. Not only did the doctor at Green Haven dislike midlevel practitioners; he also did not have the time to teach or give them the support they really needed. I do not fault the Green Haven medical director for his feelings. Green Haven was a very busy place, with very sick inmates and a lot of bloody trauma. Later on in my career, I became close friends with the medical director at Green Haven. I was able to better understand his attitude toward new practitioners and realize that Green Haven was not the place for them. After many lengthy conversations with this man, many during lunch, I felt that he was one of the best educated people I ever met. He was a pathologist for many years before taking the directorship at Green Haven and was trained by Jesuits. He has since retired to Florida. I still miss the discussions we had about medicine and religion.

When Central Office found out that I was backing out of the program, I received one of the nastiest phone calls from Central Office that I've ever received. There was shouting and some name-calling. My response was clear and unemotional. I told Central Office that I did not want to be part of their bait-and-switch program. I explained that I was interviewing students, many female and hard up for cash to pay for their college tuition. They were interviewed at a facility that was new and clean, with a great support staff, especially for new PA graduates. Once they signed on to the program, they found themselves in one of the worst prisons in the nation. Green Haven was old and dirty, and it was not made clear to them that the staff did not have time to take new grads under their wing to help and teach them. I also reminded the Central Office caller that a female PA had been taken hostage at Green Haven for many hours, a female physiologist had been physically assaulted, and a female correction officer had been murdered at there. This was not the place for a new grad, especially a female.

In a loud, clear voice, I told the Central Office person I did not want to wake up to the morning *Poughkeepsie Journal* to see headlines that a female PA was attacked at Green Haven and know that I had something to do with placing that person there. I repeated myself to the Central Office staff that it was wrong, very wrong. I believe that this was the end of the program. Albany should have had the interviews done at Green Haven with the facility health-services director there, and with a tour of that facility. I did not feel badly about the program ending because in my heart I felt that it was wrong.

That was the last time the Central Office person and I ever spoke to each other. What upset me is that this person never worked within the walls of a prison, and if he did, he never came face-to-face with a sick convict in a small exam room with a correction officer down the hall. He never experienced having a bullpen full of seasoned inmates waiting to get over on a new health-care provider. The program could have worked at the right facility.

The last facility where I did extra service was Shawangunk Correctional Facility in Wallkill, New York. It was located at the base of the Shawangunk Mountain ridge, not too far from Minnewaska State Park in the Mid-Hudson Valley. It was a new facility, very clean, spotless, and well run. Early on it was a very violent place, with frequent stabbings and attacks on staff. The red-dot team was always on the run. A red-dot team was a preselected group of correction officers that would respond when someone was in trouble. When a phone was taken off the hook for a period of time or when a correction officer would pull the pin on his two-way radio, the red-dot team would show up and resolve most matters in a timely fashion. Inmates at Rikers Island called the red-dot team the "goon squad."

It is not uncommon at Downstate to have a female officer be responsible for thirty-six inmates on a unit by herself. Backup was always available on a moment's notice. On many occasions I would prefer having a seasoned female officer on a gallery than a new male officer with no experience. I must also mention that in my years of experience, I have seen the aftermath of an encounter between an angry female officer and an inmate. If an inmate disrespects a female officer in any manner, he is quickly corrected. If a correction officer did not have the ability to pull her pin and have help come in an instant, however, the officer would be in deep shit. There was a small pin on the officer's radio that had a cord attached to it. Pulling the pin out of the radio would set off an alarm, summoning help.

When I first began doing extra service at Shawangunk, it was a nice way of doing overtime. There was plenty of time to see each inmate, and I never felt rushed to move inmates out of the overcrowded waiting rooms as I did at Downstate. The callouts were limited to about eight inmates, who would be waiting for me when I arrived. In many other prisons, PAs would have a full waiting room of inmates to see, and they were always rushed to see them before the count.

Things changed in Shawangunk when a new doctor was hired. When the new doctor starting seeing patients, the number of outside trips increased. There was an increase in CT scans and MRIs, which were done at local community hospitals, and an increase in specialty-clinic consults as well. With the increase of outside trips came an increase in the number of inmates requesting sick call. It seemed as though every inmate at Shawangunk wanted some chronic condition taken care of. Many inmates at Shawangunk were doing life sentences. They had all day and night to think about their chronic problems. I am not sure whether the new doctor was intimidated by the inmates—and God knows these were the most intimidating inmates in the state of New York—or maybe the new doctor did not want to answer grievances or was just trying to do the right thing. My concern was in sending convicts—some of whom were doing natural life, if not twenty-five to life—back into the community to a small hospital setting for something that the inmate had had for years, if not decades. Some of these chronic conditions predated their incarceration.

Early on in my career when I was on call, I would send a maximum-security inmate for an outside medical trip, and then the next day, someone from the front office of the prison would hunt me down and ask whether the outside trip was truly needed and whether it could have been handled within the walls of the prison. Not only was the cost of the trip a concern, but the risk of escape was always present.

On one occasion I was asked to follow up an inmate's urology consult at Shawangunk. He had been seen by a urologist on the street, and I had to review the specialist's recommendations and order medication that the specialist had recommended.

I think in this particular case the nurses had set me up in a joking manner. I am not sure why the inmate had gone out to see a urologist. All I can remember is the bottom line, that the specialist had recommended Viagra. At first I thought that this was some sort of a joke. I asked the inmate to have a seat, and I went out to the nursing station, consult in hand. Most of the evening-staff nurses appeared to be waiting for me and waiting for my response. They all laughed when I asked them if this was for real. It appeared to be so; a specialist wanted this felon, doing a very long bid, to have Viagra. I went back into the exam room and told the inmate that it was not going to happen. I made it clear to him that he needed to write a grievance or contact his attorney, but I would not or could not write a prescription for Viagra for an inmate.

Of course, the next day the grievance coordinator showed up at my door with a smile on his face. I told him that the decision whether the inmate gets Viagra or not was not mine to make. First of all, Viagra was not on the New York State Department of Corrections formulary. (It would be quite embarrassing if word got out to the media that Corrections was handing out Viagra to its inmates.) The second was that a memo had been sent from the medical director of the Department of Corrections to all prescribers telling them not to submit a nonformulary request for the use of Viagra because there was no indication for an inmate to be on Viagra, and it would not be approved. I never heard anything more about this dilemma.

Another incident when the grievance coordinator approached me was one afternoon when an inmate walked into my exam room demanding an MRI of his knee. He said that his bunkie had the same problem that he had and the other doctor had ordered an MRI of his knee, so he felt that he also needed one. I asked how long he'd had knee pain, to which his reply was "many years." I asked what he took for the pain, and he responded, "I don't want medication; I want an MRI of my knee." I reviewed his chart and saw that he had been in prison for many years and had never complained of knee pain or requested Tylenol or aspirin. His medical chart was rather thin compared to those of other inmates who had spent the same length of time in the prison system. I then asked him to take his pants off so I could examine his knee. He again replied, "I want an MRI of my knee; I don't want to be examined." I then looked him directly in the eye, told him to have a nice day, and left the room.

The very next day I was at Shawangunk, and the inmate grievance counselor came to the sick-call area. At first, in somewhat of an accusatory tone, he asked why I did not order the MRI that the inmate had requested. I then pulled the chart and showed him that in all the years that the inmate was in prison, he did not once complain of knee pain, nor did he ever come looking for an analgesic. The inmate would not allow me to examine his knee. "Now," I said, "is it your wish for me to send a convicted murderer serving twenty-five years to life back into the community for an MRI because his bunkie had one, and he wants one too?" The grievance counselor's attitude toward me then changed.

Another memorable inmate who complained about me was a bodybuilder, also referred to as a power lifter. The inmate came into my office and complained of having shoulder pain for many years. I asked if he had tried any medications for the pain, and he responded that he did not want any pills. I then asked how much weight he lifted and how often. His response was "a lot of weight" and "very often." I asked him if the pain limited him in his daily weight-lifting routine. He said it did not. Then the inmate requested that I send him to an orthopedic surgeon for a steroid shot in his shoulder; he knew it would work. I then asked him to take off his shirt for my examination. The convict was built bigger than Arnold Schwarzenegger. I was impressed and somewhat scared of this guy's monster body. The inmate had a great range of motion of his arm and shoulder, better than my own range of motion.

I told him that I was not going to send him out to see the orthopedic doctor and that he should cut back on the amount of weight he was lifting and the frequency and that he should try an anti-inflammatory for a few weeks. He became very angry at me. Then he demanded to see the *other doctor.* At that point I told him to have a nice day and walked out of the office (not turning my back on him, of course).

On yet another occasion, I saw an inmate who was demanding high-potency steroid cream for a chronic facial rash. When I told him it was not going to happen, he became very angry at me: "I have been getting this cream for years, and now you are refusing to order it for me?" I could have chosen my words better, but I think I responded to his demands in the same manner. I told him about the side effects of using this high-potency steroid cream on the delicate skin of his face. He did not want to hear it. Then I asked the inmate if he had ever seen the stretch marks some women get from being pregnant. The medical term for stretch marks is *striae.* Then I took him over to a mirror mounted on the wall of the exam room and pointed out multiple long striae, or stretch marks, caused by the use of high-potency steroid cream on his face.

I have actually seen quite a few inmates who have come to me with cosmetic concerns. I was doing a routine admission physical exam on a parole violator. Checking his nose, I found that he had a hole in his nasal septum about the size of a nickel. You could have put your pinkie finger in one side of his nose, and it would have come out the other nostril. This had been caused by years of snorting heroin and cocaine. The inmate reported that he had it fixed years ago when he was incarcerated in upstate New York. After being released back into the community, he admitted to going back to using cocaine and heroin. The kicker was when he asked if I would recommend that he have his nasal septum repaired again. Jokingly, I said, "Sure, of course. Have a nice day."

Similarly, an inmate once complained about me because I would not request an ear, nose, and throat (ENT) consult to have his broken nose repaired. When the inmate grievance counselor came by to see me, I told him that he needed to teach the inmate how to fight, how to keep his nose away from his roommate's fist, or how to keep his mouth shut. The grievance counselor did not know that this was the third time in the past year that the inmate had broken his nose. The inmate had had the first two broken noses fixed by the state; I knew that the state was not going to pay for the third broken nose.

That was years ago. Today, as a policy, the New York Department of Corrections does not pay for the repair of broken noses, removal of tattoos (as was the case back in the early 1980s), and scar revisions for cosmetic reasons. Tattoo removals were once done at Fishkill Correctional Facility, back in the late 1970s. Against my advice, a convict demanded to have a tattoo removed. The surgical site became infected, and the resulting scar was much worse than the original tattoo. Even though I told the inmate not to have the tattoo removed while he was in prison and I was not involved with the aftercare, I was still named in the lawsuit against the state. It should be mentioned that everyone in the medical department was named in the suit. The lawsuit was denied early on and did not go anywhere. Today any non-life-threatening surgery has to be approved by a number of people at different levels in corrections.

Granted, many very sick inmates at Shawangunk need and receive great medical care using the same doctors and hospitals in the community that you and I and our families use on a daily basis. These days, I am able to pull up the inmate's medical history on a computer. Many times the inmate's chronic problems date back years, if not decades.

One story I never forgot and that illustrates the possible dangers of sending an inmate into the community for treatment was told to me early on in my career in corrections. I am not sure what state or where it occurred. It concerned an inmate who would go out to an outside hospital on a regular basis for treatment of a chronic condition. He also was doing a very long sentence for a horrific crime. He got into the routine of always asking to use the bathroom just before the trip back to the prison. One day on this hospital trip, someone put a gun wrapped in a plastic bag in the toilet tank for the inmate to use to kill the young correction officer who had taken him on that hospital trip, allowing the inmate to escape.

CHAPTER 10
DOCTOR DEATH

When my new boss eventually returned to Downstate after his vacation, I had little to do with him. Even though he was my supervising physician, we rarely spoke. The little work that needed to be done was done by the nurses. That all changed when Downstate began to fill up with inmates. The doctor spoke very poor English, or so I thought. I was very surprised one afternoon; there was nothing to do, and I was talking to an older man who was the dentist at Downstate. He was a great resource on anything pertaining to finances and where to invest your money. During our meeting the doctor came into the dental clinic and began to ask very specific questions regarding his investments. I was awestruck to hear him speak perfect English, with excellent grammar and almost no foreign accent. His knowledge of the stock market astounded me. All along, his very heavy foreign accent, which was very difficult for the inmates and nursing staff to comprehend, had just been a ruse. I believe he used his accent to avoid many of his duties as medical director.

As time went on, Downstate accepted more inmates and began to fill up. When the doctor had to attend to the medical problems of the inmates, it was clear that he did not like inmates. Eventually the inmates and some staff would refer to him as "Doctor Death." I will explain shortly how he got the name Doctor Death. Many inmates could not comprehend the doctor because of his heavy accent. A large number of inmates were academically challenged, and many had some sort of mental illness, all of which made it very difficult for the doctor to treat their medical problems. Someone once suggested that this doctor's feelings toward inmates were a result of his cultural background.

One morning the doctor went looking for me. It seems that during the previous night while at home, he had developed flank pain. When he eventually found me, he asked if I would inject him with IV dye just prior to the X-ray technician taking multiple se-quential X-rays of his kidneys, ureters, and bladder (KUB) or just a plain X-ray of his abdomen to see if he had any kidney stones. This guy never spoke to me, and now he wanted me to inject him with IV dye? I told him he was "fucking crazy." He had the IV dye in his pocket, but I am not sure where it came from or if he had taken it from another hospital where he moonlighted. In the old days of medicine, I had heard that some radiologists would use this tech-nique when fluoroscopy was not available. (Fluoroscopy has since been replaced with the CT scan, a much safer procedure with less radiation.) I told the director we did not have the equipment or facilities available if he were to have an allergic reaction to the IV dye. A reaction to the dye could be deadly. He tried to reassure me that he would not have a reaction and it would only take a few minutes. Again, I told him he was "fucking crazy."

When I told the story to another PA who was working at Downstate at the time, he told me I should have just mixed the IV dye with some Benadryl to assure that the doctor would not have a reaction. I then told the PA that he was also "fucking crazy." As it turned out, the doctor had severe flank pain again that evening while at home. He went to a local hospital emer-gency room for treatment. While at the hospital, the director had a severe anaphylactic reaction to the IV dye that was given to him, and he had to be admitted to the hospital. If I would have done what this guy had asked me to do at Downstate, I would have killed him and lost my job and my license to work as a physician assistant.

As time passed and things began to get busy at Downstate, my boss developed a dislike for me. Work was not getting done; he spent most, if not all, of the day in his office doing nothing. The front office was getting upset that the work was not getting done and reassigned a counselor to get the medical processing on track. The counselor also quickly got upset and frustrated with the doctor.

There was another PA who worked at Downstate at the time. He was very knowledgeable and very skillful. He did more than his share of work, and most of the staff liked him and would cover for him when he would disappear during the day. I can remember many occasions when the doctor would come down to my office looking for this PA. My response frequently was that he was in the X-ray department. The doctor would leave my office and head over to the X-ray department. I would quickly pick up the phone and warn the X-ray tech that the doctor was on his way over to the X-ray area looking for the PA. When the doctor asked if the PA was there, the X-ray tech would say that he was there a minute ago and was heading over to the lab. As the doctor walked over to the lab, the X-ray tech would call the lab and give the lab tech the heads-up. When he got to the lab and asked the lab tech if he had seen the PA, the lab tech would look down the hall and tell the doctor that he must have just passed him in the hallway—he was just in the lab seconds ago. Eventually, when the PA returned to the facility, he would seek out his boss and ask him what he needed, saying that many people had said the doctor was looking for him. At that point the doctor could not remember what he had needed the PA for in the first place.

When more was expected of the doctor, I think he felt that I was the person dumping more work on him. He went from doing nothing all day to being forced by the front office to do something, which I think angered him. I chose not to spend any time with him or interact with him at all. I was afraid that some of his responses and decisions would get him into trouble. I did not want any part of his decision-making or be around him when he was making decisions.

The dentist who worked down the hall from the medical department noticed that the doctor and I did not talk much, and he asked me why. I was frank and told the dentist that the doctor hated my guts, at which the dentist laughed. He said, "This guy has no reason to hate you; you do most of his work for him." The dentist told me that I was paranoid. About two weeks later, the dentist approached me, laughing, and said that I was right on the money, that the doctor did hate me. The dentist had had a conversation with him in which the director had reported to him that he felt that I was out to get him, which was far from the truth.

As I told the doctor to his face on more than one occasion, "You are doing a great job in hanging yourself with the way you speak to and treat inmates and staff." Basically the nurse administrator ran the medical department and made all the decisions for the unit. The doctor sat in his tiny office and did nothing all day. One day the front office was very critical of a decision that the nurse administrator had made. The problem at hand had had no good answer; either way it would have been an answer with a poor outcome. More importantly, the problem, like many others, should have been handled by the facility medical director. The nurse administrator became very upset and angry at the front office for lambasting her.

From that day on, any major problems that arose were referred to the medical director. When things became busy at Downstate, there was a breakdown between the front office and the medical department. Things were not getting done, and important questions and issues were going unanswered and unaddressed. It seemed that either the doctor did not want to do his job as facility health-services director or he was incapable of doing it. I have come to believe that the former is true. The front office contacted Central Office, which was uncommon back in those days. Most difficulties were handled on a facility level; the superintendent was in control and ran the prison with little input from Albany. These days it seems that all facility problems are handled through Central Office. Back in the day, the prison superintendent, once called the warden, was the king in the prison, a very powerful position. Nothing went to central office.

When things got backed up at Downstate, Central Office sent down a doctor to talk with the medical director. His unofficial title was regional medical director. This doctor, like many people, did not know or understand what a PA did and who a PA was responsible to. This occurred early on when physician assistant were a new breed of midlevel medical practitioners. It soon became evident that the doctor sent down from Central Office did not appreciate or understand the work done by physician assistants. Other incidents later in this book will show this to be true. At some point—I am not sure why or when it happened—the director's authority to be my supervising physician was taken away from him. This was something that I had nothing to do with. When the regional medical director came to Downstate, he didn't or couldn't convince the director to work with the team to get the work done. Instead, the Downstate medical director filed a discrimination grievance with the union. He felt the medical department nurses and I were against him because of his ethnic origin. This was far from the truth. Everyone had tried working with him at first, then around him, to get the work done. I felt bad for some of the hardworking nurses who we unable to get their jobs done because of him.

I was once told by a nurse who worked with the doctor at the local hospital that he was trained and certified in advanced cardiac life support (ACLS), which I found hard to believe. The reason for my doubts is that once when an employee had suffered a major heart attack at Downstate, a nurse had run into the doctor's office, which was next to the emergency room, looking for help from him. His response was to just call an ambulance and send the person out to the local community hospital. He closed his office door and did not come out to help the nurses attending to this very sick individual. Needless to say, the nurse was very angry and upset with him.

By the time I got to the prison emergency room, the patient was in severe discomfort and her EKG had what was referred to as "camel hump" S-T segment changes, a very ominous sign. We were able to start an IV before the ambulance arrived on the scene to take her away. Back in those days, there were no paramedics and no defibrillators. She did not make it through the evening. As I told the nurse, I doubted that the doctor could have changed the outcome, and it was probably best in the long run that he had stayed in his office.

One day during a heated argument with the front office, I was threatened with a formal reprimand for not being a "team player." It was a clear case of being bullied by an administrator. I became angry and asked why the doctor was not reprimanded for not being a "team player" and assisting an employee during an acute medical crisis and then why he would reprimand me for some nonsense.

The nurse administrator became more and more upset with the way the front office covered for the doctor, and she eventually left state service. It was a sad day for all of us at Downstate, both inmates and staff. The next nurse administrator was a nurse from another facility. The position of nurse administrator was a promotion for her

One morning I was working a dermatology clinic with an outside specialist in the square area of the facility's main building. Because of the large number of chronic, severe dermatologic problems of inmates passing through Downstate, once every six weeks a local dermatologist would come in to see and treat inmates at Downstate. This man was a great dermatologist; he knew his stuff. It was kind of him to come into the prison to see inmates. Many doctors would not do that. On this particular morning, a young inmate became very sick with asthma.

Back in the early 1980s, there were not as many ways to treat asthma as there are today. Only a few medications provided any relief from the wheezing. The inmate was a young, handsome black male who was very ill with chronic asthma. He required many outside hospital emergency-room trips to treat his acute wheezing attacks, which were not controlled with his handheld inhaler. When he returned from the outside hospital, he would be kept in room J in the hospital infirmary. Room J was right next to the emergency room.

One of the treatments that was used back in the early eighties was aminophylline, either administered as a pill or intravenously. Aminophylline has a side effect that would make a person very dry and thirsty, always requiring drinking water. When anyone would walk down the hall in the prison hospital/infirmary past this asthmatic inmate's room, he would get up out of his bed and ask for a pitcher of ice water. He would hold his gold-colored plastic pitcher in his right hand and knock on the window with his left hand. The inmate would do this repeatedly, many times a day, to anyone who passed his room. He was never obnoxious or annoying. When we would speak with him on rounds, he was always pleasant and respectful. This guy was kept in the infirmary for long periods because of the severity of his asthma. On this particular morning, the inmate was not doing well; his wheezing became severe, and he was in moderate to severe distress. The infirmary nurse brought him into the emergency room and then called the doctor, who started an IV line in the inmate's left arm. The medical director was going to give an aminophylline IV, meaning he was going to inject the medication directly in the patient's intravenous line, which was an accepted treatment at that time. Today we have much better and safer ways of treating acute asthma with nebulizers, inhalers, and other oral medications.

It is very important when using IV aminophylline that the doctor, not the nurse, give it very, very slowly. The doctor needs to watch the clock and administer the drug over ten minutes. Later in the 1980s, an IV product called a microdrip was developed to administer drugs like aminophylline IV. They may have had the microdrips available in the outside hospitals, but they were not yet available to us at Downstate. A nurse came running into the square area; she was very upset and asked me to come quickly to the ER. When I got to the ER, one nurse was doing CPR on the inmate and another was using the Ambu bag, a plastic resuscitator bag used to assist ventilation, on him. The doctor was standing in the background, visibly shaken and upset. I was informed that the ambulance was on the way.

I asked for the laryngoscope to intubate the patient. For some reason I had difficulty seeing the patient's epiglottis and had difficulty intubating him. I don't think it was anxiety on my part; I think it was the position of the patient on the table. The dermatologist who was seeing patients in the square had come over to the ER to help. The ambulance finally showed up and took the inmate to a local hospital, which was about ten miles away. The inmate never made it. The facility ER nurse at the time said that the doctor was administering the aminophylline IV when the inmate just keeled over. The doctor caught the inmate as he fell forward. This was very sad, to lose a patient because of asthma.

Even today, people in the community do not take asthma seriously. They often wait too long before getting help and end up in the morgue. Asthma kills both old and young. Later in this book, you will read that the inmate's ghost still lives in room J in the hospital. I think this is the incident that prompted the inmates to begin to refer to the medical director as "Doctor Death."

A short while after things got very busy at Downstate, the doctor was transferred closer to his home—not because of his lack of medical judgment, but because Downstate was backing up with inmates who needed to be evaluated and classified. This was something the doctor felt he had not been hired to do. His transfer resulted in a geographic pay increase, much less work, and being closer to his home.

CHAPTER 11

ANTHONY JOSEPH FORTE, MD, AND THE AIDS EPIDEMIC

When things began to get busy at Downstate with the reception process, two physician assistants were added, making it a total of three, and a part-time physician was added. Anthony Forte started at Downstate as a part-time physician, working just a few days a week. His office was next to mine, and we became good friends during the many years that I worked with him. Dr. Forte looked like Robert DeNiro and had the sense of humor of Mike Myers and Mel Brooks put together. He was a very religious man who had a strong belief in God that was reflected in the way he treated others, especially sick inmates.

I can remember clearly one Wednesday, during IPC (infirmary) rounds, when all of us PAs and MDs went into F room, the room next to the dayroom, to see an inmate with the first name of Joe Joe. It was a double-bed room, but because of Joe Joe's illness he was by himself; the other bed was kept empty. He was in the bed next to the hallway window. Joe Joe was very ill, near death. His mind was very sharp, and he was well aware that he was dying. We had tried everything for Joe Joe, as had the local hospitals and

Westchester County Medical Center (WCMC). Joe Joe was treated many times out at the outside hospital for his condition. The night prior, Joe Joe had been running a very high fever, which did not come down after taking Tylenol and Motrin. He was visibly sick and in distress, emaciated, underweight, and very weak. But he understood everything that was said to him.

While on rounds in F room, Dr. Forte moved a chair over to the side of Joe Joe's bed and sat down; he was at eye level with Joe Joe. The room and the infirmary seemed very quiet that morning. Dr. Forte told Joe Joe that there was nothing more that could be done for him and that he would die soon. He asked Joe Joe if he was right with God. Dr. Forte said the time was near and that Joe Joe would be meeting God soon. Joe Joe understood all that was said and responded that he had made things right with God and that he was not afraid to die. This occurred early on before AIDS or HIV had a name.

Dr. Forte then looked Joe Joe in the eye and asked him to take a message to God when he met with him. Dr. Forte asked Joe Joe to tell God that we needed help dealing with the many inmates who were dying from this new disease. He wanted Joe Joe to say that all of us who worked with these very sick inmates were very scared, not knowing what we were dealing with. We were all afraid of getting this new unknown disease or TB from the people we treated on a daily basis. At that time no one knew what this new illness was or how it was spread. There was talk of medical workers contracting AIDS from needle-stick injuries or from blood spills. Joe Joe assured Dr. Forte that his message would get to God. Joe Joe died in the next few days at an outside hospital.

A few months before Joe Joe's death, he had become very ill. It was Christmas Eve, and I was on call and celebrating with my family at my mother's home. I will never forget that night. My beeper went off about eight o'clock. The evening nurse told me that Joe Joe was running a very high fever and was sweating profusely. I instructed her to try Tylenol and/or Motrin to bring the fever down and to let me know if his condition changed. A few hours later, the nurse called back and said that there was no change in his fever and that he was starting to hallucinate. I instructed the nurse to have him transported to Westchester Medical Center because he probably had *Pneumocystis carinii pneumonia* (PCP) and needed IV antibiotics.

After a few minutes, the nurse called me back and said that Joe Joe did not want to go to WCMC; he wanted to stay at Downstate. She said that she had told Joe Joe that if he did not go out to WCMC, he would probably die in the prison, and nobody wants to die in a prison, especially on Christmas morning. Joe Joe had responded to her that he was tired of going back and forth to outside hospitals; he said he knew he was going to die soon and that he would rather die at Downstate. Joe Joe had said that having this disease in the community was difficult; people treated you with disrespect, especially the farther north out of the city a person went. Joe Joe told the nurse that he would rather die in a place where he was treated with respect and dignity, treated like a human being, and that was at Downstate.

Later that night the nurse called and said that Joe Joe was hallucinating, speaking to some other inmate in his room. Joe Joe was in room J, the single-bed room next to the emergency room; the same room where the young black inmate stayed just before he died of an acute asthma attack.

When the nurse came to check on Joe Joe, he asked if she would give the other inmate in the room some ice water. Joe Joe said he was tired of hearing the inmate knock on the window, asking anyone who walked by to fill up his gold-colored plastic container with ice water. Joe Joe went on to describe the other inmate in the room as a young, thin, handsome black male with short, cropped hair. When the nurse told me this over the phone, the short hairs on the back of my neck stood up. I told the nurse that he had described the inmate who died to a T. The nurse had little idea who the inmate was because she worked nights and had little contact with the inmates or regular staff.

I dropped my family off at home and went in to see Joe Joe to try to talk him into going to an outside hospital for treatment. I personally asked Joe Joe about the other inmate in the room. With that, Joe Joe asked me if I would give that poor boy some ice water. He said he had been banging on the window all night asking for ice water. Joe Joe was not alone in that room.

With some help from the psychiatrist on call and some Valium, we were able to talk Joe Joe into going out to WCMC. He did have pneumonia, which resolved with the use of IV antibiotics; next time he would not be so lucky.

In 2013, a very sick HIV patient was in that same room. This inmate told the lab tech that he was not alone in the room. He said there was somebody else there with him. The patient told the lab tech that he did not tell the nurse because the nurse would call the psych department and label him as crazy. The lab tech knew of the ghost that was rumored to live in that room and came running to tell me. My most recent boss, who also knew about the ghost, went back to interview the inmate. His response to me was "Holy shit!"

Anthony Forte spoke frequently of his childhood; his father had been a successful, wealthy attorney in Manhattan. Once, while we were walking past Ferrara's Bakery in Little Italy in Lower Manhattan, Forte told me that his father had owned the building. During Forte's youth, his mother was very sick; he was cared for mostly by his grandmother. When Anthony was older, his father placed him in the New York State Military Academy in Cornwall, New York. When the academy would close for the summer months, his father would drive up to Cornwall to pick him up and take him to a summer camp in the Adirondacks for the entire summer. When summer camp was over, his father would then return him to the academy in Cornwall. Forte told me he was never at home. He had told me that his mother was very sick for a long time and that he had hardly seen her. It was a very sad day when I asked him if he had been close to his mother. He told me that one summer on his way up to summer camp with his father, he had asked his father how his mom was. His father told him that his mother had passed away a few months earlier.

Forte told me that he did very well in the military academy; he was second in his class, which included Donald Trump. I wonder if Donald Trump remembers Anthony J. Forte? After graduating from the military academy, Forte went on to Curry College in Massachusetts, where he flunked out his first semester. I asked Forte how he could go from second in his class at a very difficult boarding high school to flunking out in his first semester of college. His response was that in the military school, the doors to the study halls were locked, so you had no choice but to sit and study. In college, the doors were open, and girls and alcohol were so readily available that he could not resist the temptation. He told me it was a great first semester for the bars and women in Milton, Massachusetts.

After getting his feet back on the ground, he applied to other colleges, one of which was Howard University in Washington, DC. Howard was a predominantly black college. The university promised Forte that if he would complete a master's-level program in pharmacology, they would accept him into the school of medicine, an arrangement to which he agreed.

Forte was one of two white students in class. Once I met a doctor who worked at Fishkill Correctional Facility who had graduated from Howard the same year as Forte had. When I described to Forte what this man looked like, Forte knew exactly who he was, even before I mentioned his name. The doctor was very tall, and his right eye was off-center, tilted outward. When I bumped into the doctor again while making box rounds at Fishkill, I asked him if he remembered graduating with Anthony Forte. He could not remember him at all, which I found very strange. I then reminded him that it was a small class and only had two white students in it and asked him how he could forget a guy like Forte.

Forte told me that he had done well in medical school; he loved medicine and would read anything about it he could get his hands on. At Downstate, people would often laugh when he would walk down the hall, usually about 1:00 p.m., to the bathroom with the newest issue of the *New England Journal of Medicine*. Everyone knew that he would be in the bathroom for a while. His love for medicine and his knowledge base became invaluable when the outbreak of the HIV epidemic began. Forte's second wife often told me that Forte would spend his entire weekend reading medical journals. He would have a stack of the unread journals on the left side of his easy chair and a stack of the journals that he had already read on the right side of the chair.

Forte had few interests outside of medicine. He did not hunt, he had no hobbies, and he did not watch sports on the television. But Forte greatly enjoyed eating out in fine restaurants. When I first got friendly with him, a small group of guys would frequently meet on Tuesday nights at Uncle Chu's Restaurant, just north of the Beacon-Newburgh Bridge on Route 9D. Uncle Chu was the first restaurant in the area to offer all-you-can-eat Chinese food, but only on Tuesday nights. The restaurant was high-end and unlike the all-you-can-eat Chinese restaurants that you see in strip malls today. The waiter was a very tall and ugly Chinese man, the Chinese equivalent to our Frankenstein.

The guys who went out to eat at Chu's with Forte did just that, eating just about everything the cooks would bring out. The evening would consist of nonstop eating, drinking, and belly-wrenching laughter. The food, as I remember it, was pretty good when the restaurant first opened. The owner tolerated the amounts of food we all ate because we ran up a large bar tab, and we were great tippers. Toward the end of the evening, the group would become loud and obnoxious. By that time, late in the evening, the place would be near closing, and the restaurant would be nearly empty. We started with about four guys and grew to fourteen. The group consisted of MDs, PAs, COs, recreation leaders from the prison, and nurses. Women did not usually come out with us. It was not that we did not want women; it was like a men's night out, away from our spouses and significant others. One woman did come out with us on one or two occasions, and the guys did not seem to mind it. Many of the jokes may have been in poor taste, but I must admit I never laughed so hard and so long in my life.

Forte showed a different character away from the facility. At the prison he was all about medicine and business. On our nights out, it was like having dinner with Mike Myers and Mel Brooks. I can remember laughing so hard there were tears coming from my eyes. These nights out brought a group of men who had vastly different backgrounds, upbringings, and interests closer together. In the spirit of the college Greek fraternities, we did choose a group name, but I am too embarrassed to place that name in print in this book.

Later on in the early 1980s, when the food at Uncle Chu's began to slip, one of the recreation leaders suggested a steak house out on Route 52 in Fishkill that offered all the prime rib you could eat for $17.95. The Continental Inn, like Uncle Chu's, at first welcomed the group. We started drinking early and stayed late. The owner became concerned, however, when some of the group would eat four or five servings of prime rib. Most of us were happy with two servings, but there were those who ate a lot more. The waitresses loved us because we were great tippers, and they loved to hear our laughter. After a few weeks at the Continental Inn, you could see that the owner was becoming concerned about the amount of food we all ate. Finally, he asked that we not come back as a group.

When I returned one night with my wife, he quickly came over to me to make sure I was alone and not with the group.

From the Continental Inn, we moved to the Raccoon Saloon on Route 9W in Marlboro, which is still open but with different owners. At the Raccoon Saloon, the owner, Pat, did not care how loud we got and always welcomed us. Forte's favorite meal was *zuppa di pesce*, and he would always ask the waiter to have the cook put a steamed lobster on top of it to make it complete.

When the medical director was moved out of Downstate, Dr. Forte took over as facility medical director. Dr. Forte changed a lot about the way the medical department was run at Downstate. He expected all the PAs and MDs on staff to read and keep up with the latest medical journals. Many times he would copy articles and highlight each important area on each person's individual handout. Later in the week, he would quiz us to make sure that we had reviewed the articles that he took so much time to distribute to us. He was a great teacher, and he made learning fun. Dr. Forte also made sure the staff had what is called Journal Club. On Wednesday morning after rounds, in our group meeting a PA or MD was required to present and discuss a medical-journal article to the group. The articles had to be from a legitimate medical journal such as the *New England Journal of Medicine* or the *Journal of Emergency Medicine*, not from drug company medical journals or handouts that were used to promote products.

Dr. Forte was a well-dressed man; he liked wearing Brooks Brothers suits, suspenders, and proper bow ties, and he always had a Montblanc pen in his pocket with the snowcapped top in view. His shoes were always polished. Dr. Forte would always use his Montblanc pen when he had to "two-PC" a psychiatric patient. That was when two MDs had to sign off on an inmate who would be transferred to the psychiatric hospital against his will. He referred to the Montblanc as his special two-PC pen.

One day when I had to wear a suit for a court date, I made it a point to wear a bow tie to honor him. He made it a point to make sure that I hand tied it myself and it was not a clip-on bow tie. I also, as a joke, had a counterfeit Montblanc pen in my pocket, with the fake snowcap on the top of the pen in view. It was a knock-off that I had purchased on Canal Street in New York City. I once told Dr. Forte that if he ever found himself waking up in an ambulance or on a hospital stretcher and noticed that I had his Montblanc pen in my shirt pocket, it was just for safekeeping, because hospital and ambulance staff had a tendency to remove them from patients while they were under their care. He knew that mine was a fake, and he would roll his eyes whenever I would use it. When I finished my master's degree in 1993, Anthony Forte gave me the real thing: a genuine Montblanc pen. It made me very happy. I still have it, but I am still afraid to carry it around because someone might borrow it from me and not return it. I still and will always cherish it.

When Dr. Forte took over as medical director, the physician assistants took primary call for the facility. As a physician assistant, I took call for twenty-nine years. Then, for some reason that I don't understand, Albany took physician assistants off being on call. During the years that I was on call, the procedure worked like this: When an inmate became sick or needed suturing after hours, the nurse would call the PA who was on call to come in and see the inmate. Some things could be handled over the phone, and some things needed the PA to return to the facility to see the inmate. This was done to avoid sending an inmate to a community hospital, which was not only costly but could place the community at risk. At times the inmates did need to be sent out to the local community hospital, such as in cases of severe trauma or a life-threatening illness.

Occasionally the nurse would call the PA on call and tell him or her that there was no sense in the PA coming in because the presenting illness or trauma made it obvious that the inmate had to be transferred out. When an inmate had a severe stab wound or obvious fracture dislocation or was in cardiac arrest, the nurse would inform the PA that the inmate was on his way out to the local community hospital. When inmates were sent out without the PA coming in to see them, the next day a lieutenant or captain would show up in medical asking if the previous night's outside medical trip was necessary and if it could have been prevented. The officer would always ask why the inmate was sent out without the PA coming in first to see him. Often it was more important to get the inmate out as quickly as possible because he was in a near-death situation and time was important. Nobody dies at Downstate. Sending inmates out was a big, costly production and placed the community at risk.

Dr. Forte and the second MD were always available for backup consultation for the PA on call, or for the nurse if she or he felt uncomfortable with the PA's initial decision. The MD always had to be called when there was a death in the facility. Today many inmates receive after-hours emergency treatment at local outside hospitals.

During the early days of AIDS, PAs were frequently called in during the evening and on weekends. On more than one occasion, I can remember being called in very late in the evening by the radiologist. After the radiologist worked his regular hospital shift in the local community hospital, he would come and read the X-rays taken at Downstate. This would be late in the evening. Because of an increase in tuberculosis (TB), all new reception inmates and returning parole violators were required to have a chest X-ray done. Initially, Central Office had a problem with the fact that we were doing chest X-rays routinely on all new inmates and parole violators because of the cost involved. When AIDS and TB became more prevalent, Central Office stopped complaining.

When AIDS first began, many inmates infected with the illness would present with Pneumocystis pneumonia or PCP pneumonia.

This was a severe, debilitating, noncontagious illness; we did not know that at the time. It was a killer of many with AIDS early on in the history of AIDS.

The radiologist would see a patchy, infiltrate pattern on the chest X-ray; by this time the inmate was very sick and near death. There was no treatment at the time for PCP. The on-call PA was called in to see the inmate. Most times there was no indication on the inmate's medical chart that he was at risk for AIDS; the risks were there, but the inmate had not been truthful when the nurse did the admission history. Inmates with AIDS were afraid of being shunned by other inmates or correctional staff, so they lied about their prior medical, drug-use, and sexual history. When chest X-rays turned up abnormal, indicating PCP, it was usually too late. The inmates would be brought up to the hospital, always very sick. They were severely underweight, many times with a very high fever, and they were sweating profusely. The inmates knew that they were very sick, but they would not report it to anyone, hoping to recover and not wanting anyone to know or maybe hoping to die. At this point the inmate would be too sick to be cared for in the prison infirmary, so he needed to be transferred to a local community hospital. When AIDS first appeared and inmates were becoming very sick and dying, the local hospital did not want anything to do with them. On more than one occasion, doctors in local hospital emergency rooms hung up the phone on me when I attempted to transfer sick inmates to their care. I learned always to first ask whom I was speaking with when I called. These inmates were in need of compassionate terminal care that the prison could not give. These inmates were near death, very sick and suffering.

As time went on and some treatments became available for the inmates with HIV infections, the doctors at the AIDS Designated Center at Albany Medical College were a blessing. Whenever a difficult problem with an HIV-infected patient would arise, a phone call would provide a quick answer. Doctors from the AIDS unit were always happy to hear from the practitioners in the field and were willing to help resolve difficult problems. Inmates who had problems that could not be resolved at the local level were sent out to outside hospitals or to larger teaching hospitals. I slept better knowing I had this great resource on the other end of the phone.

On-call shifts would go from Monday morning to the following Monday morning. If Monday was a holiday, the call would change the next day. Any inmates admitted to the infirmary were the responsibility of the PA on call. The on-call PA would do the history and physical on the inmate, as well as the admission note.

Dr. Forte always made it a point to make rounds of the in-patient component (IPC), also called the infirmary or the prison hospital, on Monday mornings at 7:00 a.m. Everybody in the facility just called it the hospital. The PA going off call would have to present the inmates that he had admitted over the weekend. The PA coming on call needed to familiarize himself with the new patients on the unit. Dr. Forte was there to make sure we did not kill anyone. On Wednesday morning, the group would make rounds again to review the inmates and their care. On Friday morning, the group would make rounds for the third time in a week before the weekend in an attempt to discharge patients to free up some beds for possible weekend admissions.

Many nights, inmates would come up to the prison emergency room with vague complaints and presenting signs. It was sometimes easier to hold the inmate in the infirmary overnight to see if he became sicker or if he became better and could be returned to population. Rounds were called "stump the chumps." It was a term that went back to my days in a large teaching hospital, when the attending physician would make rounds on the (at that time) hospital wards. (Today the hospitals have private or semiprivate rooms.) The attending physician would pose questions to residents, interns, and PAs regarding the patient's illness. He would go down the line, starting with the third-year resident, and make his way eventually down to the PA. God forbid that the PA would know the answer to a question that the residents did not. That routine became known as "stump the chumps"; the residents, interns, and PAs were the chumps.

I can remember once in the ER at Cumberland Hospital in Brooklyn (now closed) when an older man came into the hospital with a large foreign body in his rectum. When the attending physician placed the X-ray on the view box, the residents and interns, many from foreign countries, had no idea that it was a vibrator. Several days later, the attending physician asked what had become of the patient: Was he admitted or sent home? The attending doctor saw the expression on my face and waited for an answer. Someone in the group said jokingly that the batteries were changed and the patient went home. Sick medical humor. When I worked in a city-hospital emergency room, I saw patients who had inserted many strange and unusual things into their rectum or penis. This habit of people inserting things into their rectum was frequently seen in the prison system.

Dr. Forte took very extensive medical histories and performed thorough examinations of all of his patients. At times, this annoyed me to no end. Downstate was a very busy place with a lot of sick people. One day I went into the emergency room to see why inmates were stacking up in the waiting room. An inmate had complained to Dr. Forte that he had had rectal bleeding and pain for the last day or so. After Dr. Forte asked the patient about three dozen questions, he proceeded to do a rectal exam on the patient. When I walked in, a nurse was helping him by holding the patient in a knee-to-chest position with the male nurse's right hand on the inmate's head, and Dr. Forte had his left hand on the inmate's thigh. While Dr. Forte had his finger in the inmate's rectum, I asked the nurse in an annoyed tone what the hell Forte was looking for. The nurse responded that Forte had lost his ring during the exam. While his finger was still in the inmate's rectum, Dr. Forte and the patient both began to laugh out loud. They both, the patient and the doctor, had tears in their eyes from laughing so hard.

When Dr. Forte was finished, he lectured me again about the importance of a proper, thorough history and a complete physical exam. I responded back to him that the most common cause of rectal bleeding of a short duration in a middle-aged patient was hemorrhoids. "Check the *Merck Manual*," I told him. I would have given the inmate a box of rectal rockets (hemorrhoid suppositories) and told him to return to sick call in a few days if the condition did not improve. I reminded Dr. Forte how busy Downstate was and that he needed to triage each case accordingly: treat what we were able to, send out those we could not treat, and move on to the next patient.

One Friday during rounds with Dr. Forte, an inmate was in the hospital dayroom on a one-on-one psych watch because he had made an attempt to take his life by hanging himself. This was a Friday before a long holiday weekend. It seems that he did not want to go to where they were going to send him; he wanted to stay at Downstate. As mentioned before, during a one-on-one psych watch a correction officer sits outside the cell or hospital room and watches the inmate twenty-four hours a day, seven days a week, until he is cured of this desire to hurt himself or until he is sent to Central New York Psychiatric Hospital.

On this particular Thursday, an administrator was passing through the hospital and asking questions about this inmate. I had suggested to this woman that the inmate—a transient inmate who did not belong to Downstate but was just passing through—should be placed in a van and driven separately, by himself, to the facility he belonged in and did not want to go to. In an authoritative tone, speaking down to me in front of the group, the administrator would not agree to do that because of the cost involved with hiring overtime for two correction officers to drive him upstate. I reminded her that it was a holiday weekend, and getting a psychiatrist to clear this inmate and release him from the one-on-one psych watch would not occur until Tuesday afternoon, if we were lucky. The inmate would remain on a watch until Tuesday, resulting in three overtime shifts a day for five days. (One-on-one watches were usually staffed with overtime officers.) I then reminded her that the cost of transporting this inmate to a psychiatric hospital would be a lot less than having him watched by a correction officer 24-7 through the long holiday weekend. I was not upset about the questions that the administrator asked, but I was annoyed with the attitude and the tone that was used. The inmate left that afternoon, we got our dayroom back in the hospital, and the overtime officer went home.

Wednesdays were lecture days; there was no sick call on Wednesday morning, and the time was used for catch-up and instruction. I remember frequently finding myself in Dr. Forte's office with him lecturing me about something. One Wednesday, Dr. Forte was lecturing me about my bad habit of not asking inmates how injuries had occurred. He insinuated that I was not interested in the mechanism of the inmate's alleged injury. He insisted that it was important in history taking and for documentation purposes. As I told Dr. Forte, many inmates were not truthful in reporting what occurred and usually said that their injuries occurred when they "fell in the shower." I told Dr. Forte that I was tired of being lied to and no longer cared about what happened to the inmate or how it happened. I said I wished I had a dime for every time I heard an inmate say "I fell in the shower." Forte again reminded me of the importance of taking a proper medical history.

Just as Dr. Forte was finishing lecturing me, the ER nurse came into his office and asked that we come to see an inmate in the ER. The inmate had been involved in some sort of altercation with another inmate. To put it bluntly, *he got the snot kicked out of him.* Cuts, bruises, and abrasions covered his body. Glancing at me first and then turning to the inmate, Forte asked him how this occurred. The inmate looked Dr. Forte directly in the eye and said, "I fell in the shower." I laughed out loud and then asked Dr. Forte, "What is the point?" Of course security would soon be there with a camera to interview the inmate in detail. Then I reminded Dr. Forte to expect the other inmate, the one who did this to him, to be up in the ER in the next few days with a shiv (a homemade knife) in his chest or back for retribution.

One Wednesday morning I was called into Dr. Forte's office for what I thought was another lecture. When I walked into Forte's office, there was the regional administrator from Albany Central Office with a perturbed look on his face, holding an inmate's chart in his hand. In the chart was a urinalysis that indicated the inmate had a moderate amount of blood in his urine. As it turned out, the inmate had died from a cancerous kidney tumor, diagnosed on the postmortem exam. The family was suing the Department of Corrections. The regional administrator said that because I had signed off on the blood work and urinalysis results and had done nothing about it, the inmate had died needlessly and the family was suing the state.

I became noticeably angry and opened the chart to show that I had listed on the problem list that the inmate had blood in his urine and that he needed follow-up at his permanent facility. I also pointed out to the regional administrator that I had placed three stars next to my entry on the inmate's medical-problem list, indicating to the next facility that this was important and must be followed up. When an inmate is received at a new facility, a nurse reviews the inmate's medical records and acts accordingly. I opened the chart to the notation on the ambulatory health record (AHR) of the nurse receiving the inmate into the new facility. She had clearly written that the inmate had hematuria, blood in the urine, and the inmate needed to be scheduled for the facility MD.

This had not been done, for reasons unclear to me. It seemed that the receiving facility had dropped the ball.

I was not angry that nothing had been done at the receiving facility; mistakes always happened. I was very angry at Albany Central for not understanding the medical record—a problem-orientated medical record (POMR)—and for trying to make me a scapegoat. This administrator was old school, and as I said before, he was unsure about what a physician assistant did and did not do. I would go so far as to say that as an old-timer, he felt threatened by the new midlevel practitioners, as did many doctors and nurses at that time. He also did not understand the POMR approach of the corrections medical record. The POMR listed problems on the problem list on the front cover, and what was being done about the problem was listed on the AHR. Angrily, I asked why the receiving facility chose not to do anything about the inmate's problem. He had no answer for that. I understand that the state settled out of court for an undisclosed amount. This occurred many years ago.

From that point on, and for many years, any inmate with blood in his urine was worked up at Downstate. Hematuria is not uncommon in males in the prison system, and many times the repeat of the urinalysis comes back as normal and is repeated again weeks later. Sometimes the inmate may need to have a CT scan done to determine the cause of the blood. Back in the day, an intravenous pyelogram (IVP) was performed—an invasive, costly procedure that had many risks to the patient, done when a patient had chronic, painless hematuria. Kidney stones can produce painless blood in the urine, as can tumors of the kidney, ureters, or bladder. While having the workup, the inmate would be held at Downstate until the cause of the blood was determined. A few cases had to be referred to an outside urologist for addition workup. Rikers Island treated hematuria differently; the medical staff there would order Vibramycin, a broad-spectrum antibiotic, twice a day for ten days, and hope the inmate would be sent to Downstate for the potentially costly and lengthy workup.

I recall another memorable Wednesday morning, early on when AIDS was infecting a number of inmates and before it had a name. We had little to help us in making the diagnosis of AIDS. It was very important to interview the inmates regarding their past history of risky behavior. Important questions about an inmate's history of IV-drug abuse, tattoos, and homosexual encounters had to be asked. During this Wednesday morning lecture, Dr. Forte was telling me that I should not lower my level of speech to that of the street or prison level, what he referred to as "the vernacular of the prison." He told me that it was important that we raise the vernacular of the inmate to a higher level, not bring ours down to theirs. I responded that it was time-consuming and difficult. I told him that the patient must understand what I was asking him. Believe it or not, at that exact moment, the ER nurse came to us and asked if we would see an inmate with a high fever in the ER. The inmate was poorly educated and appeared very sick.

During Dr. Forte's exam, he detected oral thrush—a heavy white coating covering the tongue and cheeks. Early on in the AIDS epidemic, it was an indicator that the person might be infected with HIV. It should be mentioned that thrush can also occur with other illnesses. Dr. Forte began questioning the inmate for risk-behavior factors. The inmate denied IV-drug abuse and denied any tattoos. Then Forte asked, "Have you engaged in *anal-receptive intercourse* recently?" The inmate responded by saying never, with a surprised look on his face. It was clear to the nurse in the room, and to me, that the inmate had no idea what Forte meant by *anal-receptive intercourse.* The inmate was academically and somewhat mentally challenged and had no clue what Forte was talking about.

At that, I placed my arm on Dr. Forte's shoulder and began to lecture him on the virtues of the prison vernacular. I explained to Dr. Forte that if the inmate does not understand the doctor, you will never get to the bottom of his condition. Then someone in the room turned and asked the inmate, "Do you take it in the butt?" (*Rectum* would have been a better choice of words.) With that, the inmate smiled and said, "yes." I then looked at Dr. Forte and repeated, "Vernacular." I started to laugh and mentioned to Dr. Forte that if you asked the average young inmate in prison if he used "protection"—meaning a condom—on the street, the most common response would be "I carry a Glock 19 for protection." I said that if you questioned any sexually active male teenager today if he used a prophylactic during sex, you would get a puzzled look. I used to repeat to Dr. Forte frequently, "Johnny caps and rain-coats," slang for condoms. I would remind everyone I worked with to inform the young inmates to "wrap that rascal," or "don't forget your Johnny caps or raincoats when having sex." I felt this was imperative in the prevention of HIV and other sexually transmitted diseases.

Dr. Forte's growing-up years were much different from that of many of his patients. He was not the same as the people he treated in prison; he came from an affluent family. His father was an expensive New York City lawyer. I must say that he did learn a lot early on and quickly learned about the ways of the street. It took him a short time to learn and adjust to the prison way of life. Some of what occurred in the prison was upsetting to Dr. Forte and was a real eye-opener for him.

During rounds one Wednesday morning in the mid-1980s, the discussion was about unprotected sex, various forms of sex, and the transmission of HIV. I think someone in the group had mentioned that the Mineshaft, a members-only gay club in Lower Manhattan in the heart of the meatpacking district, was closed by the New York City Department of Health. The Mineshaft was a hotbed of HIV transmission during the early days of AIDS. It was the home of hedonistic sex, the doctrine that pleasure is the chief good in life: if it feels good, do it. When he was growing up in New York, Dr. Forte had never heard of the Mineshaft and asked what it was. I had told him that the newspapers were reporting that it was a sex club where people were having casual, multiple-partner, and anonymous sex. This sparked Forte's interest, and he had more questions about the place. When the health department closed it down, there were reports that fresh semen was found on walls and on the floors. Another PA in the group brought up golden showers—when a person urinates on someone else for pleasure, and the person getting urinated on receives some sort of pleasure from it—and glory holes, multiple holes in the wall at different levels where people would insert various body parts and wait for some sort of response from an unknown person on the other side of the wall. Dr. Forte's response was "Holy shit!" Then he asked how a person goes about joining this club. One person in the group who had a great knowledge of the city said that the membership was rather inexpensive. With that Forte asked, "How do you know that?" and the group laughed.

It is hard to write separate chapters on Dr. Anthony Forte and HIV. He was the facility health-services director at Downstate at the time when HIV first showed its nasty self. Because he was well read and very interested in the appearance of this new illness, he was beneficial not only those who were infected but was also an asset to the New York State Department of Corrections. Unfortunately, that went unrecognized. The Central Office of the Department of Corrections was slow to respond to this epidemic in the prison system. Because Downstate Correctional Facility was the reception center for New York City, we were hit hard and early by this killer. Many of our new reception inmates had a history of intravenous drug abuse. A small number were homosexual males, and an even smaller number were men who had sex with other men or with prostitutes. At that time, as many as twenty thousand inmates were passing through Downstate, the bulk of whom were new reception inmates and parole violators. There were also court-return inmates going back down to Rikers for court dates and transient inmates being transferred from one facility to another.

Early on in the epidemic, the PAs and MDs doing the intake physicals on the new inmates were noticing that many had unexplained generalized lymphadenopathy. This condition was marked by swelling or enlargement of lymph nodes in more than two areas of the body. When palpating the neck region, auxiliary (armpits), and groin area of an affected inmate, you could feel hard, nontender lumps that felt like grapes under the skin in these areas. (During my training, one doctor reprimanded me for comparing tumors and skin lesions to vegetables, fruit, or other food sources. He said that he loved a particular fruit and did not appreciate it being compared to a malignant tumor. But I still like to use the comparison for laypeople.) The admission blood work that was available at the time of the physicals back in the early 1980s could not explain these unusual and frequent physical findings. We would make an entry on the problem list that this should be further investigated when the inmate arrived at his permanent facility.

At Green Haven Correctional Facility, a few of the inmates with these enlarged lymph nodes had biopsies done, but the results could not explain the reason why the nodes had gotten bigger. The biopsy reports listed nonspecific hyperplasia, a term that did not mean much to anyone. When many of the PAs and MDs at the permanent facilities questioned Central Office on what should be done to address the entries on the problem list indicating generalized lymphadenopathy and what sort of follow-up was needed, the Central Office doctor told them to ignore the entry. I will never forget that response from this doctor in Central Office. As it turned out, generalized lymphadenopathy was a clear indicator of an HIV infection and a poor prognosticator for this deadly illness. Central Office had dropped the ball.

Early on in the disease, when there was no name given to it, no blood tests that could indicate the person might be infected, and no drugs to treat the illness, no one in the outside medical community wanted to talk about HIV. The first medical conferences addressing the topic that I can remember were in the basement conference room at Saint Clare's Hospital in New York. There was no sign in the hospital lobby indicating where in the building the conference was being held. When I asked the doorman where the conference was, he whispered the word "downstairs," as if he did not want to alarm other people within earshot. Saint Clare's Hospital in Midtown had a number of outpatients coming into the hospital to get treatment for this unknown disease. There was no coffee and bagels for breakfast, no lunch purchased by the drug companies, and no free pens to be handed out. Today the companies that manufacture medications that treat AIDS offer lectures from prominent doctors in the field of infectious disease at quality area restaurants. But hospitals today still avoid signs indicating that they have HIV clinics to avoid stigmatizing the patients using the clinics.

No one in the outside medical community wanted anything to do with any inmates for any reason. On more than one occasion, doctors at local community hospitals would hang up the phone on me when they learned that I wanted to transfer an inmate to them. I would begin my phone conversation by asking the person on the other end for his or her name. They all knew I was sending them someone with AIDS who was very sick. Not until later on in the AIDS epidemic did the New York State Department of Health step in and make its staff available if a local hospital refused to provide care to these very sick individuals.

At one time, correction officers would get dressed up in white hazmat suits that would cover them from head to toe when they had to interact with inmates who showed signs of HIV infection. We called them bunny suits. I cannot forget the scene in the prison hospital when two rather tall, robust correction officers, dressed from head to toe in white hazmat coveralls, with eye protection, masks, and gloves, were escorting a very small, emaciated, under-weight inmate down the hall with leg irons, handcuffs, and a chain around his waist. The leg irons, cuffs, and chains probably weighed as much as the sick inmate did. The scene reminded me of the movie *ET*. The medical staff of MDs, PAs, and nurses seemed not to be concerned about the few inmates who exhibited overt signs of the infection. We all knew that those who became sick were only the tip of the iceberg, and there were a great many others out in the general population who were infected. We were all scared shit-less. As I said previously, we were afraid of the unknown, the silent carriers of this new illness.

When the papers first began to report the transmission of the virus to medical personnel by needle-stick injuries, the en-tire medical community became worried. In a place like a prison, there was always blood being spilled from stabbings or fights, so everyone who worked in the prison system began to feel very un-comfortable. In the back of many health-care practitioners' minds was the thought that they, too, could be infected and not know it yet. There was a constant worry about what they might be bringing home to their families. This was compounded by the fact that many of the inmates had very weak immune systems where tuberculosis (TB) flourished, which also could be spread to the staff working in close proximity to the infected inmates. Not only did TB become a challenge, but a resistant form of TB began to spread. Multidrug-resistant tuberculosis (MDRTB)—that is, TB that was resistant to all medications that treat TB—was a huge problem and concerned everybody. In 2013, MDRTB was first diagnosed in the world. TB affected staff as well, and I think that there was one death of a staff member from TB.

People who had prolonged contact with inmates had their PPD skin tests convert from negative to positive, indicating TB infection had occurred. This is not to say a person with a positive TB test has active TB, but people who convert from having a negative PPD test to a positive PPD in one year have an increased risk of developing active TB. Granted, it is not a very high risk, but the risk is higher if a person converts within a year. These people are called recent converters. In the New York State Department of Corrections, recent PPD converters are treated aggressively. Any inmate with a recent PPD conversion—a documented recent negative test that is now positive—is required to take medication, usually INH (isoniazid) and Vitamin B6 for nine months (originally six months). The vitamin is added to minimize any side effects of the INH. If an inmate refuses to take INH medication, he is placed on a TB hold. His daily activity is limited to his cell, and people who come in contact with him are also limited. Again, it is important to mention that a person who converts to PPD positive does not always have active tuberculosis but is at greater risk of developing the active disease. It is also important to say that at Downstate, as a reception center for the state of New York, all new reception inmates and parole violators who come into the state system have a chest X-ray done. The infectious-disease nurse at Downstate is very diligent in her work, tracking down suspected TB cases. The nurse constantly seeks me out to make sure that all TB issues are properly addressed and documented on the patient's chart and in the computer. One time, two nurses covering the night shift converted to a positive TB test. As it turned out, the ventilation system was the suspected reason for their PPD conversion. It was shut off during the night, for reasons unclear to me.

We were all scared shitless, seeing AIDS before it had a name. There were very sick individuals. Not knowing what they had and often being unable to make them better or even comfortable was unsettling. One of the first inmates I encountered who had the mysterious disease was a young inmate porter who was assigned to the hospital area. He was a pleasant, happy-go-lucky guy who would always say good morning to everyone. He did all that was required of him as a porter and did it without complaining. He was always eager to help the nurse and was always available to move a bedridden inmate when asked. I understood that he was doing a "skid bid"—inmate slang for a one-to-three-year sentence for a nonviolent crime. He had a wife and a young child. One weekend he was admitted to room A in the hospital, a single-bed room. He told the nurse on Saturday that he had suddenly lost the ability to walk. He denied trauma or any pain or discomfort and did not at first seem too concerned and thought that this would pass.

On Wednesday during rounds, he seemed more concerned. The neurological exam could not explain his inability to ambulate. At one time or another, a PA or MD had questioned him about risky behavior: Did you use IV drugs, have you ever slept with a prostitute, or are you a gay male? All his answers were emphatically no. One of the other PAs suggested after we left his room that he was probably unable to pay off his Super Bowl wagers and needed to get off the gallery so as not to be beat up by the other inmates to whom he owed money. Having trouble paying off wagers was not uncommon after the Super Bowl. On one Thursday, another inmate porter passed me in the hall, looked me in the eyes, and then covered his mouth and whispered to me, "The monster." At the time I did not think much about what he said; my mind was concentrating on some other problem.

On Friday morning, before making our rounds in the hospital, we were called to his room. When we entered the room, we could smell urine and feces. The inmate was in a panic, crying uncontrollably. He cried out that he had suddenly lost the ability to hold his feces and urine and was quite alarmed. The look on his face was unforgettable. An ambulance was called to have the inmate transferred to a higher level of care. We all left the room to do something else except Dr. Forte, who stayed behind to be with the inmate until the ambulance came to take him away. On

Monday morning, Dr. Forte informed the group that the inmate had passed away. Of course we all asked Dr. Forte about the cause of death. He closed the door to his office, looking somewhat upset. Dr. Forte reported that when he was alone with the inmate on Friday, just before the ambulance came, the inmate had admitted to having anal-receptive sex on multiple occasions while in prison. The inmate died from some AIDS-related infection, but it is very important to mention that at that point in time we did not have a name for what was killing young males. This inmate did not consider himself a gay man. This risky behavior was later considered to be men having sex with men. At that moment I remembered what the other inmate porter had whispered to me on Thursday, "the monster."

Early on, when AIDS first came on the scene, inmates were dying, and all we could do was make them as comfortable as possible and watch them waste away and die. Even keeping them comfortable was sometimes easier said than done. During one hot summer in the Hudson Valley, the maintenance department at Downstate had a great deal of difficulty maintaining a comfortable temperature in the facility hospital. The air conditioner ran very cold, and the many AIDS patients in the infirmary were freezing. Remember that they were very sick, underweight, and unable to get out of the hospital bed that they were in. The only way to remedy the situation was to purchase electric blankets; yes, we had to send someone out to buy electric blankets in the middle of July. Of course they were difficult to find, but we were able to purchase them at a great price. I can still picture the five or six inmates wrapped up in dark-brown blankets. The blankets were not across the bed, but instead the inmates were wrapped up like newborn babies in the maternity ward of a hospital. They looked like giant pinecones yet to open, or like cocoons with the electric cord tethered to the wall. It was like something one would see in a science-fiction movie. The inmates were wrapped from toe to neck and did not have any strength to unwrap themselves or move. Many had to be fed and cleaned by an inmate hospital worker. A bath towel was wrapped around their heads to keep them from losing valuable heat from their heads. Of course, cleaning each inmate was lengthy and troublesome. The inmate workers did not seem to mind doing this unpleasant task of helping the very sick inmates, many of whom were near death. These inmates were not trained as nurse's aides; they were actually inmate hospital porters who stepped up to the plate and helped out when they were needed. Not knowing what this new deadly illness was or how it was spread did not stop them from helping those who were in so much need. Or maybe the inmate porters did know how this illness was spread.

When new inmate patients who were admitted to the infirmary became mouthy or abusive to the nursing staff, the inmate porters would talk with them and correct them before the correction officers became involved. The common phase was "Could you tighten up the guy in room E?" There was never physical violence, just intimidation on the part of the inmate hospital porters.

During my decades in medicine and working as a physician assistant in the New York State Department of Corrections, I witnessed the onset of a new and devastating disease that took the lives of many people, young and old. I treated firsthand new cases of a disease that had no name, not knowing what I was doing or dealing with. I always lived with the fear of contracting the disease through contact with the people I treated medically. I was also always scared shitless that I would bring some type of illness, like tuberculosis, home to my family.

CHAPTER 12

MEDICAL ADVANCEMENTS IN THIRTY YEARS

I was fortunate to witness firsthand four important advancements in the diagnosis and treatment of what is now called AIDS. One of the most important breakthroughs was the discovery that PCP pneumonia could be prevented and treated with a common antibiotic, sulfamethoxazole, and with trimethoprim, commonly called by its company trade name Bactrim DS. Bactrim DS is readily available, inexpensive, and effective, and it is still used today. The only drawback is that some people are allergic to it. Many times it is not a life-threatening allergy, but it still poses a concern to prescribers.

The second important discovery or breakthrough was when the researchers were able to determine the status or condition of a person's immune system by determining the number of T lymphocytes, more commonly called T cells, in the person's blood. Today it is also referred to as the CD4 count. T-cell amounts can fluctuate on a daily basis in both healthy and sick individuals. When the number of T cells drops to two hundred or less, the incidence of opportunistic infections like PCP pneumonia or TB occurs. Before there was an HIV blood test, we were able to test a person's immune system by checking his or her T-cell count. This was not a test for HIV, but it was a good indicator—and the only indicator that we had at the time. We were advised by attorneys working for the Department of Corrections in Albany that we were not to use the T-cell counts as a diagnostic tool, which I still do not understand. We had an important tool but were unable to utilize it. Today we constantly monitor the T cells and the HIV viral load (the amount of virus in the blood of an infected individual) to determine if the current treatment regimen is working or if it is time for a medication change.

Like diabetes and thyroid disease, AIDS today has become a numbers game; we are constantly checking blood levels of T cells and viral loads, similar to checking blood-sugar levels in diabetes and thyroid levels in hyper- or hypothyroidism. Today we utilize objective parameters to monitor the disease process of each patient. We are able to determine when to increase, decrease, or change the person's current HIV medications. It is important to mention that monitoring T cells every three months is unlike monitoring diabetes, where diabetic blood sugars may be measured as frequently as four or more times daily. In some ways, HIV treatment has gotten somewhat simpler than treating diabetes. The pill burden—how many pills a person takes on a daily basis—is much smaller today than it was years ago. At one time the treatment for HIV consisted of a large number of pills—called a *cocktail*—many times a day. Today it could be only one pill once a day. This was a dramatic breakthrough, and it has changed how the disease is viewed today—not as a life sentence but as a treatable chronic illness.

It is very important to mention that HIV is still a very serious illness; we are now seeing resistance to medication as well as rare strains of the HIV virus. There has also been a trend where gay men have become more lax in their attitudes about sex because they see HIV as more of a nuisance and not a killer as it once was. According to Jacob Andrews in an article in the *New York Times* in April 2005, with the increase of methamphetamine use, there was also an increase in condom-less intercourse, known as bare backing, among gay men. I mention this because if this is occurring in the real world, you know that it is occurring within the walls of prisons across the nation and throughout the world. Methamphetamines may not be available in state prison, but there are a large number of other drugs that alter one's judgment. It is important to remember that condoms are not handed out in prisons in New York State.

There is concern in the medical community that because HIV/AIDS is now a controllable disease, we will see a return to risky sexual behavior, casual sex with anonymous partners, and sometimes multiple sex partners. What I consider the third most important breakthrough in the treatment of HIV that I have witnessed in my long career was the development of the first drug to actually attack the virus: a drug called AZT, also referred to as Zidovudine.

As you may have noticed, I use the terms HIV and AIDS interchangeably. Early on in the illness, it was thought that you might be infected with the HIV virus but without contracting the diseases it causes. Years ago, to identify someone as having AIDS, the person needed to meet certain criteria or have one or more symptom. There is a small group of people who are infected with the HIV virus but have yet to progress to getting full-blown AIDS. Today we see some patients with a positive test for the virus, a small amount of virus on the viral load, but their T-cell counts have remained normal for many years. Scientists have been working diligently to determine what sets this group apart from the others. Today an individual begins treatment early, when his or her viral load goes up and his or her T-cell immunity begins to go down. Attacking the illness early on prevents the illnesses attributed to the virus and changes the prognosis from death to a lifelong, treatable illness. This is different from what occurred early on, before the advent of viral load and T-cell testing, when all that was available to the medical-treatment teams were the signs and symptoms as to when to begin treatment.

AZT is still being used today in many treatment cocktails despite the problems associated with AZT. It had to be taken five times daily when it was first developed. That meant getting up during the night to take a dose, which created a problem. A colleague of mine told me that at Green Haven, inmates were given small battery-operated alarm clocks to wake them up during the night to take their AZT. She told me that one inmate would sleep through the alarm but it would wake up the inmate in the cell next to him. The inmate in the next cell told the infected inmate to tie a string to his toe and run the line to his cell. When the neighbor would hear the alarm clock, he would pull on the string to wake him. I guess some inmates did not mind that other inmates on the gallery knew that they were infected with the HIV virus. It seems to me it was more important to take this new medication, AZT, properly than to go home in a pine box having died from AIDS. There were, and still are, some people unable to take AZT because they are allergic to it. AZT resistance has developed, making the drug useless against some HIV viruses.

The last and most important breakthrough in the treatment of AIDS was the development of the drug Atripla. There were two very important things about this new drug. The first was that Atripla was the first successful once-a-day treatment for AIDS. A patient needed to take only one tablet of Atripla a day to fight off the HIV virus, bringing down the viral load and strenghtening the immune system, which could be objectively seen in the increase of the T cells. Atripla was a combination of three potent antiviral medications designed specifically to combat the powerful HIV virus. This was a monumental breakthrough because two different drug companies combined their HIV drugs to form one highly effective drug. Atripla works, it is well tolerated, and it is easy to take. Taking only one pill a day is a big change from taking a large number of tablets or capsules many times a day.

On many occasions, I witnessed inmates coming into the prison system very sick, many times underweight, with their T cells very low or almost nonexistent, and with viral loads in the hundred thousands; some even had viral loads in the millions. With the stable environment that the prison system provided—three "hots" (hot meals) and a cot (a place to sleep)—many had their mental illness controlled with medication and medical care. I saw many inmates put on weight so that their faces would fill out, and their T cells returned to somewhat normal numbers, with their viral-load levels going undetected. You could see in their faces that they felt better and looked better. Unfortunately, when infected individuals are released back into the street after their bid, they do not follow up on taking their psychiatric medications; then they stop taking their HIV medications and end up on the street again, very sick, both mentally and physically. Eventually they violate parole or get rearrested and find themselves back in the prison system. On more than one occasion, I found them in my office again with hardly any T cells left in their bodies and with viral loads that were through the roof. It is a vicious cycle that I have witnessed too frequently. More needs to be done to treat the mentally ill on the street. I have no idea how to do this, and I don't think anyone in politics or society in general does either, so the cycle will repeat over and over again. If society could learn to better treat the mentally ill, mentally disabled, and the chemically dependent person, the prisons would be nearly empty.

On one routine day many years ago, I was in the middle of an admission physical when I noticed a loud, harsh heart murmur. I said to the inmate, "That don't sound good."

His reply to me shocked me. "Don't you remember me, Doc? I will never forget you," he said. I started to sweat.

"When I was here the last time, many years ago, you saved my life," he said. "Don't you remember?"

"I honestly do not," I told him.

He went on to tell me that about five years earlier, when he was at Downstate, he became very ill, near death. "I had a very high fever and thought I was going to die. I was so sick I wanted to die," he said. "Because of my symptoms and the fact I had a loud heart murmur, which I never had before, you thought I had endocarditis and transferred me to the Westchester County Medical Center. As it turned out, you were right, and after many days of IV antibiotics, I lived."

Endocarditis is an infection that we do not see much anymore. Many years or even decades ago, it was seen among IV-drug abusers. Bacteria from a dirty needle are caught up in the valve of a person's heart. The person becomes very sick and develops a noticeable heart murmur. I asked the inmate what he was doing back here, and he informed me that he went back to using IV drugs again. "How could you do that?" I asked. "Drugs almost killed you, and you still went back to using them?"

With sincerity in his face and voice, he told me that neither I nor anyone else will ever understand the hold that street drugs have on a person's soul. All it takes is one hit of heroin or crack cocaine, and you spend the rest of your life trying to obtain the feeling you had the very first time you shot up or snorted. It is impossible to recreate the euphoria, but you keep on trying. You never stop, and you are never cured of your addiction; the only respite is when you get arrested and spend time in the state prison or die. That is when you are drug-free, but not free of the addiction. "The only cure for addiction is death," he said.

I remember in my training days when an old-time doctor told me that many drug overdoses are suicide attempts and not accidental, when the drug user is tired of going on with his or her life. The inmate said it is like the first time a person has an orgasm; it's something a person never forgets. "I bet you remember your first piece of ass, don't you?" he said with a laugh. "You will never forget that moment and will always try to recreate it." I worked evenings almost ten years in a drug-rehab program, detoxing people off drugs and alcohol. I'll never forget the discussion I had with this inmate. I will never look at a drug abuser in the same light as I did before this discussion.

Addiction—whether it be to alcohol, street drugs, or prescription pain relievers—is killing this nation. Making cannabis (marijuana) a prescription pain medication would make the national addiction problem grow by leaps and bounds. This country has enough people addicted to prescription pain relievers already. California thinks it would be able to tax the use of cannabis for recreational use, but this would only be a gateway to years of addiction to other drugs, and the increased tax receipts would just pay for more prisons and drug-rehab programs. I feel strongly that legalizing marijuana will bankrupt the states and the nation in the long run. The nation as a whole needs to take a long, hard look at the legalization of marijuana. Remember that marijuana is a Schedule I narcotic.

It seems that every time science learns to treat and control a disease, a new disease appears on the scene. Take heart disease, for example; it was a killer of young (fifty- to sixty-year-old) men in the 1960s and '70s. Today, after a patient has a very short stay in a local hospital and some new plumbing work done in the way of bypass surgery on the heart vessels, science can add decades to a person's life. As I explained earlier, a new disease, AIDS, which was first seen in the early 1980s, is now treatable and controllable with medication. Recently, however, a new, very scary disease has developed: MRSA infections.

MRSA infections are frequently seen in high-school wrestlers, child-care workers, and people who live in crowded conditions, such as in prisons. MRSA, properly called Methicillin-resistant Staphylococcus aureus, can be fatal. I have sent many inmates out to large hospitals, where they required aggressive intravenous antibiotic therapy. Some were septic and near death. For the most part, most MRSA cases I have seen were large, ugly boils or abscesses on the skin. The infection is spread by skin-to-skin contact. At Downstate we would place the inmates in contact isolation in a private infirmary room until the lesions dried up. There were antibiotics that were readily available to treat MRSA, but cultures had to done to determine which one to use. I would always tell the staff and inmates to wash their hands frequently with a lot of soap and for more than just a short rinse. One reason MRSA seems to be under control in the prisons now is the development and extensive use of a green cleaner called "128," or the "green stuff" as it is called in the prison system. When 128 first became available for use at Downstate, the staff was only authorized to use it in three areas: the hospital, the special housing unit, and the draft area. As mentioned before, the draft area is where inmates are held when they are coming and going from other jails and prisons. The draft area is a very busy place at Downstate, with controlled confusion requiring the meticulous processing of the worst that society has to offer. Inmates are shaved, showered, and interviewed by the psychiatric and medical nurse in the draft area.

Early on in the MRSA battle, I had two inmates who had significant MRSA infections on the same tier. Inmates live thirty-six to a gallery, with six inmates living on each tier. It was highly unusual to have two cases occur so near each other. I made it a point to tell the officer to get a bottle of 128 and have all the cells on the tier cleaned with it. He told me that he needed special permission to use 128 in any areas other than the draft, SHU, or hospital. I called the sergeant, the lieutenant, and the captain and received the same nonsensical reason. When I got the same response from a front-office administrator, I inquired who wrote the policy and how I could get hold of this person to make an exception to the rule.

After speaking with the area sergeant, lieutenant, and captain, I learned that the most feared man in the New York State Department of Corrections was "Two Bucket Chuck." He is more feared than the commissioner himself. Two Bucket Chuck is the man in charge of prison cleanliness, which products are used, and how they are used in all of the prisons throughout the state of New York. He gets his nickname from the way he teaches the proper way of mopping the floor in a prison—one bucket with soapy water and one bucket with clean, clear water to rinse. Two Bucket Chuck makes yearly visits to inspect all of the facilities. Two weeks prior to his announced visit, the prisons are made spotless, cleaned from top to bottom, like the spring cleaning my mother would do. The executive team, captains, and lieutenants follow him around the facility as he makes his inspection. God help us if a certain area is found not to be up to snuff. It has repercussions down the chain of command, all the way to the sergeant. That is a way of getting your name on the front-office shit list for a long time. God forbid if Chuck smells bleach being used to clean in the prison. (Two Bucket Chuck forbade the use of bleach in the prisons years ago, other than for washing clothing.) Nobody would ask Two Bucket Chuck if the cleaner 128 could be used in areas other than those he designated; everyone was afraid to ask him, regardless of the need. I did not push the issue after seeing the response I received from many ranking officers, many of whom were my friends. Fortunately there were no additional cases of MRSA on that one gallery. Now 128 is used everywhere in the facility, and the incidents of MRSA went down dramatically.

Before moving on to the next important disease affecting the population and staff in the prison system, I need to vent a frustration. During the end of my career I would always notice that the windows of two cells on a top tier were covered in what I thought was pigeon shit. Either pigeons or some other type of bird had made a nest above the windows, and both windows were covered with pigeon droppings. At an unrelated meeting with the front office, I voiced my concern and requested that the environmental committee see to it that the windows were properly cleaned. I became very upset with the amount of nonsense about cleaning two windows. The more upset I became, the more the people at the meeting made light of the problem and did not take me seriously. One ranking officer told the group that we had nothing to worry about because it was not pigeon shit but sparrow shit. Jokingly, he said that I did not know what shit I was talking about.

I told them that the cells with the affected windows were psychiatric observation rooms where men spend most, if not all, day breathing the fungus from the bird droppings. Some of the men were HIV-infected and had low or very low immune systems. I made it clear to everyone in the meeting that inmates housed in these cells were susceptible to serious fungal diseases such as histoplasmosis and cryptococcosis. Secondly, I told the people in the meeting room that it looked disgusting, and most importantly, the policy and procedure manual clearly states that windows should be cleaned at least once a year, in May, unless cleaning was needed more frequently. I said that the inmates who would clean up the windows needed to be instructed on how to properly clean bird droppings from the windows.

As I write this chapter, the windows are still covered in bird shit. I suspect that after this book is published, someone from the front office will make it a point to have the two windows properly cleaned. I know that after correction officers read this they will walk over to check the windows to see if, in fact, the windows are clean. I am still angry about how difficult it was to get things cleaned in the prison.

I recently had the pleasure of hearing Ted Conover, the author of *Newjack*, speak at a literary conference in New York City.

Someone in the audience asked if any good came about as a result of his book. He laughed and responded that at least the very large windows on B Block in Sing Sing have been cleaned.

One final illness that I would like to touch on is hepatitis C. Many years ago, or should I say decades ago, before it was labeled hepatitis C, a few inmates had a condition that did not fit the mold for the common types of hepatitis. These inmates, mostly IV-drug abusers, had elevated liver-function tests or liver-function studies, referred to as LFTs. The antigen or antibody tests for determining hepatitis B were negative, as were the blood tests to determine if the patient had hepatitis A. The inmates were not really sick, but routine screening blood work indicated abnormal LFTs. With no obvious reason for the spike in LFTs, they were labeled as having "non-A, non-B hepatitis," a term that was used for many years. Now that an antibody test and a viral load study (a study that tells us how much virus is in the blood system of a person infected) are available, science and medicine have labeled it hepatitis C.

Wikipedia mentions that there are now five known hepatitis viruses: A, B, C, D, and E. Hepatitis C has become a huge problem for prison systems across the nation. Many convicts, as well as people on the street in society, are infected with hepatitis C and do not know it. Only when people are arrested and placed in state prison, where routine admissions blood work is done and an increase of the liver-function studies is noticed, does the person have an idea that he or she might be infected with hepatitis C. This person would otherwise go through life not knowing if he or she were a carrier for hepatitis C.

It should be mentioned here that there is no vaccine available for hepatitis C. There are vaccines available and commonly used for hepatitis A and B. Inmates in New York State are routinely screened for hepatitis A and hepatitis B. If a person is not immune to hepatitis A and B, meaning that routine blood work does not indicate antibodies, he or she may be offered a series of shots that usually provides lifelong immunity for hepatitis A and hepatitis B. I stress the term *may be offered*. Many inmates do not accept the vaccination, nor do they accept the tetanus booster shot or the measles, mumps, and rubella shot that the state offers when they first enter the prison system.

This distrust of prison health care goes way back to the Tuskegee Syphilis Study, also called the Public Health Service Syphilis Study, which took place in Tuskegee, Alabama, from 1932 until 1972. It was a study to track the natural progression of untreated syphilis in poor, rural black men who were made to believe that they were receiving free health care. They were never told that they had syphilis, nor were they ever treated for syphilis. The program went on for years after penicillin became the standard treatment for syphilis in 1947. Only after a leak to the newspapers did the program stop. Many men died from syphilis, as did women who contracted the disease from men in the study group, and children were born with congenital syphilis. The Public Health Service Syphilis Study significantly damaged the black community's trust of the medical community, especially of white doctors and nurses. It is important to mention here that one of the pivotal people involved in the study was an African American nurse, Eunice Rivers. Participants in the study received free rides to and from the clinic, hot meals, and treatment for minor ailments, but not the penicillin that they so badly needed. To this day I hear older black inmates refer to syphilis as having "bad blood," a term that dates back to the Tuskegee study.

One thing that I must say is that the number of syphilis cases in this state is down. At one time in New York State, I can remember regularly ordering three shots of penicillin. These shots were ordered because an incoming inmate had high blood titers for syphilis and no past history of being treated. The New York State Department of Health would refer to these cases as late latent syphilis, which would require three shots of Benzathine penicillin G. I ordered a lot in my early days, but not as much lately.

Benzathine penicillin G had to be refrigerated. It was as thick as heavy cream. You had to tell the nurse hours in advance that the patient needed a shot of it. The nurse had to take it out of the refrigerator and bring it to room temperature. After bringing the medication to room temperature, the nurse would roll the vial containing the penicillin G in her hands to warm it up to body temperature. The needle used was the size of a small pipe. It was a big needle. One day, the inmate receiving the silver bullet, as we called the shot, was being a real pain in the ass. In addition to having committed a horrific crime, he was loud, obnoxious, and demanding. After the inmate received his first penicillin shot (it had to be in the buttocks), the inmate could not walk. I later learned the nurse did not bring the penicillin to body temperature but injected this thick, cold, viscous fluid into the small cheeks of the inmate's buttocks.

Going back to hepatitis C: there is a cure for hepatitis C. It is not 100 percent effective, and the treatment could involve taking pills (ribavirin) on a daily basis for anywhere from twelve to twenty-four weeks and shots of a drug call Pegasys or peginterferon on a weekly basis. The shots are not at all pleasant, and some patients have a flu-like illness for a couple of days after receiving the injection. On the street, outside of prison, people who receive Pegasys take the shots on Friday nights so they have the weekend to get over the discomfort they experience and do not miss any days at work. Of course, blood has to be drawn on a regular basis during treatment, which to me is also unpleasant. More importantly, the workup for hepatitis C requires a liver biopsy, which is both costly and painful.

When the screening test for hepatitis C first became available, the state would not allow us at Downstate, as a reception center, to test all inmates entering the New York state prison system. To this day, routine screening for hepatitis C is not done. I assume that the cost of treatment—for staffing, the expense of the liver biopsy, and the great expense of the medication—would bankrupt the state. I recently asked a nurse who was screening the new draft (new inmates coming into the state system) what criteria he used for hepatitis C screenings. He told me that he asks each inmate if he has had hepatitis C in the past, used intravenous drugs, or has received tattoos recently while in prison.

Alarmingly, the majority of infected inmates are being missed. I was always a proponent of testing all inmates coming into the state system for hepatitis C. Just being an inmate in a New York state prison places a person at risk for hepatitis C. As I mentioned previously, many people who are infected have no idea that they are, so they go on infecting others. It is also important to say that the hepatitis C virus is not spread like the HIV virus is, and for the most part, it is not spread through heterosexual intercourse. The hepatitis C virus is not found in semen. There have been cases reported in which one partner is infected but his or her heterosexual partner is not. It is my opinion, after years of working with inmates and interviewing hundreds of inmates with hepatitis C, that a common denominator among infected individuals whom I have directly spoken to is the use of intranasal cocaine. It should be mentioned again that I am talking about inmates in a state prison.

Many are very surprised to learn that passing a straw or a rolled-up dollar bill from one person to another to snort up cocaine transmits blood from inside one person's nostril to another. When several people share a straw or rolled-up dollar bill, the act of rubbing the straw end along the nasal passage during the inhalation of the cocaine transfers blood from one person to another. When a person is first told that he is positive for hepatitis C, I review all the possible means of transmission, most of which the person will deny doing. Usually when I ask if the inmate used cocaine, he remains quiet and does not say anything. Then when I ask if the inmate shared the straw, his expression changes.

Maybe this is my public-service announcement to stop the spread of hepatitis C. If you are going to use cocaine, then use a personal straw to stem the transmission of hepatitis C; don't pass the straw around. Again, this recommendation is not based on any scientific study that I know of but is based on my years of interviewing inmates who have just learned that they have hepatitis C.

Finally, I would like to mention one giant breakthrough in science that did not directly affect me, a PA practicing in the prison system: the development of DNA testing and using DNA to identify criminals.

DNA does not play a role in the day-to-day practice of prison medicine, but DNA is collected on a daily basis from inmates, new reception, and parole violators coming into Downstate. When the collection of DNA first began, we needed to collect it from the inmate's blood. An extra tube of blood was collected at the same time that a routine admission blood panel was collected.

Sitting across from where the inmates lined up to have their blood drawn for DNA, I watched a number of inmates sweat. The inmates knew that they were in trouble once their DNA was collected. The inmates looked worried; you could see it in their faces. They knew that their DNA would tie them to some unsolved crime that they committed before this prison sentence. Some were sweating in the middle of the winter, and they were stepping from one foot to another, moving back to the end of the line when the correction officer was not looking.

When an inmate refused to give up his blood for DNA testing, he was placed in the special housing unit (the SHU). At some time later in the week, an extraction team of correction officers was formed, and the inmate was brought up to the hospital area where he was held down and the blood was forcibly taken from him. The extraction team was made up of about six tall correction officers whose job was to remove inmates from a cell when they refused to come out. The team was nicknamed the Ninja Turtles because of the way they looked after they were all geared up. They were dressed in black coveralls and black helmets, and underneath it all, they had hockey padding on their legs, chests, and arms. The correction officers did not have to be big to begin with, because after they put on all the gear, they looked like monsters—very intimidating.

Corrections made it a point to have the extraction team lined up in the hall for the inmate to see on his way to the hospital. The mere sight of these guys made the inmates give up their blood without a fight. Some were so scared that they gave up more than blood. This was all done while the video camera was recording everything. Again, this was more a corrections function, not a medical one. The phlebotomist collected the blood after the inmate was held down. Fortunately the use of the extraction team to collect DNA samples was not used frequently; it was a rare occurrence. Today DNA is collected from an oral swab, not from blood.

One spring day while I was making my rounds in SHU and the protective custody unit, I was in the courtyard when an inmate yelled down to me from his window. He was being held in a SHU cell for refusing to give up his blood for DNA testing. I recognized his voice, and the two of us laughed that he was back in the state system yet again. "Yo, doc," he said. "You and I go back a long time." He went on to ask, "What's the real deal with the DNA shit?"

I responded back to him, "Harry, (name was changed) tomorrow if you do not give up your blood, you're going to get your ass kicked but good."

"No shit?" he said.

I followed jokingly with, "No shit."

The next morning he was escorted up to the hospital and past the extraction team, which he knew was waiting for him. Harry gave up his blood for DNA testing without a fight. He was then moved from his SHU cell back into regular population.

CHAPTER 13

FAKES AND FRAUDS

The greatest difficulty in prison health care is determining who is sick and who is not—who is faking illness and who is truly sick. Inmates who are seeking drugs could convince the best medical doctors that they are in severe pain. This fear clouds a professional's decision-making abilities.

Recently an angry young inmate yelled at me, "The officer kicked my ass, and nothing was done about it." He was in SHU, the box, for assault on staff. The inmate was shouting loudly so the camera could record his conversation with me. "I cannot hear from my right ear," he yelled.

I told him that he was not being truthful; I wanted to say that he was full of shit, but the cameras were rolling, as the saying goes. "Didn't you go out to the local community emergency room after the incident?" I asked. "Aren't you scheduled to see the audiologist for a hearing test?" I then asked. He said yes to both questions. "So how could you stand there and lie and say nothing was being done for you? Not for anything," I said. "You had your hands around a correction officer's neck. You should be thankful that you still have teeth in your mouth. If you would have grabbed an officer by the neck at Green Haven or Clinton, you would be enjoying the liquid diet right now."

He said that he did not have his hands around the officer's neck. I told him that I heard it from more than one officer and that he'd left scratch marks on both sides of the officer's neck.

In the end, the audiologist felt, after careful testing, that this inmate was exaggerating his hearing loss and that his hearing loss was not significant, if he had any hearing loss at all. The audiologist and I saw through this inmate's attempts to game the medical system. But all too often, inmates do manage to convince medical professionals that they have a health problem that they do not—sometimes with disastrous results. One case in point is Robert Garrow, who claimed that he was partially paralyzed by gunshot wounds that he suffered in 1973 when he was captured. As a medical practitioner in the prison system, a doctor's or PA's most difficult determination is validating whether inmates who are confined to wheelchairs really are unable to walk. There is always the consideration that the inmate may be claiming he can't walk for secondary gain.

At the time Garrow claimed he was paralyzed, having to use a wheelchair meant that an inmate would be in a less secure unit that was close to New York City. An MD or PA had to determine if the inmate could walk and chose not to, if he had a true medical condition that prevented him from walking, or if he had an underlying mental illness that caused psychogenic paralysis.

The state did attempt to cluster the elderly inmates together back in the seventies in Fishkill, New York. The Elderly and Handicapped Unit was at the Matteawan Facility, a medium-security prison on the grounds of the present Fishkill Correctional Facility. This is where inmate Robert Garrow, who was convicted of fatally stabbing a sixteen-year-old boy in the Lake Pleasant/ Speculator area in 1973, made his escape. From 1973 to 1978, thirty-two inmates escaped from the Matteawan Facility.

It was a medical doctor's nightmare. Robert Garrow, who was thought to be paralyzed and in a wheelchair, was moved to the minimum-security Elderly and Handicapped Unit (the E and H unit) at Matteawan. During the night of September 8, 1978, Garrow placed a dummy made of rags and wire in his bunk. He had with him a .32-caliber handgun when he walked out the front door of his cell. The gun had been brought into the facility in the bottom of a bucket of fried chicken that his family had taken to him. Garrow then scaled a fifteen-foot-high fence topped with barbed wire and escaped.

His escape was discovered the next morning. The security in the Elderly and Handicapped Unit was not as strict as it should have been because it was a medium-security prison. The Corrections Emergency Response Team (CERT) was brought in from Green Haven Correctional Facility. Of course the public in the local area of Fishkill and Beacon was angered, outraged, and scared. The CERT team thought that Garrow was hiding in the overgrowth near Route 84, waiting to hijack a car passing on the highway and return to the Adirondacks. Roadblocks were set up everywhere.

Three days later, Garrow jumped up from his hiding place in the overgrown weeds on prison grounds and began firing his handgun. Green Haven correction officer Dominic Arena was hit by gunfire in his leg, and the response team returned fire with shotguns, rifles, and handguns. Needless to say, Garrow was dead before he hit the ground. After this episode the Elderly and Handicapped Unit was moved to Green Haven Correctional Facility, a maximum-A security prison, and renamed the Unit for the Physically Disabled. A maximum-A or a max-A prison is the highest security rating a prison could be.

Later in my career, there were two important incidents regarding the use of wheelchairs and inmates claiming that they were unable to ambulate. The first was an inmate who claimed he was assaulted by correction officers while at Rikers Island. He claimed that he had lost the ability to walk and needed a wheelchair as a result of his injuries. The PA who was on call at Downstate and had admitted the inmate to the infirmary had trained and worked at Montefiore Medical Center in the Bronx. He had spent a number of years on the neuro/surgical unit there. He was very knowledge-able and did a great neurological exam. He was able to transform a patient's physical findings to a localized area of the brain that might have been affected. This new inmate was a challenge, and the PA took a long time in his examination. After reviewing the cervical spine and skull X-rays, and after his thorough physical ex-amination, he concluded that the inmate was, in his words, "Full of shit."

He took the wheelchair away from the inmate, and for the first few days, the inmate would just lie in bed claiming he could not walk. After a couple of days of not showering, he began to place his blanket on the highly polished floor of the infirmary. He would push himself on the blanket to the shower down the hallway, and he would wash himself on the floor of the shower. This went on for a few days, but the PA was adamant about not giving in to his demands for a wheelchair. Watching the inmate get about on the blanket, anyone would question his paralysis. One morning when the hallway was clear, the inmate was on his blanket making his way down to the shower room, when he jumped up and shouted to the correction officer at the end of the hall, "Fuck you—fuck everybody. I can walk; get me the fuck out of this hospital."

Then almost two weeks to the day later, the same PA happened to be on call again and responsible for the infirmary when he re-ceived a phone call from the draft nurse. The draft nurse would medically screen all inmates coming into the facility. She had told him over the phone that there was a new inmate down in the draft area complaining that he was unable or unwilling to walk after be-ing "thumped" or beat up while at Rikers Island. Before hanging up the phone, the PA told the nurse to send the inmate to X-ray for cervical spine and skull X-rays and then send him up to the infirmary. After hanging up the phone, he looked at me and said, "Here we go again with an inmate claiming he cannot walk."

Later in the day, the PA came up to me and was as white as a ghost. He said the cervical spine X-ray indicated a large, unstable fracture of C2, a very crucial bone in the neck. The PA said that if the inmate sneezed, he could become paralyzed from the neck down. He had the inmate placed in a cervical collar on a long backboard, and he was transferred by ambulance to the nearby medical center. After the inmate was safely transferred to the medical center, I can remember the PA looking me in the eye and nervously saying, "Holy shit!"

Once, when I took away a wheelchair from an inmate, it prompted a meeting with the inmate grievance guy, who had fielded a complaint about me. Of course, he didn't know the backstory on this particular inmate. One day at Shawangunk, a correction officer had taken me aside and said that an inmate who used a wheelchair and claimed he could not walk played softball on a regular basis. I told him to record it on a video camera, and I would take care of it. The next day, sure enough, the officer had a video of the inmate pitching nine innings of a softball game—and he was a pretty good pitcher, at that. I told the CO to take away the wheelchair, and I would make a note in the inmate's medical folder. The following day, the inmate grievance guy showed up again at my office. This time, with a slightly better attitude, he asked why I took a wheelchair away from a crippled convict. Jokingly, I shouted out like Warner Wolf on Channel Four News, "Let's go to the videotape," and showed the grievance counselor the video of the inmate playing softball. I told the grievance counselor this inmate was making me look like an asshole.

Inmates who came into Downstate the night before had to be screened by a PA the next morning. Whenever I would see an inmate with a cane or crutch, I would carefully watch the way he was using it to determine if he really needed it. Many inmates claimed they were unable to walk without a cane so they would not be double bunked upstate.

Some inmates used a cane for protection from other inmates. For example, there was a doctor who had been convicted of murder because he had allowed a young girl to die during a botched abortion in the Lower East Side of Manhattan. An officer who knew the inmate from Green Haven said the inmate needed the cane to protect himself from other inmates who knew what he had done and would punch him as he walked the long hallways at Green Haven. The officer said he had seen the inmate use the cane as a sword for protection, and it was clear to the officer that the inmate did not need the cane to walk. One day, in the emergency room at the facility, this same inmate told the ER nurse that he was a physician, with a tone of voice that demanded respect.

The nurse on duty got very red in the face and angrily responded, "A doctor would not have left the young girl to die on the abortion table like you did." She went on to say, "You are no doctor; you are a piece of shit."

During my years as a PA, I would make it a point to carefully review inmates' charts to see if canes were issued to them in their previous jails. Inmates knew if they had a cane, they would not be double bunked and would be housed on the flats (ground-floor cellblocks) to avoid using stairs. Sometimes an inmate claimed he needed a cane to walk after a fall, many times on a wet shower floor, at Rikers or after an altercation at his previous facility. None of these incidents were documented on transfer records. After my interview, I would tell the inmate to leave the cane in the corner of the room. If he persisted in claiming he needed the cane, his activities would be limited to the gallery only to avoid going up and down stairs. His meals were brought to him (by other inmates), and he was not allowed to use the gym or go out to the yard.

Downstate was built on several levels, with many stairs, and it was very difficult for someone with ambulatory problems to get around. The outdoor rec yards were built on a steep slope. When the grass was wet, it was very slippery. Because of the limited number of beds in the infirmary, and because of the number of sick, bedridden inmates we received on a regular basis, placing inmates with ambulatory difficulties in the infirmary was difficult. Inmates that were placed on gallery restrictions were to be expedited to a facility that could better accommodate their disabilities. After a few days of being unable to hang out with his buddies in the yard or the gym, and after receiving many cold meals, the inmate would almost always come back to sick call, saying all was better and that he did not need to use the cane any longer. He would hand the cane back and ask to be removed from all restrictions and returned to full activity.

Even though I routinely dealt with inmates who claimed to need wheelchairs or canes, the doctors weren't necessarily aware that this was a problem. One beautiful spring morning, I bumped into Dr. Forte coming into work about nine o'clock. I was carrying a pair of crutches and one cane from the room where I had been screening a new draft inmate. With a strange look on his face, he asked why I was carrying the cane and crutches. I laughed and said, "It's not even nine a.m., and I've already made two men walk." I told Dr. Forte I wanted to hang the canes and crutches on the wall like they do in churches in Europe after people are healed and are able to walk again. Dr. Forte had little understanding of what went on in the early hours of the morning at Downstate. Buses were being loaded up to take inmates to all corners of the state to make room for new inmates.

Not all fake medical problems in prison revolved around problems with walking. Over my years as a PA, I've seen inmates pretend to have all sorts of maladies. For example, one inmate tried to convince me he was blind. This incident began at sick call one morning, when an elderly inmate returned with a prepackaged medication he had received the previous day from me. The very fine print—and I mean *very* fine print on the package—indicated a contraindication. The inmate was angry with me for giving the medication to him. He complained about the many side effects listed on the package. The lettering on the package was tiny; I had a great deal of trouble reading it. The inmate said he had no trouble at all seeing the lettering. I indicated to the inmate that the contraindication meant nothing to him and that he could safely take the medication.

Two days later the same inmate showed up late to sick call as I was all packed up and leaving the area. He made quite a scene to the other inmates and to the officer because I would not see him. He was very loud so everybody could hear him. When I asked where he had been, he reported that he had been in the law library doing his legal work when he was called for sick call. I told him sick call was over and that I had reviewed his sick-call slip, and I told him his medical problem could wait until sick call tomorrow. He was not happy. I also went on to tell him that if he demanded an emergency sick call for a chronic, non-acute problem, I would see to it that he would get a disciplinary ticket.

About a week after this incident, the same inmate was seated in the waiting area, waiting to be called for academic testing. When the young woman came out to call him in, the inmate, in a very loud and nasty voice, told the woman he was blind, could not read, and could not be tested. He did this in front of a large group of inmates. When I heard this, I became angry and jumped out of my seat and went out to confront the inmate. In a louder voice, I told the inmate not to lie to this young woman who was trying to do her job. I told her he spent hours in the law library reading law books and had no problem reading the fine print on a medication package. The female counselor put down in his classification chart that he refused testing.

A few days later, the inmate came back to sick call with an attitude toward me. I said to him that he had some nerve—that before we met he was unable to see and claimed he was blind and that now after a brief intervention, his sight had been restored. I commented that his sight was restored to the point he was writing letters to everybody to complain about me. I told him that was no way to treat a person who had helped him regain his sight. He did not laugh.

Yet another inmate would come to sick call on a regular basis to have his heart medication renewed for his cardiac-related chest pain. He was very tall, lean and muscular. One morning during sick call, I walked past a large window overlooking the gym at Downstate. This inmate was playing basketball with a small group of inmates. For the short time I was watching him, I was very impressed by his physical condition on the court. Not once did he stop to catch his breath, unlike the other inmates he was playing with, and he had no difficulty in rebounding against the other aggressive inmates playing with him.

When I returned to my office, I reviewed his medical chart and noticed that he came to sick call on a regular basis to get his heart medication renewed. Almost like clockwork he showed up. I went on to review his chart and noticed that his electrocardiogram was normal, and that his cardiac complaints were very vague and unclear. I became very suspicious as I reviewed his medical record, so I went over to his housing location.. I still remember his location to this day. I cannot remember my cell phone number, but I can remember his cell location fifteen years later. I had the officer open his cell door, and I went in to find about seven unopened bottles of his heart medication lined up on his windowsill. All had the labels facing the same way, no bottles were opened, and there was no indication that the patient was taking this tablet. I confiscated all his medication and returned the bottles to the pharmacy. I took my time and wrote neatly in his chart what I had witnessed in the gym and the fact that the inmate was hoarding medication in his cell.

The inmate did not waste any time in complaining about me. He filed a grievance stating that I had no right to enter his private cell. Later that week he came back to sick call demanding his heart medication back. When he claimed that he needed the tablets for chest pain, I became angry and told him he was full of shit. I explained to him and everybody listening how I had watched him for a good length of time playing basketball with no shortness of breath or chest pain. I told him that if he persisted in complaining about chest pain, I would limit his level of physical activity, restrict him from strenuous activity such as going to the gym and the rec yard, and would suggest a full cardiac workup when he got to his permanent facility upstate. He turned and walked away from me. Both of us were angry, and all the correction officers and other staff could see it in our faces and hear it in our voices. I think he was trying to use his size and demeanor to bully me.

Later that week while I was having lunch with my boss and the other PAs at Downstate, the grievance counselor came up to our table in the officers' mess hall. With a grin on his face, he asked if I had told an inmate that he was full of shit. My quick response was "On more than on one occasion." Then I thought for a moment and asked what had brought this to his attention. It turns out the inmate had written to Central Office to complain about my choice of words. Central Office had contacted the superintendent at Downstate, who had passed the complaint to the deputy superintendent. He had then passed it on to the grievance counselor, who was supposed to hand it to my direct supervisor. If I had known what the inmate was convicted of I think my choice of words would have been a lot more different.

Fairly often I was called upon to treat inmates who were legitimately deaf or were faking deafness. One such encounter began early one morning when a screening nurse approached and said that a sign-language interpreter was coming in to help us communicate with a deaf-mute inmate. As a result of a lawsuit against the state, a signer was always available from another facility, about fifty miles away, to help interview deaf inmates who were able to sign.

Before the lawsuit happened, I would write questions for the inmate on a piece of paper. He would either nod his head or write his answer back. The Department of Corrections learned the hard way in a federal court that this was in direct violation of the Americans with Disabilities Act (ADA) and the Rehabilitation Act of 1973.

Later in the morning the screening nurse noticed that I was speaking with the inmate who had claimed that he was deaf and needed a signer. When I called the inmate to my interview room, I had recognized him, as he had me. We knew each other for too many years through the prison system. I caught him off guard, and he forgot that he had told the draft nurse that he was deaf. Our meeting was sad, though, because both of us recognized that we were aging. He said that he was back on a parole violation, police contact, after spending twenty-two years in the system.

When the nurse saw the two of us talking, she became very angry: first, because we were talking like old high-school buddies, and second, because she had gone through great trouble in getting the signer to come over from Eastern Correctional Facility to interview this inmate. As it turned out, when he was young the inmate had lived with two people who were deaf and knew how to sign, and they had taught him how to sign. Many deaf people do not sign. He used his ability to sign to his advantage while in prison. He could hear and speak clearly, but to get special placement, he would fake his hearing loss and utilize his signing skills to fool the staff. Unfortunately for him, some staff members in the prisons knew him and knew he could speak and hear. Because of his many years in prison and his ability to communicate with the deaf, he became an advocate for the hearing-impaired and an adversary to the New York State Department of Corrections.

On the other hand, there were a number of inmates who would fake their hearing loss to get additional privileges or to be placed in facilities closer to their homes. The term that the audiologist would use on the consultation form was FOHL, spelled out in capital letters. It stands for *Functional Overlay of Hearing Loss.* Some thought it meant *Faking of Hearing Loss.*

The most difficult thing about providing medical care within the walls of a prison is determining who is truly sick and needs attention and who is faking a medical illness for secondary gain. In the back of my mind, I always worried that an inmate was faking an acute illness so he could be taken to an outside hospital emergency room to meet his family and friends in the ER waiting room. When I was on call, I would make it a point to come in to see and examine most inmates who required treatment at an outside hospital emergency room. I bet that there is nothing more frightening for two young correction officers than to walk into an outside hospital waiting room with a convicted felon, only to find a room filled with his family and friends waiting to visit with him on a prearranged acute illness. It is just a matter of time before something goes wrong and someone gets hurt. Someone could get injured, whether it's someone unrelated to the convict, the correction officers, or maybe some bystanders waiting to be cared for in the emergency waiting room, or the emergency-room staff might be shot in an escape attempt.

Not a day goes by without an inmate demanding a controlled medication. Many inmates claim they have a seizure disorder to obtain Klonopin, which is a longer-acting, better type of Valium. I always love to question the parole violators who will be returning to the street soon as to when their last seizure was. When they claim their last seizure was recent and that their seizure disorder is poorly controlled with the current dose of Klonopin, they always ask that I increase it. I love to tell the inmates that it is my responsibility to contact the New York State Department of Motor Vehicles to yank their driver's license so they will not have a seizure when driving a car and hurt someone. In New York State, a person has to be seizure-free for two years to operate a motor vehicle. Of course then the inmate's story changes.

Just today an inmate reported to me that he was getting phenobarbital for his seizure disorder. He claimed that he has been getting phenobarbital since the age of thirteen; his last dose was just before he was arrested. I had checked the computer prior to seeing the inmate and noted that this was his third bid, the third time he was convicted for criminal sale of a controlled substance. This did not include his parole violations. The computer did not list that he was on phenobarbital, since he has been frequenting Downstate Correctional Facility since 2006. When I asked the name of his doctor on the street, there was silence. "I don't remember," he finally responded.

"You mean to tell me that you have been seeing a doctor on the street for more than fifteen years, and you cannot remember his name?" I asked. I then asked him where he had the prescriptions filled.

He said, "At CVS in Manhattan."

"Where in Manhattan—what street?" I asked.

He could not remember. He became angry, and so did I. I told him that I didn't believe him, and he became indignant and asked me why. I then went on to ask him what he was convicted of, knowing he was a drug dealer and would not answer me. Then I asked him what he was convicted of on his second bid. He did not admit that he was convicted for drug sales, and finally I asked what he was sentenced for the first conviction. Again he did not answer. I told him that I had trouble believing a three-time loser who was on a controlled substance when he couldn't remember the MD or pharmacy that was giving it to him on the street.

In a loud voice, he shouted that his family was going to hear about this and that I was going to be sued. I told him that if he was smart, he should use a different lawyer than the lawyer he used for his last three convictions.

One must understand that it takes me longer not to give an inmate what he claims or demands. Phone calls have to be made, and documentation has to be clear and neatly written to avoid being questioned by someone at a later time. Many times it would be much easier and quicker just to give the inmate what he wants.

On another morning as I was making my way down the hospital hallway, I heard a young inmate screaming and crying very loudly. He was sitting on his hospital bed, closest to the hall in room H, holding his head in his hands and complaining of a severe headache. He appeared to be in serious pain. As I made my way down the hospital hallway, I stopped and asked the male nurse covering the infirmary what the patient's problem was. With somewhat of an attitude, the nurse responded that the inmate was looking for narcotic pain relief for a headache. I asked the nurse what the inmate's blood pressure and pulse were. Now, with more attitude, the nurse responded to me that the inmate was drug seeking. The nurse had yet to check his vital signs and was not familiar with the inmate's condition. I quickly reviewed the transfer records, which indicated that the inmate had end-stage AIDS (a term that you do not hear as frequently anymore). His T-cell count, also referred to as a CD4 count, was not available yet. His transfer summary from Rikers indicated that he had a very high cryptococcal titer. Highly elevated cryptococcal titers are variable, but because the inmate had AIDS, one of the differential diagnoses is cryptococcal meningitis. Not a good diagnosis to have. This guy was not faking his illness; he was truly very sick.

I took a thermometer and blood-pressure cuff and went in to see the patient. His temperature was slightly up, his blood pressure was moderately elevated, and his heart rate was tacking away (the medical term for a fast heart rate or tachycardia). Looking at his vital signs and the amount of pain that the inmate was in, I arranged to have him transferred to Westchester County Medical Center in Valhalla. I was somewhat upset with the nurse because before he had even checked the inmate's vital signs, he had labeled the inmate as drug seeking. Granted, the inmate did have a long history of IV-drug abuse, and drug seeking is very common among inmates and drug abusers. However, anyone could see that this guy was in a lot of pain and true discomfort. The inmate did not last long in the outside hospital and died a few days later from cryptococcal meningitis. He was not faking his illness.

Dealing with convicted felons has always been difficult. Here I deliberately use the words *convicted felons* or *convicts*. There has to be some relation between the words *convict* and *con*, as in con man. Obtaining a straight, true answer to a medical question from a convict is at times difficult. Just obtaining a brief medical history can be long and painful. Something as simple as questioning an inmate about his asthma can be frustrating.

A common interview goes like this. "How long have you had asthma?" I ask. Frequently, the inmate responds, "A minute," which is street slang for "a long time." I once told an inmate that I was going to lock him up for a minute if he did not answer my question properly. Then I ask the convict when was the last time he used his asthma rescue inhaler. The common response is always "at Rikers Island." At this point I start to get a little annoyed with the inmate. I repeat the question in a louder voice: "When, not where, was the last time you used your asthma pump?" The next question I need to ask is how often the inmate is using his inhaler. (It is important to determine if the inmate is abusing his rescue inhaler or using it more than he should.) The inmate always responds that he uses his pump only when he needs to. I ask the inmate why he would use the inhaler when he did not need to. Then I ask the convict how many times a day he uses the asthma pump. He usually says, "When I am wheezing." At that point I threaten to take the inhaler from the inmate and have the inmate brought up to the facility hospital when he needs to use the pump so the nurse can monitor the use of the inhaler and avoid abuse and overdose. I have seen inmates abuse asthma inhalers to the point of near death. I tell the inmate that before the nurse allows him to use the rescue inhaler at the medication-room window, the nurse will check to see if the inmate is truly wheezing.

Before I am finished evaluating the inmate's asthma, I have to check his breathing using a peak flow meter (also called a peak expiratory flow meter). I am not fond of using the peak flow meter because of abuse potential, as there may be a false reading of a peak flow because of a poor effort by the inmate. The peak flow monitor test is very subjective and is based on the patient's cooperation. Unfortunately, Central Office requires that all new inmates have a peak flow baseline. Before I administer the peak flow test, I look the inmate in the eye and tell him to breathe as hard as he can into the peak flow meter. I ask the inmate clearly if he understands me and repeat to the inmate to blow in the peak flow meter as hard as he can. Then the inmate blows a two hundred on the meter, but four hundred is the least amount I will accept. The measurements are related to the age and height of a patient. (I was mostly dealing with young athletes who should be able to blow much higher.) The inmate is trying to prove that his asthma is severe and that he cannot breathe.

These inmates are bodybuilders or basketball players who are in great physical shape. I know that this inmate is jerking me around, and I begin to get angry. I then ask him if that is the best that he can do. I offer him one more chance. If he does not get above four hundred on the peak flow meter, I restrict his physical activity—no gym and no yard. When he learns that he will not be able to lift weights, play handball, or work out in the rec yards, he wants a third attempt at the peak flow meter. I look the inmate in the eye and tell him I am not in a game-playing mood today.

It is going to be a hot day in the Hudson Valley, and there is no protection from the sun in the yards; the gyms are hot, smelly, and poorly ventilated. I would be wrong to let an asthmatic person exercise if he cannot breathe as reflected by his effort on the peak flow meter. I tell the inmate to sign up for regular sick call to be reevaluated.

Besides trying to con me about how ill they are, inmates sometimes try to con me into authorizing unnecessary surgery. For instance, one busy morning when I was trying to get caught up on my work, I was asked to drop what I was doing to see a cadre inmate in the emergency room—or I should say the triage room—for acute abdominal pain. I walked in to find an inmate resting comfortably on the stretcher, with blood pressure of 110/70 and a pulse of sixty. You don't forget these things. After a careful examination, I was sure the inmate had a small left inguinal hernia that had reduced by itself. The inmate claimed the pain was unbearable with a pain-scale level of nine, with ten being the worst. This was not reflected in the patient's face or examination, but he was clear in stating that the pain had started that morning and was severe.

After my exam I looked at the inmate's chart. I try to do this after my initial evaluation so I am not swayed by what other practitioners might have written about this inmate. I was correct in my assessment; the inmate had a small hernia and was on the waiting list to see the surgeon. I was firm with him and told him he needed to wait for treatment of this non-acute, non-life-threatening chronic condition. With that, the inmate sat up and demanded to be sent to the local community hospital emergency room to have the surgery done. Again I was clear that the local community hospital emergency room would send the inmate back to the prison and suggest follow-up at the regular surgical clinic. At that, the inmate became angry and demanding: "I go home in two weeks and want the surgery done before I go home."

The inmate wrote a grievance about his displeasure at having to wait to see a surgeon. The tax-paying public of New York State should be able to see the grievances that inmates write complaining about the care they receive in the prison system. It would make a great series on reality TV. I often think of the veterans of this country who wait weeks, if not months, just to see a physician or a physician assistant.

CHAPTER 14
MEMORABLE LAWSUITS

O n more than one occasion, an older, seasoned inmate would shout out to me or to other staff, "I am going to see your ass in Foley Square," after he learned that he was not going to get what he thought he deserved or demanded from medical. Foley Square is the location of the federal court in Lower Manhattan, where lawsuits are brought by inmates, or for inmates, against the state of New York. Because the state cannot oversee lawsuits against itself, all lawsuits against the state are heard in the federal court system. Cases from the Lower Hudson Valley and New York City are heard in the federal courthouse in Foley Square. Many, if not most, of the lawsuits related to medical treatment that inmates have brought to date were judged by the federal courts not to have merit.

James Flateau, who was the spokesman for the Department of Corrections for many years, was quoted in a January 2003 article in the *Poughkeepsie Journal:* "The inmate's perception of interpretation of his medical care is based more on his desires or demands rather than his or her medical needs." Convicted felons can be very demanding and very litigious. They have all day long with nothing better to do than to think of ways to sue the state of New York. It is very important to note, and as I am going to discuss, some of these suits not only did have merit but also changed the way medical care is provided in New York State, and throughout the country, in some cases.

Brown v. Coughlin

The most memorable suit in my thirty years involved the Department of Corrections and an inmate named James Brown. Back when physician assistants were on call at Downstate, it was my week to cover call and be responsible for any inmates admitted to the infirmary during the weekend. With Dr. Anthony Forte in charge, he insisted that infirmary rounds were made on Monday, Wednesday, and Friday mornings at 7:00 a.m. The PA on call would present and discuss the new cases to the group so the PA covering for the upcoming week would have some understanding of the patients in the infirmary and their medical conditions. Dr. Forte would make sure the medical needs of the inmates were being met. Medical rounds never took long and were very important in providing direct care to the inmates in the infirmary.

On one Monday morning, after a weekend when I was covering call, there was a young, skinny inmate in room I, with his bed next to the window along the infirmary hallway. I remember the nurse calling me Friday night after the inmate was admitted from the draft area. This particular inmate was a new draft from Rikers Island. The nurse requested that I allow her to move the other inmate out of the room that the new inmate occupied. She explained that the new inmate smelled so bad that the other inmate was becoming ill. I asked her to be more specific about the origin of the smell, and she just said, "You will see it all on Monday morning." I just thought it was poor personal hygiene at the time and did not give it any more thought.

When Monday came, I had forgotten all about this inmate. During rounds, we entered room I, where the inmate was. The smell was disgusting and nauseating. Some of us in the group thought it was the smell of pseudomonas, a common, very foul-smelling bacteria. The inmate had a long leg cast, a plaster cast going from his groin down to his toes.

I asked the inmate why he had a cast on his leg and when the cast had last been changed. The inmate reported that a year ago he had fractured his femur and that a cast had been applied at that time. I again asked him when the cast was last changed. He said that the cast had not been changed since it was applied one year ago. I asked him again if that same cast had been on his leg for an entire year, and he said yes. I asked if he ever went back to the doctor at Rikers Island to have the leg and the cast checked, and his response was that they never called for him. I asked if he ever went to the medical department asking for help. The transfer record indicated that the inmate had been a no-show for the orthopedic clinic on more than one occasion. "Did the smell of your leg make you think of returning to the medical department to have the cast checked?" I asked the inmate.

At that point I realized that the inmate was academically challenged. I began to get angry and asked the inmate if any of the other inmates in the dorm or the correction people at Rikers Island had noticed the bad smell. "Didn't anyone else suggest that you go to medical or even take you there?" I asked. "Did any of the people or your family who came to visit you notice the stench? I don't believe that no one told you to go to medical to have that cast checked, or that no one called the administration on your behalf." The only person who had showed any interest in this inmate was the lawyer who represented him in the medical malpractice lawsuit against Rikers Island and Downstate Correctional Facility.

After meeting with the inmate, the group of PAs and MDs making rounds met in the hallway outside of his room. After a short discussion about what to do next, such as ordering X-rays of his entire leg and calling an orthopedic surgeon in to see the inmate, I turned to the group and said that we were in deep shit. No way will there be a good outcome to all of this for both the patient and us, I said. I turned to Dr. Forte and said that we should not have accepted this case from Rikers Island. He should have been sent back to Rikers for them to resolve up this big problem. Dr. Forte said to me, "If they did nothing for this inmate in a year, what makes you think that they would fix the problem now?" Maybe it was a blessing that the inmate was transferred to somewhere where something would be done about his leg. I told Dr. Forte that it was very important that he contact Central Office in Albany to inform management of the problem that we inherited. The front office at Downstate should also be brought online, because whatever the outcome, it would not be a good one for the inmate. I also turned to the group and told them all to write neatly on the chart and print their names under their signatures so the attorneys could identify everyone involved in the treatment at Downstate. "We are all going to Foley Square on this one," I told them. "We'll take the Downstate station wagon down to New York City, have lunch at Wo Hop in Chinatown (not too far from the courthouse), and then dinner at Luna's in Little Italy after testifying." I had a bad feeling.

Within minutes of the inmate being taken to the X-ray department, the X-ray tech called and was upset about the smell. "You've got to do something about the smell," she said, "and the X-rays of the bones don't look that great either."

The inmate came into Downstate on Friday night and was seen by an orthopedist the following Wednesday. It was very difficult to find orthopedists in the community to see our inmates. It was very difficult to find any outside specialist to see any inmates, for any reason. The cases were difficult, the inmates were more difficult, and the reimbursement was not worth all the effort. Having a convicted felon shackled with chains in your waiting room did little to reassure your regular patients.

The local orthopedist was a kind man and a true Christian. He understood that there was a need to see the incarcerated. He would come into Downstate on Wednesday mornings to help out and see orthopedic cases. He did not do it for the money; I know he did not get much from the state for seeing inmates. Not only are specialists poorly paid to treat inmates, but it can take months to get their money. The PAs and MDs at Downstate appreciated him for taking time from his busy orthopedic practice. Unfortunately, some inmates did not see it that way.

The outcome was not good for this inmate. He had to have his leg amputated from above the knee. A leg prosthesis was made for him. The rehab took many months.

A few years later, Dr. Forte was served with papers indicating that he and the staff and administration at Downstate were being sued in federal district court for malpractice against the inmate, for the amount of $4 million. Dr. Forte was visibly upset. I think that this was the first time that Forte was sued for malpractice. When he showed me the papers, I responded, "I told you we were in trouble no matter what we did and that we were all going to Foley Square." I reminded Dr. Forte that we had done nothing wrong. Unfortunately, in the court system of this country, not doing anything wrong means nothing.

The trial took two weeks; it took a noticeable toll on Dr. Forte. He was on the stand for many days, for long periods. From what I learned from people who were in the courtroom at the time, the lawyer was tough on Dr. Forte, and he took it personally. Early on in the litigation, the lawyer asked Dr. Forte if he remembered the case. Dr. Forte laughed (to himself) and said, "Of course I do. I remember it like it was yesterday. PA Darnobid said that we are all going to Foley Square on this one." The lawyer requested that Dr. Forte be more specific. Dr. Forte informed the court that during medical rounds on Monday morning, just moments after meeting with the inmate for the first time, PA Darnobid told the group of PAs and MDs that the outcome in this case would not be a good one, and that whatever we did, we would still end up in federal district court. I am not sure if he told the court about having lunch in Chinatown and dinner in Little Italy during his testimony. A correction counselor was also called on the stand to testify, and he was also asked if he remembered this particular case. With a smile, he responded that he clearly remembered Darnobid saying to write neatly and clearly and that we were all going to Foley Square. After a day of testifying in New York, Dr. Forte, the correction counselor, and the deputy superintendent at Downstate all called me and said that they were looking for me and that I should be called to testify any day.

A high-powered law firm from New York represented the inmate. Dr. Forte said to me that not once did he see James Brown wear the leg prosthesis in the courtroom. The leg prosthesis, which Dr. Forte had taken so much time and trouble to have made for him, was never worn by the inmate in the courtroom during the trial.

The attorneys for the inmate flew in an expert-witness orthopedist from California to testify against the state. From what I understand, the state's lawyers did a fantastic job in defense of the state and Dr. Forte. The last question the state's lawyer asked the orthopedist witness was if he would have accepted the case if he was in his own practice. He clearly said, "No, I would have sent the inmate back to Rikers Island. Dr. Forte was foolish to accept this problem case from Rikers Island." Remember that Dr. Forte felt strongly that we could have done a better job providing care for the inmate than the medical team had done for him at Rikers and that getting the inmate out of Rikers was important in getting his leg fixed. After two weeks of testimony, the jury was about to decide on the outcome of the case. Just before the case went to the jury, the lawyers for James Brown approached the state's attorneys and requested $600,000 to settle this case out of court. We learned later that the inmate had also sued New York City/Rikers Island for $6 million but had settled on $400,000 in an out-of-court settlement. I guess they wanted more from the state because we were the ones who had amputated his leg.

It was my understanding that if the state had settled out of court, the opposing lawyer, the inmate's lawyer, would have had all of their costs paid by the state. In other words, the cost of flying that high-powered orthopedic surgeon first class from California, putting him up in a fine New York City hotel (rumor had it that it was the Waldorf Astoria), and feeding him would have been paid for by the state. I wonder what the lawyer charged the state for each photocopy that he had made in regard to this case. After hitting the state up for the attorney fees, the lawyers would have taken one-third of the settlement. Someone also once told me that if a jury decides in favor of the person bringing the lawsuit but the jury only awards that person one dollar, the prosecuting lawyers are still able to collect all of their costs from the state. The lawyers would get more than half of the settlement after they added on their costs and additional fees.

The lawyers for the state stood fast and felt that they had a good chance of winning the case. They turned down the out-of-court settlement offer and went for broke. After a couple of days of deliberation, the jury ruled in our favor and felt that there was no malpractice involved. The inmate was doing a short bid (short prison term) for some stupid crime. He had gotten lost in the so-called cracks of the prison system, specifically Rikers Island, and as a result had been injured and lost his leg. I sometimes wonder if someone is looking after him now that he is on the street.

Dr. Forte was never the same after the inmate's lawsuit. He took much of it personally and felt somewhat responsible, as he always had, for the care of all the inmates at Downstate. The front-office staff at Downstate, the superintendent, and his deputy seemed more supportive of the medical department and Dr. Forte after the two weeks at Foley Square. Their attitude toward the professional medical staff changed noticeably.

The local orthopedist stopped coming to see inmates at Downstate. The time he had spent away from his practice for the court case making depositions and traveling to New York City to testify had been costly, a huge headache, and a financial burden. For what he was being reimbursed, seeing orthopedic cases in the prison was not worth the headache. Not having him help us with orthopedic cases was a great loss for us and for the inmates at Downstate.

Milburn v. Coughlin

The next memorable lawsuit was at Green Haven Correctional Facility in Stormville, New York. Louis Milburn sued then corrections commissioner Thomas Coughlin. The lawsuit alleged that the medical care given to inmates at the Green Haven Correctional Facility was poor, at best. It was a class-action lawsuit that was filed in September of 1979 by the Legal Aid Society of New York against the New York State Department of Corrections. The lawsuit claimed that the state violated inmates' constitutional rights by providing grossly inadequate and unresponsive medical care to inmates held in Green Haven Correctional Facility. Both parties in this case, the New York State Department of Corrections (the defendant) and the inmates at the Green Haven Correctional Facility (the plaintiffs), agreed that it would be in the best interest of all parties involved to have the issues resolved without additional litigation, so they agreed to a stipulation for entry of final judgment. A stipulation for entry of final judgment is an agreement between parties that settles the case. Both parties involved agreed that there was no need to send this dispute to a full and lengthy trial for a jury to render a decision. The judgment was entered by the court without a trial.

The court-appointed physician overseer described the care as "wretched" in 1999, as quoted by a *Poughkeepsie Journal* news reporter, Mary Beth Pfeiffer, in an article that appeared on January

6, 2003. As I understood it at the time, the main and important problem was that the appointments for outside medical-specialty consults were being made by a secretary who had little medical-specific training. The second and more important problem was that there were not many outside providers in the local community who were interested in seeing inmates. The reimbursement rate did not cover the cost of seeing each inmate, the payment took months to get, and God forbid if the state budget took months to pass, because it would hold up payments for months. In addition, having shackled inmates with armed guards in a waiting room did not sit well with other waiting patients. These inmates could be nasty, demanding, and litigious. If they felt that they were not getting what they thought they deserved, they would sue.

This is not to say that there were not sick inmates at Green Haven. There were plenty, but the demanding inmates were antagonizing the small group of local doctors who had a sense of moral obligation to provide care to inmates.

Three important things occurred as a result of this lawsuit. First, the medical care of the inmates at Green Haven improved; it could not have gotten any worse, many said. Staffing got better, the housing for the disabled improved, access to physicians became much easier, and there was an increase in availability of medications. Second, new inmates arriving at Green Haven were handed a paper outlining what they were medically entitled to, as a result of *Milburn v. Coughlin*, and whom to complain to if they felt their medical needs were not being met. And third, the federal court system placed Dr. Robert L. Cohen as an overseer of the direct patient medical care provided at Green Haven. He was placed at Green Haven to make sure that conditions of the lawsuit were being met by the state. Dr. Cohen had graduated from Princeton, had gone to medical school at Rush Medical College in Chicago, and had trained in internal medicine at Cook County Hospital. He served as a federal court monitor, overseeing medical care for convicts in Florida, Ohio, New York, and Michigan. All this oversight was a result of lawsuits from inmates against each state mentioned.

It is important to mention here that the federal judge who heard the case, Robert J. Ward, was the same judge who decided the case against New York State in *Negron et al. v. Peter Preiser*, the commissioner of the department of corrections. In that case, the Department of Corrections was relieved of the responsibility of providing mental health care and medical services to inmates under its control, and the responsibility for the care of mentally ill inmates was given instead to the New York State Department of Mental Hygiene.

As I write this, the use of prescription narcotics for chronic pain is high at Green Haven. I wonder if this was an end result of *Milburn v. Coughlin*. Are inmates being given narcotics because the physicians are afraid of litigation and the *Milburn v. Coughlin* lawsuit?

Estelle v. Gamble

I would be wrong not to mention the most important landmark case in corrections history across the nation, *Estelle v. Gamble*. J. W. Gamble, an inmate of the Texas Department of Corrections, sued W. J. Estelle Jr., the director of the Department of Corrections in Texas, for the medical care he received after sustaining an injury while working on a prison work detail. Inmate Gamble claimed that he was subjected to cruel and unusual punishment, in violation of the Eighth Amendment of the US Constitution. In this case, under the settlement order, the state of Texas agreed to specific measures to improve the health care to inmates in their prisons. The case occurred in Texas, and New York State had nothing directly to do with it. However, the decision had, and still has, a great impact on health care that is provided to inmates nationwide, in federal, state, and local prisons.

The case was decided on November 30, 1996, in the US Supreme Court. The district court dismissed the complaint, but the court of appeals overturned it. This case is monumental because it was a claim of a violation of the Eighth Amendment of the Constitution of the United States. The state of Texas was accused of deliberate indifference to the needs of its inmate population because of alleged acts, or because of acts of omission, by the medical staff. Did the medical practices in the state of Texas for inmates rise to the level of *cruel and unusual punishment?* According to the decision dated November 30, 1976, Gamble was seen by the medical staff on seventeen occasions within three months of his injury, but an X-ray of Gamble's back was never taken. It is important to state that not all claims against prison authorities violate the Eighth Amendment of the US Constitution. Inmates, like people in general society as a whole, can sue in the regular courts for malpractice in a tort claim.

Early on in my career, old-time inmates reminded me about *Estelle v. Gamble* on more than one occasion, when they thought they needed some medical procedure or treatment and felt I was remiss in not providing them with it. They would shout out, "Remember *Estelle v. Gamble*," or in a loud voice they would say that I was deliberately indifferent to what they thought was a serious medical need. Today's inmates don't have a clue about what *Estelle v. Gamble* was and what it means to their rights for access to medical care. I think the bottom line of *Estelle v. Gamble* is that the states must provide staffs that meet minimum standards of diligence and competence and that caseloads and facilities must be adequate.

Clarkson v. Coughlin

The fourth and last case that had a direct impact on my career as a PA in the New York State Department of Corrections was *Clarkson v. Coughlin*, which was entered as a judgment on June 12, 1996. The federal district court found that the New York State Department of Corrections was not offering sufficient services to the deaf and hard-of-hearing inmates in its custody. This was in violation of the US Constitution, the Americans with Disabilities Act (ADA), and the Rehabilitation Act of 1973. What was very important in this judgment was the finding that prisons must provide *reasonable accommodations based on disability*, which became the mainstay for inmates with disabilities in the New York State Department of Correctional Services.

The plaintiff, Doris Clarkson, was a woman who had been deaf since childhood and who communicated using sign language, specifically American Sign Language (ASL). She was incarcerated at Bedford Hills Correctional Facility, a New York state prison for women in Westchester County, not far from New York City. The state knew that Clarkson needed a sign-language interpreter, but she was never provided with access to one. While at Bedford Hills, Clarkson was administered an HIV test without her knowledge or informed consent. The state alleged that she had a psychiatric condition, but the medical staff did not evaluate her properly because no sign-language interpreter was available. During parole board meetings, she was not provided with a sign language interpreter for interviews.

A number of other inmate plaintiffs were listed in this suit, including an inmate named Mark Brock at Downstate Correctional Facility. Brock had been completely deaf since birth and communicated primarily through ASL. During his time at Downstate, inmate Brock was not provided with the services he needed, despite his obvious hearing impairment and his direct requests. According to the lawsuit, Brock was not able to write English well and was not given access to a qualified sign-language interpreter. Because of this, he was not able to explain his medical problems to the medical staff and could not participate in Alcoholics Anonymous meetings. At that time there was a woman who was familiar with sign language at Downstate. She was not fluent in ASL and was not a qualified interpreter, however, and Brock was unable to make himself understood by his counselor or anyone else at Downstate, according to the suit. There were also many other hearing-impaired inmates in the custody of the New York State Department of Corrections at a number of other prisons throughout the state who were also involved in this class-action suit.

As a result of *Clarkson v. Coughlin,* a formal mechanism was established in the prison system by which inmates could discuss their individual needs for reasonable accommodations, based on their disability. Because of *Clarkson v. Coughlin,* closed captioning had to be added to televisions and to films so that deaf and hearing-impaired persons could follow the programs. Visual fire-alarm systems—bright flashing strobe lights—had to be added at Downstate. Special telephones that use electronic transmission of text were made available—telecommunications devices for the deaf (TDD), which allow deaf people to communicate via the telephone with deaf or hearing people who have access to this same service. In addition, shake-awake alarm clocks were made available to wake up inmates who were not able to hear the COs yell out in the mornings.

Today, before a hearing-impaired or deaf inmate is interviewed, a qualified sign-language interpreter has to be brought in. The use of amateur interpreters, especially other inmates who are able to sign, is forbidden during medical visits. This assumes that the inmate is able to sign and understand sign language. I am not sure if the state teaches sign language anywhere in the system.

One offshoot of *Clarkson v. Coughlin* is the availability of an ATT language-translator service. Either by using a speaker-phone or an extra extension phone, we are able to communicate with inmates who do not speak English. Spanish-speaking, monolingual inmates are not so much a problem because of the number of Spanish-speaking health-care workers available in the prison. The problem arises with so many others from small countries who find themselves in prison and unable to communicate with anyone. It becomes a big problem for these inmates who come from countries where tuberculosis or other communicable diseases are common. It seems that ATT has translators available for just about every imaginable language in the world. I understand that ATT offers eight different dialects of Chinese alone, and I have personally used a number of them. I think that ATT has foreign-speaking individuals contracted throughout the country who could be available at a moment's notice to translate; they just need to be near a phone. I guess that they are located somewhere in the country where the labor rate is low and where there is an abundance of foreign-speaking individuals. I was told it once cost the state $2.50 a minute, and I'm not sure what it costs the taxpayers now. Without this service, providing medical care to everyone in the prison system would be impossible. Thank God we do not need to use the translation service often.

A few years ago, a foreign-born inmate from an Asian country who did not speak or understand English committed suicide. During the investigation it turned out that the inmate had been screened by a psychiatric worker the day before and was deemed not to be at risk for suicide. The family was quite upset and questioned the state whether a translator had been used, because the inmate did not speak or understand a word of English. It was my understanding that the state settled out of court for a lot of money. Now there are green cards in all the interview rooms at Downstate explaining to all providers how to access the ATT translator service.

On a very busy day, several years ago, an inmate pretended that he could not understand me, indicating that he spoke only Spanish. I did a quick check and noticed that this was his fourth state bid, and nowhere did it list that he did not speak or understand English.

I called the senior counselor and asked if he had a problem. Her response was that he had been tested in English and had tested quite well. I became angry for a moment and told the inmate I didn't have time for his bullshit and to get out of my exam room. Of course, I made it a point to document this incident with neat handwriting in his medical chart.

Negron v. Preiser

With the help of the Legal Aid Society, Valentine A. Negron and a group of inmates at the Matteawan State Hospital in Fishkill, New York, brought a lawsuit against the then commissioner of the New York State Department of Correctional Services, Peter Preiser, in October of 1974, challenging the constitutionality of certain conditions of their confinement.

The inmates alleged that the conditions of the isolation cells in ward 3 at the Matteawan State Hospital violated the Eighth Amendment of the US Constitution. The inmates claimed the use of isolation/seclusion cells constituted cruel and unusual punishment. The complaint alleged brutality, excessive use of physical restraints, and the unauthorized dispensing of psychiatric medication by prison guards. According to what I have read, the judge, Robert J. Ward, did not believe what the inmates claimed about the conditions at Matteawan. During the court proceedings, he summoned a driver and a car to drive up to Fishkill to see the facility firsthand on that same day. At the time of his visit, he saw inmates in cells without toilets but only large, open tin cans. There was no toilet paper in the cells. He also witnessed inmates drinking from a community cup through a straw placed through the window in the door. During the trial, an inmate testified that he was confined to an isolation strip cell, wearing only his underpants, for five months. The court declined to hold that the conditions of the isolation cells violated the Eighth Amendment.

Negron v. Ward

Valentine A. Negron and other inmates brought this lawsuit in October of 1978 for an incident that occurred in June of 1975. Negron's first suit was in October of 1974. Now he found himself as a patient or an inmate on ward 3, the same ward that he had complained about in 1974 in his lawsuit against Commissioner Peter Preiser. The crux of this new lawsuit questioned whether Negron had been placed in an isolation strip cell because he was severely mentally ill or because of behavior reasons. Benjamin Ward was the commissioner of the New York State Department of Correctional Services at that time.

After a disruption on ward 6 at the Matteawan State Hospital in Fishkill, a group of inmates were moved from ward 6 to ward 3, a psychiatric ward. Ward 6 was an open dormitory ward where inmates were permitted to leave during the day for work details, for institutional programs such as school, and for occupational programs. The inmates were allowed to have recreation and associate with the other general population inmates at Matteawan. The inmates in the group were placed in seclusion, in solitary confinement in a strip cell. Each inmate was stripped to his underwear and locked in a cell containing only a mattress and maybe a toilet. The seclusion order was signed by an unlicensed physician who was not a psychiatrist. The jury found that the plaintiffs were kept on ward 3 solely for punitive or disciplinary reasons, not because they were mentally ill. The jury awarded each plaintiff $125.

This reminded me of the great movie *One Flew over the Cuckoo's Nest*. It was based on the novel with the same name written in 1962 by Ken Kesey. The movie was filmed at the Oregon State Hospital in Salem, Oregon. The lead character in the movie was Randle Patrick McMurphy, played by Jack Nicholson. He was a recidivist, antiauthoritarian convict serving a short bid for statutory rape. Even though he did not show any overt signs of mental illness, he was transferred to a mental institution for an evalua-tion. McMurphy learned that because of his antisocial behavior, the nurses and doctors had the power to keep him committed in-definitely, longer than his sentence. In an attempt to correct his antisocial behavior, electroconvulsive therapy (ECT), or electric shock therapy, was administered. Finally, at the end of the movie, to control McMurphy's sociopathic behavior, he was given a frontal lobotomy and left in a somewhat comatose state.

The movie was made in 1975, about the time of the lawsuits against the state of New York because of the conditions at the Matteawan State Hospital. The movie *One Flew over the Cuckoo's Nest* is considered one of the greatest American films. According to *Wikipedia*, in 1993, the film was deemed "culturally, historically, or aesthetically significant" by the US Library of Congress.

Dunleavy v. Wilson

This suit was brought against Malcolm Wilson, the governor of the state of New York at the time, regarding the treatment provided for the mentally ill who are in the prison system. The judge felt that the plaintiffs, Dunleavy and other inmates, had an incorrect understanding of the statute, article 16 of the New York Correction Law. The word *treatment* (in regard to the mentally ill) does not ap-pear in article 16. The correction law only provides for the care and custody of inmates, not for the treatment of the mentally ill. As I understand it, back in 1975 the state of New York was not ob-ligated by the correction law to provide treatment for the mentally ill. The plaintiffs in this case, George Dunleavy and James Clifford Wilson, appeared before the district court *pro se*—without the as-sistance of an attorney, unlike in most of the other cases. It is my feeling that these and other lawsuits, as well as the media's cover-age of the trial at the time, made the state legislature recognize the obvious need for a change.

In 1976, article 16 of the New York Correction Law was repealed as it related to the treatment of the mentally ill in the Department of Corrections. It took the responsibility of providing psychiatric care for inmates away from the Department of Corrections and transferred it to the Department of Mental Hygiene. Standards were established for the operation of special housing units, which were formerly called isolation cells. On January 1, 1977, the Department of Mental Hygiene opened the Central New York Psychiatric Center on the grounds of the Beacon complex, and it was relocated to a portion of Marcy State Hospital. In September of that same year, Matteawan was closed forever. In a number of other states, the prison system would become the largest provider of psychiatric health care.

PART 3

A Day in the Life

CHAPTER 15

CORRECTIONS TODAY

Every day for almost my entire career, I had to pass through an area called the "trap" at Downstate. It is the area in front of CHQ (central headquarters) where an officer sits in an enclosed window area, opening one door to let you into the trap from the free world and then opening another door to let you out of the trap into the world of a maximum-security prison. Downstate Correctional Facility is a max-A facility. On the wall inside the trap, there are pictures above the glass of all the superintendents who have worked at Downstate since it opened in 1978. I hate to say it, but I worked for each one of them in the past thirty-five-plus years.

One does not need to pass an examination to be superintendent in a New York state prison. This is unlike most municipal police departments where you must pass a civil-service examination to become chief of the department. In corrections there is not an examination for superintendent or for senior correction counselor. A common theme that you hear in corrections is that "you serve at the will of the commissioner." You need to be in the right place at the right time. In the past, some line officers have questioned superintendents' abilities and qualifications to supervise security staff. There always seems to be resentment coming from captains, lieutenants, and sergeants that they need to pass a very demanding exam to get their positions. Not only do they need to pass an exam; they are ranked according to their grades, with the person with the highest grade being promoted first.

I started providing care for the inmates in Building 1 at Downstate, the extended classification building, after the regular doctor passed away from lung cancer in 1995. The doctor was a friend and colleague; he was a pleasure to work with. I did not realize what a difficult job this guy had in dealing with the very sick inmates in Building 1. Looking back now, I understand what a great job he did in a very difficult situation.

Downstate is made up of five main buildings. Building 4 is for the cadre inmates: inmates who cook, clean, cut the grass, and work in the libraries. Buildings 2 and 3 are for reception and classification of new inmates, and Building 1 is dedicated to extended classification. Building 1 also houses the special housing unit (SHU), also called the box; protective custody (PC); and a gallery where the mentally ill are clustered together. This gallery is referred to as the forensic diagnostic unit (FDU).

When I started in 1978, inmates were referred to as *felons*, but we were told not to call them *felons* but *convicts*. We went from calling them *convicts* to *inmates* years later. In 2013 we were instructed to refer to the inmates as *offenders*, not as *inmates*. Recently we were told to go back to calling them *inmates* and not to use the term *offender*. I always liked the term *felon*; it reminded me of the old movies.

CHAPTER 16
FORENSIC DIAGNOSTIC PSYCHIATRIC UNIT

As I said earlier in the book, the Department of Correctional Services (DOCS) was once responsible for providing care for its mentally ill inmates. But because of the inadequate job the department did, the responsibility was taken away from DOCS many years ago and given to the New York State Department of Mental Hygiene. Now at Downstate and throughout New York State, prison inmates are treated in units called either *satellite psychiatric units* or *forensic diagnostic units* (more commonly referred to as FDU). Each unit is headed by a unit chief, who could be a social worker or psychologist; many have PhDs, but a PhD is not required. The unit is not headed by a psychiatrist. I think the reason physicians do not run the units today stems from the limited number of available psychiatrists decades ago. Many psychiatrists in the prisons were foreign trained, many had difficulties with the English language, and many were unlicensed. This was many decades ago, during the 1970's and early 1980's. Today there is a larger supply of licensed, well-trained psychiatrists. The early psychiatrists in state hospitals had enough to do to practice psychiatry, let alone run a unit. Early on, many psychiatrists relied on staff nurses to suggest diagnoses and medications for the treatment of the sick inmates on their units.

It is very important to mention again that prisons have been replacing the government-sponsored public psychiatric hospitals in the last forty years. You can check the psychiatric population in the state's mental hospitals and compare it with the number of inmates in the prison system in the 1970s and see a dramatic shift in the years after 2000. It is a lot cheaper to provide psychiatric care within the walls of a prison than in state-run psychiatric hospitals. New psychiatric medications did have some effect on the number of psychiatric hospitals closing but not totally.

If properly diagnosed and treated in the prison, many inmates are more likely to successfully reintegrate into the community. My office is two doors down from the FDU discharge planner. A very hardworking registered nurse makes sure that mentally ill inmates receive proper placement and care when they are released to the street. I have worked with this woman for years, and I know that not only is she very good at what she does but she is also very sincere in doing what is right for each individual. What is heartbreaking to her is when, after all the work she has done, the inmate returns to Downstate after only a few months on the street.

One spring Saturday morning when I was on call for the facility, I received a phone call from the nurse covering the ER. He was dealing with an inmate whom he described as very large, hostile, and very angry. The nurse told me that the inmate had a bizarre look in his eyes, and he appeared ready to hurt himself or someone else. The nurse asked if he could give him a shot of Haldol to avoid anyone getting hurt. I felt uncomfortable in giving permission for that, so I told the nurse I was on my way into the facility. The nurse said I should make it quick because this guy looked like he was going to go off any minute now. I mentioned to the nurse that if he had to prevent the inmate from hurting himself or someone else, he could have the correction officers place the inmate in a Reeves stretcher.

A Reeves stretcher is a long, strong plastic-roll type of carrying stretcher with long plastic slats sewn into it; it also has a number of belt straps around it. It provides a great way to restrain someone from hurting himself. The use of camisoles, commonly referred to as straitjackets, was forbidden in the prison system. I felt uncomfortable using chemical restraints because I was not properly trained in their use and was very concerned about everyone's safety. Because the inmate had an extensive psychiatric history, I told the nurse to have the psychiatrist called in. On Saturday mornings a psychiatrist saw new inmates who had arrived Friday night.

The inmate was a very tall man and all muscle, very intimating. It was my understanding that he was an ex-marine. I reminded the nurse to keep the inmate on his side so he would not aspirate (throw up) and choke. It took seven of the largest correction officers working at Downstate that morning to restrain the inmate. When I arrived at the ER, they all looked as if they had had a great deal of physical difficulty; their faces were red and their uniforms out of place. We placed the inmate on a stretcher and rolled him down the hall across from the nurse's station into the dayroom, where he could be watched until the psychiatrist came to see him.

About a half hour later, a short man with a large mustache, dressed in a sport coat and tie, approached with his finger pointing at me. In a heavy foreign accent that was difficult to understand, he began to sternly lecture me about the use of physical restraints on inmates. The others, nurses and correction officers, began to laugh. When he finished his rant, I calmly informed him that I would have the restraints removed by the correction officers before he went in to see the inmate. I also informed the doctor that the inmate was very upset and violent, for reasons we could not figure out. I told the doc that the inmate had a great deal of hate for psychiatrists, especially psychiatrists who had difficulty with the English langue. I also said he was not fond of foreigners The psychiatrist looked into the dayroom and saw this giant of a man thrashing about on the stretcher, trying to get out of his restraints. I went on to inform him that if the restraints were removed before he went in to see the inmate, the inmate would no doubt kick the shit out of him. I told him to look into the inmate's eyes to see his anger—to look at the size of him and see his strength. After hearing my reasoning, he saw where I was coming from and my honest concern. When he spoke next, his voice stuttered, which made the group laugh. After the psychiatrist interviewed the inmate at a distance, he came back to the nurse's station and began to write his note in the patient's chart. I asked him if the restraints should be removed, and his reply was "not yet." The inmate was transferred to a local hospital emergency room for treatment.

Looking back on this case, I think that the inmate had a psychiatric disorder and was already on some type of antipsychotic medication ordered by the mental hygiene department at Downstate. It was felt that he had ingested PCP or angel dust (Phencyclidine), either by snorting it or taking it orally. What we observed that morning was PCP psychosis. With PCP psychosis, people often display dramatic mood swings, anxiety, paranoia, and aggressiveness. Violence is common, and people exhibit strength and aggression that are uncontrollable. I think that the PCP exacerbated his preexisting mental disorder, and because he was on some type of psych medication, the combination caused this PCP-induced psychosis or made it much worse and uncontrollable. The inmate did not make it through the day; he died later that morning in an outside hospital emergency room. The combination of his mental instability, the psychiatric medication that he had already taken, and taking PCP on top of all this caused convulsions, coma, and respiratory arrest.

The severely mentally ill at Downstate are housed in twelve of thirty-six cells on a gallery. These cells were once referred to as the "strip cells," meaning that the inmates have no belongings or anything in the cell that they can hurt themselves with. At one time they were stripped down so they were butt-ass naked, but, as mentioned before, now they wear a very heavy cotton smock commonly referred as a Barney Rubble (from the *Flintstones* cartoon) suit. Today, to have an inmate in a true strip cell, you better have a good reason, or he must have a mattress and a smock on. The name has also been changed to observation cells. The old-timers still refer to them as strip cells and are always corrected by the front-office staff.

The regular cell doors in these twelve cells have been replaced with cell doors with large, very thick glass windows to allow correction officers to better watch the inmate when he is placed on suicide watch, commonly referred to as "one-on-one watch." When the inmate is deemed to be at risk for hurting himself, an officer is placed outside the cell to watch the inmate twenty-four hours a day. Many times correction officers are held over from the night shift, on overtime, to sit and watch one particular inmate for eight hours straight. Some of the night officers volunteer for the overtime, and some are stuck, meaning that they have no choice but to work the eight hours of overtime.

A problem arises if the night officer did not sleep before his regular scheduled night shift. After working an eight-hour night shift, he is then required to sit in a chair and do nothing but watch another person for an additional eight hours. The gallery is dark and dimly lit. I always think of a young officer with small children who has spent the day at a lake or the ocean beach and then comes to work his eight-hour evening shift and gets stuck for another eight hours watching an inmate sleeping. You know that he is tired from playing with his kids all day at the beach. After working his regular eight-hour shift, he is exhausted.

There once was a plan to turn the dorm in Building 1 into a unit better suited for psychiatric patients. The dorm was a wide-open, very large room that could be converted into a proper psychiatric unit. This never happened. The state took a prison that was designed as a release center and tried to make it a psychiatric facility. It just did not work.

On a couple of occasions, the one-on-one watch correction officer had been found fast asleep at his post. The suicidal inmates are watching the officers who are sleeping. If prisons are going to be psychiatric hospitals, they need to be retrofitted to meet the needs of these patients. If three inmates are on a special watch, I have seen three officers sitting outside of three cells watching each individual inmate. On one occasion when I was on call, I placed an inmate on a one-on-one special watch in the hospital. I was criticized by the nurse administrator at the time for inappropriate use of an infirmary room. She said the inmate should have been placed in a strip cell in the psych unit, rather than wasting an infirmary bed for a non-medical problem. I was told this in a somewhat angry tone in front of the group of PAs and MDs making Monday-morning rounds.

I responded to her and the group that he had been in a strip cell on a special one-on-one watch when he made the second sincere attempt to end his life. In the infirmary there are bright lights and interactions with staff to keep the officer awake. It is very hard for anybody to work sixteen hours straight. Sitting in a chair in a dark area with little interaction with anyone for eight hours, after having worked eight hours already, is tough.

I recently saw on television that a prison somewhere in this great country of ours used closed-circuit television cameras. One correction officer was able to monitor the behavior of six inmates who were in strip cells or isolation cells. The officer was not far away from the area and was able to respond quickly if an inmate attempted to hurt himself. I understand that at one time at Rikers Island, specially selected and trained inmates were used to watch suicidal inmates. Using inmates to watch fellow inmates on suicide watch has since stopped.

After working in Building 1 for more than two decades, I am impressed with the level of care and insight shown by the correction officers on the psych unit. I receive phone calls all the time from the COs when someone is not behaving quite right, such as not bathing, eating, or leaving his cell. I frequently rely on their judgment because they see the inmates for long periods throughout the day.

There is no psych staff stationed on the unit. On occasion, if the inmates are agreeable, they are brought out for an interview with the psychiatrist, psych nurse, or clinician (a social worker or psychologist). There have been a few times in the past thirty-five years that I trusted the judgment of the correction officers more than I trusted the judgment of some of the staff. The psychiatrist would only spend about a half hour with the inmate, maybe a couple of times a week if the inmate was agreeable to come out of his cell for an interview. The correction officer would be with this inmate on the unit for eight hours a day.

I would seek out the regular officer on the unit before making my rounds to find out what was happening, what needed to be addressed, and who needed to be seen. Many officers knew inmates from their previous state bids. Many times the officer in the bubble (the officer's station) would greet me by saying, "Do you know who is back?" I would always check with the CO on the unit about a certain inmate and ask him, "What's the real deal?" before going down to the cell door to speak with the inmate. "Is the inmate the real deal, or is the inmate faking mental illness?" I would ask the correction officer on the watch or in the bubble.

I know that some have criticized me for relying on the judgment of staff who had no formal psychiatric training, but believe me, their input was very valuable. Their input is important, and I think that they should be part of the treatment team. It has been suggested, I think at Rikers, that correction officers be part of the treatment team and be there when inmates are interviewed by the FDU staff at team meetings. I know that confidentiality may be an issue here. But how much confidentiality is there when officers are already standing next to a violent, hostile inmate during the interview? At the risk of assault, do you leave mental-health staff alone with inmates taken out of an observation cell? Recently a special chair that is bolted to the floor was added to the interview room. The inmate is handcuffed to the chair and is unable to move out of it.

I have seen all sorts of mental problems in the FDU during my time at Downstate. Below are some examples:

One morning the correction officer shouted out to me through the glass of the officers' station, "Be careful—we have a finger painter in cell 17." Inmates who spread their excrement on the walls of their cell were referred to as *finger painters*. I guess you can call that sick corrections humor, a way to deal with difficult situations. Although not common, it does happen with the mentally ill inmates. I have been told that some inmates who are not mentally ill spread their feces on the walls of their cells or on themselves to make a point. I think about what it would smell like on a hot summer day. The heads-up by the correction officers is important. I can only imagine what it would be like to look through the cell-door opening and come face-to-face with an inmate covered in his own excrement without being forewarned.

On another occasion during my rounds, the correction officer asked if I checked cell 18. I told him I just looked in the cell quickly, and the smell made me turn away. He then told me to go back and check the windowsill to see the little snowmen the inmate had made with his feces.

On one beautiful spring day, there was an inmate in a strip cell in the dayroom of the infirmary. Back then the inmates had nothing to wear in the strip cells, so he was bare-ass naked. The correction officer on the one-on-one watch was a new jack who had gotten stuck working a second shift of overtime and was assigned to watch this inmate to make sure he did not hurt himself. The officer sat in a high chair looking into the dayroom. The inmate proceeded to squat down and defecate into his open hand without losing eye contact with the officer watching through the glass. The inmate then began to eat his own feces, watching the reaction of the correction officer. The medical term for this behavior is *coprophagia*. The new officer became visibly sick, turned white, and wanted to throw up. He called his supervising sergeant and told him to come quickly because he was very sick. A replacement officer was quickly found for the post and the new jack left the facility, never to return to corrections.

Sometimes smearing feces can lead to physical illness in the inmate, as happened with an inmate who was spreading feces on his body; he was obviously severely psychotic. I was very concerned, as this behavior had been going on for days. I asked why he was not transferred to an acute-care psychiatric hospital, but I did not receive an answer. After the weekend I went up to check on him as requested by the weekend nurse. Because he was rubbing his eyes with his feces-covered fingers, the nurse was concerned that he might have developed conjunctivitis or an eye infection. Of course, then Central New York Psychiatric Center would not take him because he had an eye infection.

During one hot summer, an inmate on a watch took feces and spread it all over his face. He was very sick mentally, although I bet some in the psych department may have felt that this was a behavior problem—that the inmate was acting out. While making rounds on the unit, I told the watch officer that this gave a new meaning to the term *being shitfaced*. Similarly, I laughed when a clinician, a psychologist, once told me an inmate was only being manipulative when the inmate inserted his entire index finger into his rectum and then licked it like a Popsicle. A few days later, he was on his way to New York Psychiatric Center to be admitted for closer observation.

I remember a story once told to me by a correction officer who had spent many decades on the job. He was on a one-on-one watch on the psych unit, observing an inmate who had claimed he was crazy. At that time the inmate was in a true strip cell with no clothing or bedding. The old-timer was watching this inmate when he began to spread his own feces on the window. This, the old-timer said, did not upset him. After the inmate was finished painting his window with excrement, he said to the officer, "I told you I was fucking crazy." The officer quickly responded back to the inmate, "If you are fucking crazy, you will lick the shit off the window." The officer told me that he was sorry that he put that idea in the inmate's head, especially after the officer had eaten his lunch. The officer told me that after the inmate ate his excrement, the officer "tossed his cookies" (medical slang for throwing up your last meal).

A few days after hearing this story, I was making my rounds on the psych ward where inmates were in strip cells. An inmate got my attention and told me his toenail was coming off. He said he had banged his toe many months ago and now the toenail was about to come off. I told him to take his sock off so I could take a look at it. The toenail was almost completely off, hanging on by a thread. I told him to leave it alone and that it would fall off in the next day or two. I also said that he could see the new nail growing in behind it, pushing it off. He demanded that I take him up to the hospital and remove the toenail. I tried to reassure him that the nail was going to fall off by itself very soon. When I turned my back, the inmate yelled to the correction officer that he needed to see mental hygiene right away because he was going to hang up (hang himself) because he was not getting medical attention for his toenail, not getting what he demanded. I walked away, knowing the inmate was already on a suicide watch.

In July an inmate was forcibly removed from a cell upstate and transferred to an observation cell at Downstate. During my rounds on the psych unit, I noticed that the inmate was noticeably agitated, very loud, and angry. He told me that during the cell extraction, his wrist had been broken. The wrist was not tender or swollen, and the inmate had full range of motion of the hand and wrist. I told the inmate that I would get an X-ray in the morning since the X-ray tech had already left for the day. Well, that was not good enough for the inmate. Shouting, he demanded to be taken out of the facility to a local hospital emergency room to have an X-ray done. I had a great deal of concern about taking a violent inmate who would cause difficulty, for sure, out of the facility to a hospital in the outside community. I did not want him or anyone else getting hurt. I could not reassure him or calm him down. He began to get more verbally abusive. He shouted out that if I did not take him out to the local hospital, he would insert anything he could get his hands on into his penis. Remember that he was already in a stripped cell.

I went back to my office and checked the computer to learn that in the past year this guy had had to be taken to the local hospital on three different occasions for inserting foreign objects into his penis. That night at dinner, he took the foil covering off the four-ounce juice container, rolled it up tightly, and inserted it into his penis. The foreign body was up his urethral shaft. (They use special paper forks and spoons on the unit to prevent inmates from breaking up the plastic and either swallowing it or placing it somewhere it does not belong.) The next morning an X-ray of his wrist was done at Downstate and it appeared negative. The foil paper was in his penis.

Another bizarre behavior that I have witnessed on more than one occasion is head banging. This occurs when inmates vent their frustration by banging their foreheads against the cell door, wall, or cell window. Not only is this upsetting to witness, but the constant sound of someone banging his head against a very hard surface makes the person witnessing this behavior sick himself. One day, again in the hospital dayroom, I saw an inmate—whether he was mentally ill or not, I do not know—who charged the large, thick window headfirst, like a freight train hitting a wall. The inmate would bounce off the window and fall to the floor. He would do this repeatly. The window has a crack in it to this day. People watching in the hallway would turn their heads just before he made contact with the glass. It was painful to watch.

When I called the psych department, I was told that a clinician (a social worker or psychologist) would be down to talk with the inmate. I was somewhat upset and responded that I wanted a psychiatrist and a nurse with a syringe of Haldol as soon as possible. I said that if that could not be done, my next phone call would be to the superintendent. The inmate could not continue doing this. "We are going to need the blood emergency response team (BERT) to clean up the dayroom," I told the psych department. "It is just a matter of time before this guy starts gushing from his head from where he is repeatedly banging it against the floor and walls."

I witnessed another sort of self-destructive behavior one day when I was called to the ER to check on a recent leg wound. An inmate had taken a razor blade and cut a very deep—and I mean deep—incision in his calf, down to the bone, to try to remove a metal rod that had been implanted years ago when he broke his leg. I was told he was suffering from a mood disorder. I would have considered that diagnosis until after I spent some time talking with the inmate and realized the rod was in his other calf. He had cut the wrong leg. The more I spoke with the inmate and confronted him, the more his thoughts and speech became disorganized, a condition commonly referred to as "speech salad." He was not making any sense, just rambling on. I doubt that the diagnosis of mood disorder was the correct one.

Mood disorders are a category of mental illnesses that describe a serious change in mood. Illnesses under the mood disorder umbrella include, but are not limited to, major depression and bipolar disorder.

I wonder what Daniel St. Hubert's diagnosis was when he first came to the New York state prison system and what his diagnosis was when he was released back on the streets with no medication and no psychiatric follow-up. St. Hubert allegedly fatally stabbed a six-year-old and critically wounded a seven-year-old in an elevator in Brooklyn not long after being released from the New York State Department of Corrections. Many times his antipsychotic medication was stopped because he was refusing to take it.

While in court, inmates are led to believe that they will be placed in a minimum- or medium-security prison according to the crimes they were convicted of. When they sit down with mental-hygiene staff, however, they learn that if they take psychotropic medications, they will be sent to a maximum-security prison. Some minimum and medium prisons have limited mental-hygiene services, from what I have been led to believe. Of course, their response is that they do not need the medication, and they say, "Please take me off of it so I can go to a minimum or medium prison."

Another reason mentally ill inmates, as well as mentally ill people in general, refuse or do not take their psychotic medication is because of a condition called *anosognosia*. Their mental illness limits their insight into the existence of their mental illness. The *Merriam-Webster Dictionary* describes *anosognosia* as "a prominent feature of schizophrenia and bipolar disorders where a person is unaware that he or she is sick." People with this condition don't feel that they are mentally ill and therefore feel that they do not need to take medication. They do not have the insight to recognize that they suffer from mental illness, have psychosis, or suffer from bipolar disorder. This is not the same as what happens when mentally ill people start to feel better after starting medication and falsely believe that now they can do without it.

With anosognosia a person suffers from a mental illness but is unaware of the existence of his or her disability. This condition is commonly seen with Alzheimer's patients who lack the awareness that they have Alzheimer's and insist that nothing is wrong with them. Because of anosognosia, there is a high level of medication noncompliance and rehospitalization in prisons and in the general population on the street.

At Downstate Correctional Facility the specific diagnosis of mental illness is typically deferred at the time the inmate is admitted to the prison. I'm told this is because the psychiatrist needs more interview time and many sessions with each inmate to make a proper diagnosis. I understand this, but as I was trained decades ago, the transferring diagnosis or past medical psychiatric history is crucial and should be included in the admitting diagnosis. If the admitting practitioner did not agree to the transfer diagnosis, he or she would write something like this: *adjustment disorder with history of psychosis.* Or he or she would say the diagnosis is something such as *psychosis by transfer summary* and rule out mood disorder. In doing this, the admitting doctor makes it clear that his or her admitting diagnosis is based on the patient's past history and was not made by the brief interview the practitioner had with the patient. It would be like seeing a new patient with a history of hypertension, but the day you meet him, his blood pressure is normal, and then you say that he does not have hypertension and stop all of his hypertension medications. In a matter of time, his BP goes up again.

Back in the early days of Matteawan, when an inmate was deemed psychotic at Clinton Correctional Facility in Dannemora, New York, the inmate was "two PC'ed," meaning that two doctors at Clinton felt the inmate needed to be placed in the mental hospital at Matteawan and both physicians signed a document saying so.

The inmate would then be sent to Matteawan, where he was evaluated by Dr. Sweeny, a psychiatrist. After two days at Matteawan, the inmate was returned to Clinton Correctional Facility. The judge in the lawsuit against the Department of Corrections, *Negron v. Preiser*, in its closing statements, questioned whether Dr. Sweeny was so good that he was able to cure these inmates in a couple of days and return them to Clinton Correctional Facility. Or were the two psychiatrists at Clinton Correctional Facility wrong in their assessments of these inmates? I think that it was the very long bus ride down from Dannemora to Fishkill that cured these inmates. This was commonly referred as *bus therapy*.

Here is an example of the type of behavior that might earn an inmate a psychiatric evaluation: One morning, a bizarrely behaving inmate was waiting outside my door waiting for sick call. Just before I was to see this inmate, the correction officer came into my office and closed the door. He reported to me that the next inmate I was going to see was "shot," and "not mentally there, the porch light is flickering, both oars are not in the water." The officer went on to tell me that when this inmate walked into the mess hall for a meal, the other inmates would quiet down and pay attention to this inmate's bizarre, somewhat entertaining behavior. The large dining hall, with many inmates sitting down to have their meals, would automatically quiet down when this inmate entered the room. When inmates in a max-A prison dining hall suddenly become quiet as church mice, it makes the correction officers very uncomfortable, knowing something is about to happen. They all reach for their radios to pull their emergency-alert pin, alerting all security that they need help. It was obvious to anyone that this inmate was seriously mentally ill. Judging by his bizarre behavior, I doubt that he had a mood disorder.

I recently had a discussion with a psych nurse whom I had worked with for years. She voiced the concern that the diagnosis and a patient's medication did not match. Both the strength and the type of medication the inmate was on did not match the diagnosis. This was a problem when referring inmates to community treatment centers upon release from the prison system. The accepting facility would frequently ask if the patient had a diagnosis of adjustment disorder, but the discharge medication indicated that there was something much more seriously wrong with the inmate.

I wonder if mood and adjustment disorders in inmates had increased while the number of psychotic and severely depressed inmates has decreased. Has the number of mentally ill inmates being transferred to the Central New York Psychiatric Center for inpatient treatment decreased? Has the state shifted providing acute psychiatric care to the prisons? Is this a reflection of the trend in society where psychiatric hospitals are closing?

In July of 2012, Heather Yakin wrote in the *Times Herald-Record*, a local newspaper serving the Hudson Valley, that over the past few decades the state and counties have closed psychiatric hospitals and scrimped on mental health, with the result that more and more mentally ill people are ending up in jails. I wonder if the decrease in funding for the mentally ill is now being filtered down to the New York State correctional system

The Diagnostic and Statistical Manual of Mental Disorders (DSM) was developed and published by the American Psychiatric Association back in 1952 and has been updated numerous times. The first two classifications that are important to my discussion are called Axis I and Axis II disorders. Axis I is a psychiatric diagnosis, and Axis II includes mental retardation, personality disorders, and maladaptive personality features and defense mechanisms. In 2013 a new edition of the DSM was again released, and the Axis I and Axis II classifications had been eliminated, but the disorders still exist.

Before 2013 Axis I disorders included psychotic disorders, with the main ones being schizophrenia, delusional disorders, mood disorders including bipolar disorder (which used to be called manic-depressive disorder), and anxiety disorders, which range from phobias to panic attacks. The difficulty I found with an Axis II diagnosis was that some did not consider it a mental illness. Axis II patients are the head bangers, inmates who sit in their cells and constantly bang their heads against the wall. Inmates who will swallow anything they get their hands on were also referred to as Axis II. For instance, an inmate from Downstate recently spent five weeks at Putnam Community Hospital, at a cost of over $1 million, for swallowing everything he could. While in the outside hospital, he swallowed the entire length of IV tubing. Also included in Axis II were inmates who cut themselves, also referred to as self-mutilators.

Two recent cases come to mind: a swallower and a self-mutilator. An inmate was sent out to a local hospital after he swallowed a battery. Don't ask me where he got a battery in jail; I don't know. There is a good chance he brought it in from the county jail. The battery was removed in the outside hospital using endoscopy; a long surgical instrument is placed down the throat while the person is sedated, and the foreign body is pulled out through the mouth. The inmate was then returned to Downstate. Shortly thereafter, the same inmate swallowed a cigarette lighter and again had to be taken to an outside hospital to have it removed using endoscopy. I am not sure what the ethical way to treat inmates who harm themselves is. I hope that my writings bring this debate to the general public and society.

Around the same time as this incident, I watched the new Batman movie *The Dark Knight Rises*. The villain in the movie had a mask strapped to his face, covering his mouth. I asked myself if it would be ethical to use a mask like the one in the movie to prevent this inmate from swallowing anything put in front of him. Think of the cost of transporting an inmate to an outside hospital and the cost of an operating room to remove the foreign objects from his stomach, let alone the risk of general anesthesia and perforation.

Then there was an inmate who was in an observation cell and spent the night sharpening a small button on the concrete wall. The next day he cut himself with the sharpened button, which required him to be taken to an outside hospital for seventeen sutures. This action was considered a behavior problem and not mental illness. I get annoyed when the front office lectures me about being punitive to inmates, and then, on the other hand, the staff knows that inmates, some of whom would previously have been classified as Axis II, are being held in observation cells for thirty days, sometimes longer.

Another self-injurious inmate purposely cut his wrist. He cut a tendon and a small artery. It was a bloody mess, to say the least. I do agree that he had some sort of personality disorder. After a lengthy interview with the inmate, I learned that this type of behavior was quite common for this individual. He said that he spent sixteen months at the Central New York Psychiatric Center on his last bid.

As I was rereading the manuscript for this book a year after I wrote it, I was asked to check on an inmate just back from the community hospital, where he had had abdominal surgery to remove bits of floor tile that he had swallowed earlier that week. The surgical scar on his abdomen was healing nicely, and he appeared to be doing well mentally. He seemed upbeat and somewhat happy. Later that afternoon he was brought up to the facility hospital, gagging as if something was stuck in his throat. He appeared quite uncomfortable and in some distress. We could not figure out what he had swallowed this time. Then the sergeant looked down and noticed that the zipper to the inmate's pants was missing. We all thought that he had been in an observation cell without his clothing. The X-ray at the local hospital confirmed that the inmate had swallowed the zipper to his pants.

It was once written that Axis I patients suffer personally, not those around them; on the other hand, people who live with and deal with Axis II patients suffer, not the patients themselves. Now that Axis I and Axis II have been combined in the DSM, it makes this statement obsolete.

I must say again that I am very impressed with the young psychologists and social workers who treat the worst of the worst on a daily basis. Their dedication and patient concern is admirable. Many are highly skilled, but some lack the experience in working with inmates in a maximum-security correctional setting. Many get to work earlier than they are supposed to and leave much later then they should. Their work and dedication will not be forgotten by me or by God.

Recently I began to reconsider my views about the Department of Mental Hygiene and what appeared to me as the ratcheting down of the incidence and treatment of mental illness in corrections. I stopped expecting that seriously mentally ill inmates will be moved to a psychiatric hospital quickly where appropriate acute care can be given, as it has been in the past for many years. My opinion was reinforced this past week.

One Tuesday morning I was informed by a nurse that an inmate who was in an observation cell had to be taken out to a local hospital because he had a broken nose and multiple broken teeth. I was interested to see how an inmate in an observation cell had his nose broken and his teeth knocked out. On my rounds I visited the psych unit on 1D and questioned the regular officers who work the unit on a daily basis. I asked the staff about the inmate's behavior before this episode. The correction officers' common response was that he is "truly shot, truly mentally ill." Most of the officers felt that this particular inmate was severely mentally ill. He was not faking his mental illness. I learned that he had been in an observation cell for two weeks. I went on to learn, after speaking with someone in the psych department that he was psychotic and was not taking any antipsychotic or any other medication. I was unable to determine what the treatment plan was. Was he just going to be kept in an observation cell on no medication until he got better? Or was he going to be transferred to Central New York Psychiatric Center?

On Tuesday morning, he was in an observation cell in the prison hospital on a suicide watch. On Wednesday afternoon, I spoke with the dentist who had made two attempts to evaluate the inmate's broken teeth. He said it appeared to him that the inmate was severely mentally ill and would not allow the dentist near him. The inmate would not speak to the dentist or acknowledge that he was in the room. He would lie on a mattress on the floor with his head covered.

I asked the psych department early on Thursday if the inmate would be transferred to Central New York Psychiatric Center. I knew that if he would not be transferred today, Thursday, the next chance of him going would be the following Wednesday. I don't understand why a hospital does not accept patients on Fridays. You only have four days to become mentally ill in the prison system. That means that the inmate would spend the next six days without any medication, lying on a mattress on the floor, on suicide watch. The first excuse for not sending the inmate to Central New York Psychiatric Center was that he was not medically cleared to go. I don't understand why inmates have to be medically cleared to be transferred to a psychiatric hospital. In addition to psychiatrists, who are physicians, there are medical doctors at Central New York Psychiatric Center to address the patient's medical needs. The inmate did not have any communicable diseases. His severe mental illness was preventing him from receiving proper medical attention. If we did not address his severe psychosis, we would never be able to address his broken teeth or nose.

My response to the psych department chief was that the inmate had been seen at a local hospital emergency room, treated, and returned to us. The local community emergency room said he was fit medically to be transferred. I also said that he was medically cleared by me to go to Central New York Psychiatric Center. The inmate's severe mental condition needed to be addressed before his broken nose and broken teeth could be addressed. In his current mental state, he would not allow anyone to be near him. His violent behavior was what got his teeth knocked out and his nose broken.

On Friday morning I bumped into a sergeant who had worked overtime the night before and who was responsible for the hospital where the inmate was being kept. The sergeant approached me and was concerned that the patient on the watch had become very agitated during the evening, talking to himself, pacing the floor, and pounding his fist. The officer was concerned that if for some reason he needed to go into the inmate's room, the inmate or officers might get hurt. Again I approached the psych department, and the staff now told me that that the inmate was not transferred to Central New York Psychiatric Center because the inmate was refusing to be seen by the dentist. He was refusing to see the dentist because he was psychotic. It did not matter if he saw the dentist at Downstate or not. The inmate was unable and unwilling to have medical treatment because of his severe psychiatric condition. He needed acute inpatient psychiatric care. Leaving him in an observation cell for weeks only made his condition worse. I didn't understand why someone in Central New York Psychiatric Center did not understand this. There are dentists and medical doctors at the Central New York Psychiatric Center who could help him after he was given psychiatric care.

My concern was not with the FDU staff at Downstate; as I said before, they are highly trained, dedicated, and skilled at what they do. I work with them on a daily basis and am proud to work alongside them. My concern was and is with what I refer to as the *gatekeeper* in Central New York Psychiatric Center, who puts up roadblocks and obstacles to having inmates transfer there. Getting inmates transferred to a psychiatric hospital where the inmate needs a higher level of care is becoming harder to achieve.

Why and how this inmate's nose and teeth were broken is not for me to determine. I was not privy to the results of the investigation, nor was I asked for my opinion. If excessive force was used on this inmate, it has to be determined by the inspector general (IG).

A common joke at Downstate is that the Central New York Psychiatric Center will not take an inmate who is not eating. He is not eating because he is truly paranoid that the prison staff is putting poison in his food. Instead of accepting the inmate for treatment in the psychiatric hospital, the center expects the local facility to get a court order to hold the inmate down, stick a tube down his throat, and force-feed him. I can see this being done for inmates who are not eating in order to make some sort of political statement, but when the inmate is mentally ill, paranoid to the point that he is not eating, I think that force-feeding is wrong, and the patient should be in a psychiatric hospital, not in a strip cell in a prison. If the inmate is not eating for other reasons, I have no difficulty keeping him in a prison.

One time a severely psychotic inmate who was not being medicated and was repeatedly banging his head against the cell wall was not transferred to an acute-care psychiatric hospital because he complained to the psych nurse that he had a headache. "You want me to send this inmate out for a CT scan of his head?" I asked the nurse. All the radiation a CT scan provides will not stop the inmate from banging his head. With the number of psychotropic medications available to treat acutely ill inmates in a psychiatric hospital, I cannot understand why they would not accept him for treatment. I always wonder if more inmates are civilly committed to psychiatric hospitals on the street upon discharge from Downstate than are committed to our Central New York Psychiatric Center.

I became angry at a psych nurse who requested that I order a diet supplement called Ensure for an inmate who was not eating because of severe psychosis. She said that he was going home in two weeks and would be committed to a psychiatric hospital on the street upon discharge from prison. My response to her was that he needed to be transferred to an acute-care psychiatric hospital now and not dumped on a city hospital in two weeks. "Keep him alive on Ensure until he goes home?" I asked the nurse. I was annoyed.

With more and more mentally ill people finding themselves in the prison system, we need to fine-tune how we treat them and also find better ways to treat them. Correction officers need training on how to treat the mentally ill if the Department of Corrections is going to be the major provider of mental health care in New York State. More training needs to be done. There was a time when the officers on the psych unit would travel to Central New York Psychiatric Center for in-service training. This is no longer the case. In fact, there was recently an official inquiry by Broome County district attorney Gerald Mollen. (Broome County is where Binghamton, New York, is located.) To paraphrase DA Mollen, "Interactions with the mentally ill are the most difficult tasks of police work." Mollen said in his conclusion that it was essential that police officers be appropriately trained to respond to arrestees who are mentally ill. This does not change when the mentally ill find themselves in a prison. NYPD has announced special police training in how to handle emotionally disturbed persons (EDPs).

The following story illustrates why better training in dealing with the mentally ill is essential for correction officers.

One morning the inmates were lining up outside my office door for their psych medications, and a new officer, recently transferred to Downstate from the upstate region, saw an inmate who was talking to himself. It appeared to me that the officer wanted to impress the attractive young nurse who was about to begin giving out medications. In a loud voice, the officer asked the inmate if he was crazy or if he was stupid. Before you knew it, they were both on the floor, and the red-dot team was responding to the area. As

mentioned before, the red-dot team is a preselected group of correction officers that responds to fights and assaults on staff.

After the inmate was cuffed, he was moved to the box (SHU)
for assault on staff. Shortly after, the psych clinician went over to
the box to check on the inmate, which is customary at Downstate
when someone is newly admitted to the box. A short time later, the
inmate was transferred from SHU to the psych department observation cell (a strip cell) by the same officer t who had started this
commotion to begin with.

I believe that the officer was not properly trained to deal with
the mentally ill inmate. As I told him later, when he asked the inmate if he was crazy or stupid the officer should have realized that
the inmate was in the crazy line waiting for his antipsychotic medication and not in the stupid line waiting for stupid pills. I always tell
new staff members to step back and take a good look at the inmate
that they are treating. Look in the inmate's eyes and check his facial
expressions. Many have obvious signs of mental illness. Be aware of
their behavior; these patients may need extra time to understand
your questions and where you are coming from.

I recently read that in the state of California, the Department
of Corrections is the largest provider of mental health care in the
entire state. Society has moved the mentally ill out of the psychiatric hospitals to the streets and now to the prison system. Prisons
are becoming the new psychiatric hospitals of the future.

In September of 2012, a press release by The Joint Commission
named Central New York Psychiatric Center a "top performer."
The mental-health commissioner wrote in the article that the New
York State Office of Mental Health strives for excellence, quality of
care, and accountability. The Joint Commission is a United State-
based nonprofit tax-exempt organization that accredits more than
21,000 health care organizations and programs in the United
States

The same day I read the article, there were ten inmates on suicide watch at Downstate. The corrections officers who were watching these inmates were overjoyed with the amount of overtime available to them just for sitting and watching suicidal inmates. One inmate was being watched in the dayroom of the infirmary for more than three weeks. All the inmates do to occupy their time is to sleep on a mattress on the floor. This occurs for weeks on end.

I can remember back in the day, not long ago, when the trips to Central New York Psychiatric Center were more common. The regular trip officer would bring a brown paper-bag lunch, made by the kitchen for the inmate. It was referred to as the inmate's "happy meal" by the trip officers, the two regular officers who routinely took inmates to Central New York Psychiatric Center. While in the facility emergency room waiting for the paperwork to be completed to take the inmate to the mental hospital, one officer would open the brown paper bag and drop a cigarette in the bag, in front of the mentally ill inmate, making sure the inmate saw him place the cigarette in the bag. The officer would explain to the inmate that the cigarette was the happy meal toy. Just as with a little child on a long car trip, he would tell the inmate that if he behaved, ate all of his lunch, and did not act up, the officer would let the inmate smoke his one cigarette after he finished all of his lunch. To a psychotic inmate, a cigarette means a lot.

One day a very large inmate, known to all to be severely mentally ill, had numerous nonspecific complaints and wanted to be housed in the facility hospital. He was lying down on an emergency-room stretcher and was taking up valuable space. It was a Wednesday, and I remember it being a very busy day. There were no beds available in the infirmary, and I expected that this guy was going to be a problem because of his size and the degree of his mental illness. At that moment a seasoned colleague of mine, another PA, walked into the ER and whispered something in the inmate's ear. After the inmate heard what the PA had to say, he sat up, reported that he felt much better, and requested to return to his regular cell. We were all amazed at this sudden recovery.

I cornered the PA in the hallway outside the ER and asked him what he had whispered into the inmate's ear. He laughed and said that he told the inmate that he would not be able to smoke in the infirmary. I asked how he knew that the inmate smoked, and he again laughed and said to take a look at his fingers—they were severely stained with tar from smoking cigarettes down until there was nothing left to hold.

Not only would the inmates on the mental-health unit kill for a cigarette, but I found that the inmates in solitary confinement had the same need to smoke. These guys would smoke anything. On more than one occasion, I yelled down to the CO that I smelled something burning on a tier. It turned out that an inmate was smoking toilet paper rolled in the shiny paper that the toilet paper came wrapped in. I never smoked, so I don't really understand the addiction to it.

One day an incident occurred that illustrates the allure of cigarettes for inmates. It began when the correction officer asked me to check on an inmate in the psych ward. He was obviously jaundiced, not eating, lying in a fetal position on his bed. He refused to walk up to the hospital; he just wanted to be left alone. I would not have known about his condition if not for the gallery officer. From what I learned, he was giving his food away to other inmates on the tier. Then the other inmates were avoiding him because he was yellow. He had also lost about thirty pounds in about three months, which was significant. He was mentally ill in addition to being severely physically sick. At first he refused to walk up to the hospital because he knew he would not be able to smoke there. I told him if he would not walk up to the hospital, I would have other inmates carry him up on a stretcher.

On examining him I found there was a very large mass in the right upper quadrant of his abdomen. We talked him into going to a local hospital for a CT scan of his abdomen. Before he was back in the facility hospital, the radiologist at the local hospital called and wanted the inmate to be returned as soon as possible. The mass had caused blockage, and no food was passing through his intestine. It was determined that he needed lifesaving surgery, but he refused to be transferred back to the local hospital by ambulance. The inmate was not able to eat because of the very large mass in his abdomen. To convince the inmate to go to the local hospital, I had to promise him that during the ride to the hospital in a state van, he would be given one cigarette and allowed to smoke it. In front of the inmate, I asked a nurse (who was a smoker) to hand the CO one of her cigarettes to give the inmate later. The inmate agreed to these terms, thankfully, but he refused treatment again once he got there.

The local hospital had their psychiatrist see the patient and determined that he was not capable of making reasonable decisions. The psychiatrist at the local hospital suggested a court order because of this severe mental illness. The inmate later passed away.

One morning, I was called to check on an inmate in the psych ward. The person reported to me that an inmate in an observation cell had swelling on his upper lip. I found the inmate in the cell with no clothing or smock on, just bare-ass naked. He had this glazed look on his face, staring out into space. He had spread feces all over his cell and on himself. With the help of the watch officer, I determined that the inmate caused his lip to swell up by slapping himself in the face with the palm of his right hand. It was obvious to anyone that the inmate was severely psychotic. When I reported back to the mental-hygiene person who had asked me to see the inmate, I became quite upset, especially when she questioned me about not doing anything about his lip swelling. His problem, I responded, was not his lip swelling but the fact that he was severely mentally ill and was hurting himself. He was not on medication for his mental illness, and he had been covered in feces for the past few days. This occurred during a hot, very humid summer.

What really upset me was the fact that he was not scheduled to be transferred to the next level of psychiatric care, to the Central New York Psychiatric Center. I was told that Central New York Psychiatric Center does not accept sick inmates on Fridays. I became more upset and said to this person, "You mean to tell me that here it is Thursday morning, and the inmate will sit in his cell covered in shit until maybe Monday? His swollen lip is not the problem here; his severe psychosis is."

Sometimes it is unclear whether an inmate's unusual behavior is the result of a physical disorder or injury or a mental disorder. For example, this past week I was stopped by the correction officer in the main lobby on the way into work at 6:30 a.m. He said that there had been a problem with an inmate during the evening, and he had been placed in the dayroom, a room in the infirmary that we utilize to observe inmates. The CO reported that the inmate was highly agitated and very assaultive and that it took five officers to place him in the dayroom. He said if I needed to go in to see and examine the inmate, I would have to call the watch commander to get a number of correction officers to stand by in case the inmate went off. I went up directly to the infirmary without taking off my jacket to see what was going on.

The night officer told me the inmate had been struck in the head by another inmate the previous week, and the psych people believed his violent behavior was a direct result of his head injury. The officer told me that they (not sure who he meant by *they*) wanted me to send the inmate to the outside hospital for a CT scan of his head. The history was very sketchy. Was the head trauma one or two weeks ago? Did the inmate have a history of this type of behavior before? Was this behavior something new?

After further questioning, I learned the injury occurred about two weeks ago. The inmate had been seen in the local hospital ER, where he was deemed not to have a serious head injury and was returned to the prison. The psych department was putting a great deal of pressure on me to send this inmate out again for another CT scan of his head. The more they insisted, the more I resisted. I was told that the inmate had never displayed this type of behavior before and had no psychiatric history. I told the duty nurse that I felt very uncomfortable sending this very bizarre, hostile, and agitated inmate to an already overburdened local emergency room. I had a great deal of apprehension that someone outside of corrections would get hurt. If he did have a bleed in his brain or a hematoma, it should have showed up before now. Having five correction officers forcibly take this inmate out of the facility was out of the question, as far as I was concerned. When the PA who was covering the infirmary came in, she was able to speak with and examine the inmate. We thought because she did not wear a uniform and was a woman, the patient would be a little more responsive. After a thorough neurological examination, the PA was confident that the inmate's behavior was not caused by the head trauma from two weeks earlier. The inmate did not need the amount of radiation that a CT would require. The inmate was also examined by an optometrist who felt that the inmate had a minor refractory error but did not exhibit signs of increased intracranial pressure.

The psych department persisted in demanding that the person be sent out for a CT scan. A third PA who had been working in an emergency room for more than a decade—and in the emergency room where the inmate would be sent—came in to evaluate the inmate. He also did a very thorough and lengthy exam. His concern was that the inmate was severely psychotic, a concern that the other PAs and I shared. He called the psych department and reminded the staff that a psychiatrist is a physician, and if he was so concerned about this inmate, he could order the CT scan. As it turned out, the psychiatrist had not even evaluated the patient yet.

Next, my boss became involved and did an extensive review of the inmate's past medical and psychiatric history. It turned out that this behavior had occurred a number of times before, and the inmate had been hospitalized in a psychiatric hospital on more than one occasion. When I was questioned by the front-office staff about this particular inmate, I stated that we truly felt this inmate did not need a CT scan but instead needed aggressive treatment in a psychiatric hospital. I also stressed the fact that this should happen sooner rather than later, before he or a staff member got hurt.

My point in all of this, the bottom line, is that Downstate is not a psychiatric hospital. It was not designed to be a psychiatric hospital. I have been reminded not to call our infirmary a hospital. It is not a medical hospital. Conversely, Central New York Psychiatric Center is not a prison. It was not designed to be one, and it will never be one. I am able to send inmates out to a community hospital when they become medically sick and I am not able to care for them in the prison infirmary. What becomes of the mentally ill when acute psychiatric care cannot be provided at the facility level?

Another day I was called to the facility emergency room to see an inmate who was housed in the psychiatric unit. He had told the officer that he had severe chest pain and needed to be brought up to the facility hospital. When I walked into the emergency room, I could see from the inmate's face that he was in severe pain and was very uncomfortable. He reported the pain started on the left side of his chest and traveled down his left shoulder. These are classic symptoms of a myocardial infarction—a heart attack, in other words. The EKG confirmed that the inmate was having a heart attack. After giving him an aspirin and a nitroglycerin tablet, the inmate felt better and wanted to return to his cell. I told him that not only was he not going back to his cell, but he was going to be transported by ambulance to the local community hospital. He then became angry and told the nurse that he was going to refuse to be taken to an outside hospital. He demanded to be allowed to return to his cell. He said that he had the right to refuse treatment and to refuse to be kept in the facility hospital.

Then I became angry and told him that he did have the right to refuse to go to the local hospital ER, but he had no choice on where he was going to be housed in the prison. I angrily told him that if he were to drop dead in his cell, the code-blue team would have to run out with the defibrillator and a very heavy medical-treatment bag with a small oxygen tank in it. I told him that if he was going to die, it would be in the prison hospital, near the equipment needed to resuscitate him back to life. "No way am I going to put the staff at risk, running up and down stairs with this equipment, because you are being an asshole," I said.

The Protestant chaplain was called in to convince the inmate to be taken to the local hospital, where it was determined that the inmate did have a significant heart attack.

Many years ago a cocky male nurse received a phone call from the gym correction officer in Building 3. Back in those days, each gym had a correction officer assigned to it. The officer reported to the male nurse, who was covering the emergency room, that an inmate was down on the gym floor having what the officer thought was a seizure. The nurse told the correction officer to walk the inmate up to the hospital after he was finished seizing. A few minutes later, the officer called back and told the nurse that he thought the inmate was finished seizing and it looked like he was now dead. Since this incident, nurses, PAs, and MDs have to run out to see the inmates who pass out. This is how the code-blue policy began.

Recently I voiced my concern about the length of time inmates spend in observation rooms. When I voiced my concerns to the psych department, the response was unsettling; the person calmly said that it was not unusual to keep an inmate in an observation cell for up to thirty days. I responded that I doubted that at Central New York Psychiatric Center an inmate is left in an observation cell for thirty days. I doubted that Central New York Psychiatric Center had observation cells.

I also get upset when the psych staff asks why medical conditions of some mentally ill inmates are not being treated. In a somewhat short tone, my response is that if you cannot cure this person of his paranoia, do you think he will accept treatment for his medical condition? As I said before, when they ask why I cannot control the pain of a bipolar person, I respond that if they are unable to treat his bipolar disorder, what makes them think I can control his chronic pain? I have seen many psychotic patients refuse treatment for many serious, life-threatening medical problems like insulin-controlled diabetes or severe hypertension.

About two weeks prior to this incident, I called an inmate up to the infirmary to be interviewed by my boss. I told my boss to look at his facial appearance, to look him in his eyes, and to talk to him about his past psychiatric history. Then I told my boss to ask the inmate why he had stopped taking his antipsychotic medications. The inmate was clear and said he wanted to go to the shock program to decrease the amount of time he needed to spend in prison. He had been told that because he was on psychiatric medication he would be denied the shock program. Just by looking at the inmate's face, anyone could see he needed to be medicated. I then asked my boss to interview the inmate and ask the inmate who had told him this.

Later that same day I was speaking with another PA, someone I have worked with for decades. She reported that she was concerned when a senior counselor approached her and told her that a number of inmates were being coded as less severely mentally ill than they appeared to be, in order to get better placement—or should I say quicker placement—in facilities upstate. The question is, were they being talked out of their mental illness.

Aggressive behavior in the mentally ill is another major problem. There have been numerous attacks on people by the mentally ill on the streets of New York City. One reason is that the attackers have stopped taking their psych medications. In April of 2012, without warning, a man plunged a knife blade into the temple of Officer Eder Loor of the NYPD. Officer Loor and his partner had told the man he had to be taken to a hospital, as his mother had requested. The mother of the attacker had called the police to inform them that her son was bipolar and schizophrenic and that he had stopped taking his medications.

In the late 1990s there were multiple incidents involving individuals with untreated mental illness becoming violent. Andrew Goldstein, who was twenty-nine years old at the time, pushed Kendra Webdale to her death in front of an oncoming NYC subway train. The *New York Times* reported that Mr. Goldstein had been discharged by North General Hospital in Harlem because the state's reimbursement for twenty-one days of treatment had expired, and there was no financial incentive to keep him there. He stopped taking his psychiatric medication and failed to report to the outpatient treatment center. As a direct result of this, Kendra's Law was passed. It is a New York state law concerning involuntary outpatient commitment. Kendra's Law does not require that patients be forced to take their psychiatic medications, however.

In another case shortly after Kendra Webdale's death, Julio Perez, age forty-three, pushed a man onto the subway tracks. The victim later lost his legs. Julio Perez had been discharged from a psychiatric facility with little or no medication.

Many, if not most, of the homeless in New York City, the people you see lying on the streets and sleeping in doorways, suffer from mental illness and are not receiving proper treatment. Some of these people are potentially violent and could strike out at anyone. As fewer inpatient mental-hygiene beds are available, we are seeing increasingly more mentally ill people wandering the streets of New York City. Many of these mentally ill individuals end up in the New York state prison system. After they are released from the prison system, the mentally ill inmates find themselves where they started. They are back on the streets, with no psychiatric treatment, no medication, and no follow-up.

Violent behavior is not just a problem outside of prisons. In the *New York Times* on May 21, 2014, Michael Schwirtz reported that attacks by mentally ill inmates on civilian staff were climbing at Rikers Island. The attacks were mostly on health-care workers. These severe attacks resulted in staff suffering facial bruises, broken bones, and eye injuries. Schwirtz wrote in his article, "Many health-care workers argued, as have leading mental health experts, that jails like Rikers Island are not equipped to handle inmates with serious mental illness."

In addition to the mentally ill, other special groups of inmates require a considerable amount of time and special care. A small number of inmates have organic brain syndrome (OBS), but the number appears to be getting larger each year. This is a physical disorder that causes impaired mental function. It does not usually include any psychiatric disorders. The cases we see in the prison system today are caused by chronic drug or alcohol dependence, which results in permanent brain damage, once referred to by a comedian as "daim bramage." Remember the old television commercial in which a speaker would say, "This is your brain," while the camera zoomed in on an egg? And then the speaker would say, "This is your brain on drugs," while the egg was broken in a sizzling frying pan.

Other common causes of chronic organic brain syndrome are head trauma resulting from a car, motorcycle, or bicycle accident or from Alzheimer's disease. The medical term is *traumatic brain injury* (TBI). Commons signs and symptoms of TBI are impairment of memory and judgment, agitation, and confusion. Just think about your college days of heavy drinking, but it does not go away the morning after. These inmates are placing an additional burden on the already overburdened Department of Corrections. These inmates tend to be victim prone and need special placement.

Across Route 84, Fishkill Correctional Facility has a special unit for inmates who exhibit symptoms of Alzheimer's disease. There is also a special-needs unit, called the SNU, at Clinton Correctional Facility to deal with inmates with OBS. From what I understand, that unit is full, and there is a waiting list to get inmates into this unit. Until room is made for them, these inmates languish in regular prisons.

One last group of inmates also falls through the cracks of the system. They are inmates who are academically challenged or have mental retardation. These inmates need someone to watch over them. One inmate who comes to mind is an academically challenged person who told his mother and his family doctor for years that someone had left something in his stomach after he had his appendix removed. His mother was a nurse. Nobody believed him because he was slightly mentally retarded.

One morning about twenty-five years ago, the radiologist was reading films in the X-ray reading room just outside the physical-exam area. He asked me to take a look at a chest X-ray. It was alarming; anybody could see a pair of Kelly forceps in the inmate's abdomen, left behind after a surgical procedure. The radiologist was as amazed as I was. He told me that in a court of law, all the attorney would have to do was place the X-ray film on the view box in the courtroom. It was an automatic million-dollar settlement for the person with the forceps left in his abdomen. No words would need to be spoken in the courtroom.

In those days, a million dollars was a great deal of money. Back when I was in training, the chief of surgery at Brooklyn Hospital would hide instruments during a surgical procedure. When he finished the procedure, he would question the surgical tech if the count was correct (that all the instruments used in the procedure were accounted for) before closing the patient. If the tech said the count was correct and he could close the wound, he would shout out, "You're fired!" (as Donald Trump famously said). He would ask the person to leave the room and ask for another surgical tech to come in to finish the procedure.

After seeing this amazing X-ray, I called the inmate out to the exam area and asked whether he had had any abdominal surgery. He informed me and the radiologist that during his teens his appendix had burst, and he had needed major abdominal surgery. The inmate had a long surgical midline scar from the center of his chest to his pubic area. When I told him that the surgeon had left something behind during the surgery, the inmate, who appeared mentally challenged, was not one bit surprised. "I know that," he said. "I have been telling my mother and the doctor who did the surgery that for years, and for years no one believed me. I may be retarded, but I am not stupid." He explained that when his body was in a certain position he could feel the forceps. The inmate was transferred to his permanent facility where he could have the surgery to remove the forceps.

I have also seen many inmates who were very sick, directly or indirectly, as a result of their years of drug abuse. A few weeks after the Kelly forceps case, the radiologist again called me into his reading room to look at an abnormal chest X-ray. The findings on the chest film, the radiologist said, were consistent with that of a person with mesothelioma, a cancer caused by exposure to asbestos. From what I remember of my studies regarding cancers of the lung, asbestos particles are very tiny, smaller and lighter than a speck of dust. Once airborne, the particles remain in the air for a long time, unlike dust particles, which (as we all know) fall to the ground. The asbestos particle is then inhaled into a person's lung where the cancer response occurs. The smaller the asbestos particle, the deeper into the base of the lung it travels.

I called the inmate up to an exam room, and I told him that he might have a mass in his lung, as was indicated by his chest X-ray. I was amazed at his response. He said that he had worked for an asbestos abatement company, removing asbestos from old buildings in upstate New York. He said the pay was great and that he had been able to maintain his expensive cocaine habit because of it. He also told me that he was waiting for the day to be told he had lung cancer. He said for the past few months he had not been feeling right and had developed a chronic cough.

Interestingly, he said that when he worked, he and his partner would not put on the proper clothing—white bunny suits with special masks—so as not to inhale the toxic asbestos. He said the proper procedure to get all gowned up took too much time. He and his buddy would just do a few lines of cocaine before starting work, at lunch, and as a coffee break in the afternoon. He said he knew that someday his cocaine habit, and the fact that he had not taken the asbestos abatement job seriously, would come back and bite him on the ass. He also knew that being a chain-smoker made the possibility of getting asbestos-related cancer much greater. He was a young guy and had a long life ahead of him. I know that I would have been devastated to learn that I had serious lung cancer. I was very surprised that he did not seem even a little upset. This inmate, like most inmates at Downstate, was transferred to a more permanent prison upstate where treatment was started. Remember that Downstate was and is an inmate reception center.

I choose to mention this at this point in my memoirs. Chemical dependency is a form of mental illness, and it is becoming more widespread, encompassing all ages and many different forms of dependency. It is seen with high-school kids smoking marijuana as a gateway drug and in the elderly who are dependent on prescription medication. What is important is that many people who have some type of mental illness tend to self-medicate with alcohol, street drugs, or prescription medications to control their mental illness. After they are arrested and convicted and find themselves in prison and unable to control their mental illnesses as they did on the street, they begin to unravel. On the street they shop around for doctors and get prescriptions for oxys (oxycodone), perks (Percocet), morphine, or Dilaudid. Many claim they have a seizure disorder to obtain Klonopin, which is a longer-acting, better type of Valium.

Recently a new drug called tramadol, trade name Ultram, has appeared on the market. Not a day goes by without at least three or four inmates asking me for tramadol. The *Physician Assistants' Prescribing Reference* (PAPR) lists it as a non-narcotic opioid drug. It has since been changed to a Schedule IV narcotic. The inmate frequently complains of severe back pain and claims that the only drug that will relieve his pain is tramadol. After I tell the inmate no, he is not going to get tramadol, I check his history of drug abuse. Nine out of ten times, there is a history of opiate abuse on the street. Tramadol does not mix well with the psychiatric drugs called selective serotonin reuptake inhibitors (SSRIs), which are prescribed for depression or anxiety. Mixing tramadol with an SSRI-type medication could lead to serotonin syndrome, which is not common but can result in death.

There was a very famous lawsuit back in 1984, when an eighteen-year-old Bennington College freshman named Libby Zion died as a result of serotonin syndrome at New York Hospital. On November 28, 2016, the *Washington Post* published an article labeling it "The Case That Shocked Medicine." Tramadol did not play a role in the death of Libby Zion, but other drug interactions caused the serotonin syndrome that cost her life. Any doctor who did residency in this country knows about Libby Zion because her death led to changes in the training of young doctors and the number of hours they are allowed to work in one week. The legacy of this case was the issue of resident work hours and supervision. The outcome of the litigation was highly critical of the hospital and led to the formation of the Bell Commission in 1989, which recommended that doctors in training work no longer than eighty hours a week and no more than twenty-four hours in a row and that they receive significantly more on-site supervision from senior physicians. Tramadol should not be used with people with a seizure disorder or with those who have had seizures in the past. The PAPR book, under warning/precautions, writes that it should not be given to drug abusers. I get upset when a former drug abuser asks me for tramadol, and many inmates refuse to take their psychiatric medications so they can be placed on tramadol.

At a drug addiction conference in Brooklyn, I voiced my concerns about tramadol to a group of doctors and PAs. At first they all chuckled; the group then said I needed to switch the inmates to the long-acting tramadol. According to the group, the long-acting tramadol does not give a person the desired rush that the short-acting tramadol does. These medical professionals said that once they switched patients to the long-acting tramadol, the requests for it stopped.

I wrote to Central Pharmacy asking that tramadol be taken off the formulary, or at least that it be switched to the long-acting type. Central Pharmacy never got back to me; short-acting tramadol is still on the formulary. Inmates still line up to ask for it, and I bet many prisons in the state use short-acting tramadol in very high numbers. I guess that short-acting tramadol is a cheap pain reliever. Not taken into consideration is the fact that sick-call lines are longer because of inmates demanding tramadol and that because it is administered on a one-to-one pill line—when a nurse gives out one tablet at a time to each inmate—makes its use labor-intensive. I understand that some hospitals, especially large teaching hospitals, have taken tramadol off their formulary altogether. I know that when I go to work on Monday I will have at least three inmates demanding tramadol for chronic, unbearable back pain.

Another new drug that is subject to abuse in prison is a stimulant referred to as "bath salts." I first encountered someone who was abusing the drug one day on the psych ward during my rounds, I looked into a cell and saw a young, skinny black male who was bare-ass naked by his own choice. He was shouting out the window of his cell at the top of his lungs. Nothing that he was shouting made any sense. He was truly acting psychotic. I was told that he was suffering from an adjustment disorder.

That same day a lieutenant stopped me in the hall and told me that he had gotten a heads-up that at Rikers Island they were seeing more and more use of bath salts—the informal slang term for a new type of drugs found on the streets that is making its way into the prison system, Bath salts are stimulant drugs that mimic cocaine, LSD, or ecstasy. Bath salts cannot be detected by drug-sniffing dogs, and they are not detected in typical urinalysis. The problem is that this drug may cause suicidal thoughts, combative or violent behavior, and hallucinations, and in this particular patient, I believe it caused him to be psychotic. This inmate did not have a psychotic or mental history; he lived in the cadre building, and he had not been a problem to anyone. I suspect he obtained the bath salts on a recent visit.

Yet another problem related to the prevalence of mental illness in state prisons is the potential of a mentally ill inmate to disrupt the lives of the inmates and staff who must interact with him or her. The following is a case in point.

The afternoon after our Christmas office party years ago, I was doing an admission physical examination on a new inmate.

Toward the end of my encounter, the inmate made a disturbing comment, in a loud voice, about the female officer standing in the office doorway. The comment was in regard to a sexual act. It was a very bizarre and off-the-wall comment. Then the inmate began to say bizarre things about a male officer who had just entered the room. Again the comments were bizarre and alarming, and all relating to sexual acts. Fortunately, both officers could see by the look in the inmate's face that he was severely mentally ill.

Unfortunately, the other inmates in the waiting area were not so understanding. The waiting room got uncomfortably silent after this inmate's outbursts. They were waiting to see what would happen next. I went over to the phone in the waiting room and called the head of the psych department. I informed this person that this inmate needed to be removed from the general population, both for his own protection because of his obvious mental illness and because his off-the-wall comments were going to get someone hurt. I was told that he had already been screened by a clinician and found to be OK for the general population. I said that someone needed to interview the inmate again and to take a second look at his behavior. I told this person that it was clear to even a blind man that this inmate needed to be placed in some sort of protective area because of his bizarre behavior. I angrily said that I was too busy to put this inmate back together after someone beat the shit out of him after he made bizarre comments because of his mental illness.

After he was reevaluated, the inmate was moved to an observation cell. During his stay in an observation cell, a nurse was interviewing an inmate across the hall from him, and she had difficulty hearing what the inmate was saying. She asked this inmate to speak up. The inmate who had recently been admitted because of his bizarre behavior shouted out, "Speak up, you stupid nigger." This is something no one should say, especially in a prison. With this loud, offensive comment heard by many, officers on the unit responded to the gallery. Thank God both men were locked in and could not get at each other.

The inmate was placed on lithium and Remeron. Lithium is used for mania in bipolar disorders, and Remeron is used for depression. In a few days, the inmate was discharged and placed in the general population. A few days later in the hospital bullpen, a holding area in the hospital area where inmates wait to get medication, this same inmate shouted out across the room to another inmate that his mother was a "fucking whore." It was the morning medication run and the bullpen was overcrowded with inmates, most of whom were unstable with some sort of mental illness. It is the worst area in any facility for a fight to break out. By the time the correction officers got everything under control, it was a big mess. Thank God no one was seriously injured.

Recently there was another incident at Downstate illustrating how one mentally ill inmate can disrupt prison life. I was walking on the gallery for my rounds when I noticed a nauseating smell; the officers were directing large fans to blow the smell away from the center of the gallery. One of the inmates on an upper tier, noticeably psychotic, was not flushing his toilet after his bowel movements. The feces were up over the rim of the bowel like a mountain, I was told. The other inmates and gallery porters were tired of cleaning up after this inmate. The officer told me it was the third time in two weeks he had done this. It was clear the inmate was psychotic to the point he would not flush his toilet.

What upset me was that we were unable to control this inmate's psychosis and that the psych department did not believe he was sick enough to be transferred to a psychiatric hospital. His mental illness was causing him to be physically sick. He had a history of diabetes and hypertension and was not taking his medication. In other words, this psychotic inmate would not be transferred to Central New York Psychiatric Center because he was not taking his medication for hypertension or diabetes. He was not taking his medication because he was severely paranoid about the medication and the people giving it to him. His paranoia was not being controlled, and his hypertension and diabetes were getting worse.

Years ago, other inmates on the gallery would set an inmate's cell on fire to get the inmate moved off their unit. I repeatedly heard stories that inmates would set the cells on fire with inmates in them when they snored loudly for long periods. In this case, however, the other inmates on this gallery did not burn the psychotic inmate out of his cell because of the smell; they began to look out for him by flushing his toilet. The other inmates on the unit knew he was sick and would yell out to the gallery officer to open his cell so they could go into it and flush his toilet.

No two days making rounds on the psych unit are ever alike. One day I had to visit an inmate who had tried to hang himself the night before. Although he had a long history of being a difficult inmate, I never had a problem with him. I told him I found it odd that he was in an observation unit. I said to him, "I do not believe that you are crazy." I knew that on Friday he had returned to Downstate from court in New York City. I asked if he had been hit with additional time while out to court.

"On the contrary," he said, "I am going to be turned loose in six to eight weeks."

Looking the inmate directly in the eyes, I said to him, "Then why did you try to kill yourself?"

The inmate's response was somewhat sad. He said that he had been in jail since 1986 and was afraid to go home or back to the streets. "Too much has changed," he said. "It ain't the same on the streets as it was before I was arrested and sentenced. I am going to kill myself; if not here in prison, then when I get home."

"How could I stop you from doing this?" I asked.

"You cannot," he responded back to me. "You can keep me in a stripped cell under direct observation by a correction officer, but someday, somehow, I will do it."

The next day he was transferred back to his prison upstate. I don't know what happened to him. I am afraid to ask.

In December of 2012 we had a busy week. While an inmate was being taken out of his observation cell to be moved to Central New York Psychiatric Center, as he came down the stairs he punched the inmate porter directly in the nose. The inmate did not resist being taken down by the officers, but he was yelling and screaming all the way to the facility emergency room. The inmate was crazy, but not crazy enough to have punched an officer in the nose. If he had struck an officer, his next trip would have been to the local community hospital emergency room to have his face put back together. I kept on thinking that if the patient would have suffered a broken nose, then Central New York Psychiatric Center would not have accepted him and he would have languished in an observation cell at Downstate for many weeks.

Another case involved a mentally ill inmate who was classified 1S, meaning he was very mentally ill and assaultive to staff. He was being shuffled from one prison to another and was just passing through Downstate. Again, I don't understand why he was not taken by van directly to his next facility. I don't understand why he was not taken directly to Central New York Psychiatric Center instead of being bused around the state. While in an observation cell, he first refused to come to the square to be strip-searched prior to getting on the bus. The CO did note that the inmate was acting somewhat strange. After agreeing to be processed, the inmate was brought to the square area, which is a very busy place very early in the morning. Inmates are strip-searched before going down to the draft area one floor below. There are a lot of inmates and a lot of correction officers in the draft area. There is also a lot of movement, with inmates coming and going into the facility and being transferred out of the facility. Sergeants and lieutenants are always available on-site to make sure things move quickly and safely.

Very few unusual incidents occur in the square; it runs like clockwork. Security does a great job of keeping a highly volatile area under control. A few months earlier, an inmate had smashed a correction officer in the nose for no apparent reason. The inmate was not of sound mind and just did not want to be transferred. On this particular day, this transit inmate was acting bizarre, not listening to directions. I was told he had a strange look in his eyes. The correction officers were eager to get the buses loaded and were not interested in writing misbehavior reports. The COs tried to calm the inmate down, but it appeared that he was going to make a run for the exit door when they confronted him. The inmate cocked both his fists in a fighting position and was just about to hit a lieutenant. This inmate was a big guy and would have caused pain and damage to this lieutenant's face. The lieutenant was a nice guy, pleasant to work with, and treated everyone fairly and with respect.

When the inmate got into the fighting position, he had to be brought down, and he was dropped to the floor by a number of correction officers. In doing this his femur was broken (the femur is a large bone in the leg that goes from the knee to the hip). The inmate was transported to Saint Luke's Hospital in Newburgh and then transferred to Westchester County Medical Center, where he had surgery to correct the fracture.

CHAPTER 17
A GREAT TRUE CHRISTMAS STORY

I thought that my writings were finished but as time went by, I felt I needed to add to my work. On a Christmas Eve I remembered an inmate who has passed through Downstate on more than one occasion. Again, like many I have met in my many years, his crimes were not serious but more related to his mental illness. Because of his mental illness, he was homeless. Those who have passed through Penn Station have probably seen this individual but never paid much attention to him. He was not a stupid person; he was smart enough to purchase the cheapest train ticket available at Penn Station, which enabled him to sit or sleep in the restrictive seating when he needed a better place to stay when the weather got cold. He was never nasty or demanding to me or others. He became angry when people, other inmates, or correction officers made him shower. If you gave him a cigarette, you were his friend for life.

When he arrived at Downstate, he appeared normal, or mentally stable, to some extent. For some reason he took his psychiatric medications at Rikers Island but stopped taking them after being at Downstate for a few weeks. After those few weeks, he regressed and spent his days just lying in bed. When his mental illness became worse, he would not shower.

I would make it a point to go up on the tier to check on this inmate. One day I was able to see that he was jaundiced and his abdomen appeared distended. The other inmates on the tier said that he had stopped eating and coming out of his cell altogether. When I called out to him through his cell door, his only request to me was for a cigarette. I arranged to have the inmate brought up to the infirmary, and then he was sent out to a local emergency room. As it turned out, he had an obstruction in his bile duct, which was correctable.

He spent many months at Downstate and was released back to the street. He did not spend any time at the homeless shelter, as he had agreed to do. He would end up back at Penn Station, by his own admission. This guy came back to Downstate again just before Thanksgiving. It was remarkable how healthy he appeared. It was also remarkable how clear and normal his thinking was. His color was good. I commented to him about how good he looked, and he admitted to me that he was taking his psychiatric medication at Rikers Island. He laughed and said that he wanted to spend Thanksgiving at Downstate with his friends. I think he meant it. The staff at Downstate had a way of looking out for the needy.

As time went on, he again began to refuse his psychiatric medication, and the cycle started all over again. He returned to spending the day in bed, not coming out for his meals or to watch the television with the other inmates. During my rounds one day, I made it a point to check in on him. The other inmates on the tier told me that he had stopped eating again as before. When I got him to come to the cell door, I could see that he was very jaundiced and his abdomen was again distended. He had to be carried up to the infirmary again.

I was not sure whether there was a relationship between the inmate refusing to take his psychiatric medications and his physical illness. It was probably just coincidental; one could not be related to the other. He agreed to go out to the community hospital for a CT scan of his abdomen. It showed a tumor in the upper right quadrant of his abdomen, which was causing an obstruction. After continuing to refuse treatment at the outside hospital, he was returned to Downstate. Arrangements were made to have him transferred to a long-term medical facility at Fishkill Correctional Facility. The tumor in his abdomen was growing larger, and he was still refusing to take his psychiatric medication. I thought his time with corrections and New York State was numbered, but I had been wrong before. I didn't think he was long for this world, and I didn't think it mattered to him whether he lived or died.

When I heard he was going to be transferred, I stopped by his hospital room, J room in the infirmary, to see him off. He was different, extremely happy about something. You could see it in his face and hear it in his voice. He said, "Do you know what the doctor and reverend did?" The doctor was the facility health-services director, and the reverend was the Protestant chaplain at Downstate.

I thought to myself, here it comes. The inmate is not happy about something and I am going to hear all about it.

"They found and contacted my mother. She was in Atlantic City," he said with joy in his face and voice. "She came to visit me yesterday with her sister. I have not seen my mother since 1996. We talked for three hours. It was so good to see my mother again," he said. He was very happy. He was like a child on Christmas morning.

I spoke with the nurse covering the infirmary about his visit. When the correction officer told the inmate that he had a visitor, he did not get dressed or get up from the bed, knowing he had no one who would visit him. Then the correction officer told him that his mother was here to see him, and he responded, "Don't fuck with me, and leave me the fuck alone." When he heard his mother's voice, his demeanor changed. When he saw his mother's face, he cried.

He repeated to me that he had not seen his mother since 1996. This inmate had had a normal life. He was in the army at a young age and was stationed in Germany as a gunner in a tank division. At age twenty-five, the signs of schizophrenia set in. He has been in and out of mental hospitals and prisons ever since. He is not an angry or hostile individual. When he is compliant on his anti-psychotic medication, he is quite personable. The nurse said his family was very happy to see him again and truly concerned about his health. They were appreciative of the care he was receiving at Downstate. The last thing he said to me was that he did not mind being moved to Fishkill. He said that they had treated him well when he was there in the past. I told the infirmary nurse that he was one of God's children, and we will be judged on how we treat him (my boys are tired of hearing that from me).

CHAPTER 18

SUICIDES

I t is a known fact that suicides in prisons are common. The suicide rate at Downstate has made the front page of the *Poughkeepsie Journal* on more than one occasion. After being sentenced in the local county jails and in New York City, inmates are brought up to Downstate for their initial processing into the state's prison system. It finally sinks in that they are going to spend the next many years of their lives in prison. Some will spend most of their lives in the state prison system. Not getting depressed about their situation would be abnormal.

All inmates getting off the buses when they arrive at Downstate are screened by a nurse and by a mental-health clinician. The following day the inmates are screened again by a nurse and another mental-health clinician. Do inmates fall through the cracks? I don't think so. Do inmates go on to commit suicide after being screened? I have seen it happen. An inmate is locked in a cell for the better part of the day, for the rest of his life, and has little to think about. I think that being guilty of the crime or wrongfully convicted has little to do with the person's suicide risk.

When a suicide occurs at Downstate, five different agencies investigate. Each person involved has to tell what happened to five different pairs of investigators. The facility has its own investigation; the state police are there promptly, asking the same questions; the inspector general's office comes in the next few days, along with the Department of Mental Hygiene investigators; and finally the commissioner of corrections comes in, all to investigate the suicide. The same questions are asked over and over again by different people.

One morning, a correction officer with years of experience in corrections, but little experience in a reception center, was short one inmate. He was in the square area where the entire galleries of thirty-six inmates were scheduled to be processed. When he was asked where the inmate in cell 14 was, he became very defensive and a bit angry. I took the CO aside and gently informed him that most likely the inmate was still back on the gallery, sleeping in his locked cell, and that the officer should go back to the gallery to wake him up and bring him to the square for processing.

The CO was not happy with my suggestion and developed an attitude toward me. Then I became angry with him and told him that if the inmate were hanging up in his cell, the officer would be screwed and would have to tell his story to five different agencies, explaining why he only brought thirty-five inmates up to the square to be processed and not thirty-six. The correction officer then seemed to get my drift and returned to the gallery to find the inmate fast asleep in his cell.

The three worst things that can happen to a correction officer, or to any staff member during his or her career, are the following: (1) a suicide on his or her watch or of a person he or she is responsible for, (2) losing his or her facility keys, and (3) getting caught with a cell phone in the prison. These are the three *don'ts* of corrections.

Suicides affect everybody in different ways. One morning a young inmate was found hanged in his cell by a rookie correction officer, one with less than a year on the job. The officer was in the dental office and was being consoled by members of the medical staff; he was quite shaken up. No way could this young officer have been able to stop this inmate from taking his life. He was in the wrong place at the wrong time, as the saying goes. He was quite shaken up for two reasons. The first was that he had found this young person hanged in his cell, dead. The second was that he knew that because he was a new officer, on probation, he would automatically lose his job. He was a young man with a young family and had been out of work for a long time before getting this job in corrections. He needed the job to feed his family. In the end the officer lost his job.

I routinely make rounds in the forensic diagnostic unit (FDU), where the severely mentally disabled inmates are housed. Many are in strip cells (observation cells) on anything from a one-to-one watch (one officer watching one inmate) to a one-to-three watch (one officer watching three inmates). These are the inmates considered to be at high risk for hurting themselves. I have to make it a point to ensure that the inmates in these observation cells are eating and are not on a hunger strike. I have to eyeball every inmate who was moved over from the special housing unit (SHU) to the observation cell.

Inmates can be held in observation cells for many weeks on end, which annoys me to no end. I let my boss know my strong feeling that if the inmates' conditions cannot be controlled with medication within a short period of time while on watch, or if the inmates refused oral psychiatric medication and the psychiatrist is unwilling to use injectable medication, then the inmates should be moved to a proper mental-health hospital, the Central New York Psychiatric Center in Marcy, New York. The issue always arises that perhaps the inmate is faking mental illness and is there for behavior reasons. I can understand the frustration of the psych department. I also must mention that inmates who are not psychotic could have a severe mental disease that could lead them to commit suicide when isolated for long periods.

As mentioned before, Building 1 is where inmates who have special needs at Downstate are clustered. It is called extended classification. Inmates placed here have special needs and need to be placed in specific prisons upstate that are able to provide the services they require. The needs may be for medical reasons or psychiatric problems. Sometimes they may have intellectual disabilities, academic challenges, or hearing or visual impairments, or they might have difficulty with the English language. Older inmates are placed in Building 1 until an appropriate facility is located where the inmate can be placed. Inmates with moderate to severe Asperger syndrome are housed in Building 1. Building 1 is where the protective custody unit is, as well as the special housing unit.

Inmates are frequently held in extended classification for many months. There are no programs, or what corrections calls *programming*, available for these inmates. The inmates are just parked in Downstate, spending most of the day in front of the TV watching Jerry Springer or playing cards. I wish I had a nickel for every time I walked on a unit and heard Jerry Springer on the television shout out: "You are the father!" It seems to be the most watched TV show in the prison.

Because there are many challenged individuals in Building 1, many of whom are incapable of administrating their own medications, they must be rounded up and escorted to the center building for the nurse to give each inmate his own medication on a one-on-one basis. It is also referred to as DOT therapy, meaning *directly observed therapy*, also referred to as *the pill line*. At Downstate it is commonly referred to as *the med run* for short or *medication run*. The line consists of fifty to sixty inmates and occurs four times a day. The inmates are walked down a long tunnel and up a narrow staircase by one officer. They are placed in a waiting area called the bullpen. I was never happy with this situation of marching inmates with difficulties up to the hospital and placing all of them in the bullpen.

I often asked if it wouldn't be safer to have the nurse bring out the medications to Building 1. The usual response was that I placed too many inmates on one-on-one medication. I would get angry at this and ask that person to look at each inmate in line and tell me which inmate he or she thought was capable of taking his own medications in his cell. Actually, it is a sad thing to watch each day, so many inmates who are unable to care for themselves. You can see it in their faces, in how they walk and conduct themselves. Frequently, an inmate in another building overdoses on his self-carry medication, either because he is stupid or because he wanted to take his life.

After a medication overdose, the first thing that is done is to review his medical record to see which practitioner gave the inmate the pills he overdosed on. At one team meeting, after an inmate took twenty Naprosyn tablets, I asked the group what asshole gave that inmate twenty Naprosyn tablets. I knew, as well as everyone in the group knew, that it was me.

Each morning we did a.m. draft screening—that is, reviewing medication with inmates who had just arrived at Downstate the night before. One day my boss, the medical director, asked how we knew if an inmate was capable of taking his own medication properly. The first day the inmates are at Downstate, their schedule is very busy. I told my boss, "You have about one minute to look straight into the inmate's face, look him in the eye, and make a decision if he is or is not able to self-medicate. Then you hope and pray that he will not overdose on something you gave him."

After the inmate takes his pills on the pill line, he opens his mouth in front of the nurse, sticks out his tongue, and moves it around to assure the nurse that he did not cheek his medication. A great example of this is in the movie *One Flew over the Cuckoo's Nest* with Jack Nicholson playing the role of Randle Patrick "Mac" McMurphy. I have seen severely mentally ill inmates come up after having lunch, still chewing their food, stuff their pills into their mouths, and then open their mouths with this disgusting mess in it to show the nurse that they swallowed their pills. It is not a pretty sight.

Just down the Hudson from Fishkill is the West Point Military Academy where *The Long Gray Line* was made famous. Up the river is Downstate Correctional Facility where *The Long Pill Line* was made famous.

One morning I was making rounds with my boss and had to interview an inmate on 1D who was on a hunger strike. He had not eaten or drunk anything for many days; it was a true hunger strike. When we approached the cell, we could see that the inmate was highly agitated and angry. When I asked him why he was not eating, he said that the officers were putting poison in his food. I asked why he was not taking his psych medication, and he said that the nurses were putting poison in his medication. He was refusing to allow the nurse to check his vital signs and his urine. Checking urine for ketones is a good indicator of whether a person is eating or not. When one does not eat, the body breaks down fat into ketones, which show up in the urine. I asked him why he wasn't allowing her to check his urine, and he angrily said, "To piss, you need to drink fluids, asshole."

His point was well taken. I told him that if he did not eat that they were going to force-feed him.

More angrily he shouted back, "I have been strapped down to a table, had my head held down, a tube was shoved down my nose, and I was forced-fed in the past. You need to check my records. I have been through this before." His last words to me and my boss were "Go fuck yourselves."

It was not the first time an inmate had told me to go fuck myself, but this man was very angry, agitated, and hostile. After thirty-five years of dealing with mentally ill inmates, I must admit that he did impress me as being sick. I was scared that he could become violent, and I knew he really wanted to hurt himself. Later that morning I briefly spoke to the psychologist who was caring for this inmate. She thought that the inmate was not mentally ill but had a behavior problem. OK, I thought to myself. The inmate was moved to another facility, bus therapy.

CHAPTER 19
THE BOX

Solitary confinement in the prison system goes by many names. At Rikers Island it is referred to by staff and inmates as *the bing*. I hear old-timers refer to solitary confinement as *the hole*. It was also called the hole in the movie *Each Dawn I Die*, with James Cagney and George Raft. I think that term goes back to the days of Eastern State Penitentiary in Philadelphia. As mentioned before, in the New York prison system, solitary confinement is referred to by the front office as SHU, or the special housing unit, but inmates and regular staff call it "the box." It is no longer called *solitary*, as it was in the old-time movies.

In the old movies, the cells in solitary confinement are behind a locked door. At Alcatraz, to get to the barred cell door, you first had to open a very thick, large door with a small window. An inmate was locked in twice. This had to have a great negative effect on the mind of the inmate.

Access to the solitary unit at Downstate requires that you pass through many locked double doors. To get to the courtyard outside of SHU, you need a special key that unlocks double doors. You open the door to enter a small area, then you lock that door behind you, and then you unlock a second door into the courtyard.

Once in front of the SHU door, you need to be buzzed into another small room, called a trap, where you sign in. Once the CO sees that you have signed in, he opens the second door, allowing you into the SHU.

Security is very tight, and every activity by inmates and correction officers is slow and purposeful. This is done to avoid assault on staff. You are probably wondering, what about assault on inmates by staff? Again, every action by staff, both security and nonsecurity, is recorded on video cameras. There are fifty-three cameras, to be exact. I think that new inmates on the unit do not learn this for a while. Inmates are not let out of their cells without first being handcuffed. The solid door has a small hole with a door that allows the inmate to stick out both his hands to be handcuffed. After being cuffed, he is told to step back into his cell, and the door is opened by another correction officer in the bubble, who watches all of this on closed-circuit TV. Once handcuffed, usually behind his back, the inmate is told to walk backward out of his cell.

If it is shower day, the whole procedure is repeated for the shower area. Every six cells have a separate shower with a bar gate in front of it, again with an area where the inmate pushes his hands through to be cuffed and uncuffed. It is a very long and arduous process that is repeated for each inmate in SHU, three times a week on shower days, or when the inmates go outside for their hour of daily recreation. Before inmates go outside for rec, they are all patted down, and their shoes are checked for contraband or maybe a razor. It is a big production, and I try not to get in the correction officer's way when I am on the unit making my rounds. The officers are very focused on doing their jobs when dealing with inmates out of their cells. These are very dangerous inmates, so the officers do not take their eyes off them when they are out of their cells.

The fifty-three cameras on 1E watch over thirty-six inmates when the unit is full. These cameras record everything that goes on: what is said to the inmates and what inmates say to staff. I learned that at Green Haven an inmate once got under the skin of the MD making rounds, and the MD was recorded telling the inmate to "eat shit and die." The MD was reprimanded, from what I understand. Inmates in the box tend to be nasty and belligerent and often use foul language with staff. Many inmates are doing very long bids, and many have committed horrific crimes such as murder, rape, and kidnapping. A few inmates in SHU are young punks who don't know when to shut up and to keep their hands at their sides. A smaller number of inmates do something stupid on purpose to be placed in the box so they will have limited contact with correction officers and other inmates. They want to do their state bids segregated from the rest of the prison population and will do what it takes to be placed in the box.

Today when an inmate from SHU is moved through the facility, he is cuffed from behind and escorted by an officer and a sergeant. It is announced on the radio that a SHU inmate is being moved. All inmates in hallways or waiting areas that the SHU inmates pass through have to stand up and face the walls until the inmate passes. There is no eye contact between SHU inmates and other inmates in the facility.

I recently watched a reality television show in which a film crew had recorded the goings-on in a state prison in the South. When a SHU inmate was being moved through the prison, a black cloth bag similar to a pillowcase was placed over his head. This was done for two reasons. One was to keep the inmate from spitting on staff. The second was to prevent other inmates in the facility from seeing who was being moved and to prevent eye contact with other inmates, either friend or foe. This was not being done in New York state prisons, to my knowledge.

Many years ago, a correction officer was escorting a SHU inmate to the main building by himself, without a sergeant. The inmate was cuffed from behind. While the officer was escorting the inmate, walking behind him up a narrow staircase, the inmate kicked back and hit the officer in the face. When the officer fell backward, the inmate repeatedly kicked the officer in the face and head with his state-issued boots. The officer suffered serious injuries to his face and head. He has not been able to return to work and is permanently disabled as a result of his injuries.

Fortunately today, with the special doors that have sliding-glass windows, inmates are unable to throw human waste on staff as they did years ago. I am required to eyeball each inmate in the box, giving each inmate a chance to voice any medical concerns that he may have. If they need more attention, I ask the inmates to submit a sick-call slip to the officer so I can see them the next day with their medical chart in my hand. The most important thing I do while making SHU rounds is to make sure that no inmate is decompensating because of the pressures of being locked in a cell for twenty-three hours a day. Many inmates who do not have any psychiatric problems before going into the box develop them after long weeks of confinement. I am not the only one required to make SHU rounds; the psych department also has someone seeing each inmate daily, the clergy visit the box on a regular basis, and different levels of security make rounds on the unit. The superintendent of the facility makes regular rounds on the unit as well.

One day an inmate complained to an administrator that I would not allow him to keep his special, *doctor-ordered(?)* red designer sneakers. I was called down front by the administrator and questioned as to why I was being so harsh in regard to this inmate's request (demand). I was more than somewhat upset and showed it. I felt as if I was being called on the carpet. "The state's policy on special sneakers is very clear," I told them. The *Policy, Procedures, and Guideline Manual* (PP and G Manual) was more than clear. But then I told them that with an e-mail from either the superintendent or the deputy superintendent, I would make sure that the inmate got his special, bright-red sneakers.

The administrator responded back, "What policy? What are you talking about? I checked the policy book, and there is no policy for special-issue sneakers."

Fortunately, before I had gone up to the front office, I had made copies of the state's policy on special footwear. I handed each a copy of the policy, to their surprise. I never heard any more about high-end sneakers from the front office again. It is my understanding that in many prisons and jails, one inmate will kill another inmate for his beautiful high-end sneakers. Inmates will kill for anything. It makes sense to me. I can see why the policy is important.

On one busy morning, years ago, the phone rang in medical records. The registered nurse who answered said the superintendent wanted an inmate X-rayed to see if he had swallowed two screws. I was going to tell the nurse that I would see and interview the inmate later that morning when I went out to Building 1. Before I could get that out of my mouth, the nurse repeated what the person on the other end of the phone was saying: "because the superintendent is in charge of a paramilitary department, the superintendent can order X-rays on inmates." I am not sure who this person was.

I thought to myself, is this what they teach superintendents at Superintendent Training School? I was taught in PA school that you must see and interview a patient before ordering any X-rays or lab tests. If the superintendent could order X-rays, then why was the superintendent calling me? I was also taught that ordering X-rays to look for things in a person's body for a nonmedical reason could be considered assault. I could understand ordering an X-ray if the person was sick from what he had swallowed and if the person was agreeable.

Later that morning I made my way up to the psych ward to see and interview the inmate. He was very agitated, very loud, and verbally abusive to everybody, and he was pacing back and forth in his cell. When I asked the inmate if he had swallowed any screws, he told me to go fuck myself and would not agree to have any X-rays done. What went through my mind next was somebody ordering the extraction team to forcibly remove the inmate from his cell, carry him up to the X-ray department, and hold him down on the X-ray table so he could have his stomach X-rayed. I thought to myself that they might as well order X-rays of his nose and jaw at the same time, knowing that forcibly re-moving this inmate against his will meant that he was going to have something fractured. I wanted to have a psychiatrist see this inmate, possibly sedate him, and then re-interview him when he calmed down. Before any resolution of this problem happened, he was transferred to another facility.

It is crucial that I mention the important role the clergy or chap-lains play in the prison system. Often they are able to defuse situa-tions that could result in injury to inmates and staff. Whether it is a Catholic, Protestant, Jewish, or Muslim chaplain making rounds in the facility, he or she provides an invaluable service to both the inmates and staff of the prisons.

Late one Friday afternoon, I received a phone call from the lieutenant in charge of the SHU. He said that a cell-extraction team was over in SHU and was about to physically remove an in-mate from his cell. He said he was calling me to come over to the unit and to be available in case someone got hurt. I told him that I was on my way, and I asked him to page the Protestant chaplain who was covering that day to also have him respond to the area. The lieutenant really did not want to hear this; he just wanted to go in and forcibly remove this inmate with the cell-extraction team.

I told him that it was Friday afternoon, and it was 2:40 p.m. If there was one thing I didn't want on a Friday afternoon in the springtime, it was working overtime doing "use of force" paperwork.

When I arrived on the unit, the extraction team, about six large officers dressed in black riot gear, was waiting in the wings. Along with the extraction team, a correction officer was recording all of this on videotape to document that proper procedures and techniques were used to prevent anyone from getting hurt, and to document any injuries. The inmate had a razor-sharp top from a sardine can that had been part of last night's dinner, and he was holding it to his neck, threatening to cut himself up. It would have been a bloody mess. The inmate had a history of mental illness and had cut himself in the past. The extraction team was going to take the can top away and then move him to a strip cell over in the psychiatric unit, where he would be under constant observation. We were going to hurt him to prevent him from hurting himself.

You are probably wondering how this inmate had gotten a sardine can in his cell. So was I. The inmate was on a kosher diet, and sardines were a part of this diet. I was very surprised that sardines were part of an inmate's diet. The officer who gave him the tray with the sardine can on it should have checked the tray and taken the can of sardines, opened it, and scooped it onto the dish. He should not have allowed the inmate to have the empty can, which could be used as a weapon. Unfortunately he did not remove the can.

Just after I arrived on the unit, the Protestant chaplain walked up right behind me. His first question was "How did he get a can top in SHU?" We all walked away from the cell door to allow the chaplain to speak with the inmate alone and in private. After a short time, the inmate gave the can top to the chaplain, and the inmate was escorted to an FDU cell for mental observation. No one was injured, no use-of-force forms had to be filled out by medical, and I left work on time to enjoy the beautiful springtime afternoon in the Hudson Valley. The Protestant chaplain had come through again; he was a valuable asset at Downstate, to both security and medical. He always came through in the pinch to prevent people, both security staff and inmates, from being injured. He was also a great go-to person to speak with sick inmates and to contact families on the street if the need arose.

That same morning I had an encounter with another nasty inmate. He was verbally abusive and demanding—just not a nice fellow. When I did a background check on this man, I learned that he was doing eighty-three years to life, and his first parole hearing would be in 2082. Not only was his parole officer not born yet, neither was the parole officer's father or grandfather. His complaint, one of many, was that when the emergency services unit (ESU) from New York City Department of Corrections at Rikers Island had handcuffed him, the cuffs were too tight, causing numbness to both hands. He also was unhappy about riding alone in a box inside a van. He became angrier when I told him that I could not help him. He demanded a cane and then yelled profanities at me when I told him that I had watched him on numerous occasions walk across the courtyard and go up and down the stairs without any difficulty whatsoever. I said, "No cane." He was a very dangerous man, and yes, he did scare me. But I did not want to see the cane wrapped around someone's head.

After being called a motherfucker, piece of shit, and cocksucker and being told to go fuck myself by more than one inmate, I went home to my wife, who asked what kind of day I had. I responded as I always do: "Wonderful; how was yours?"

CHAPTER 20
PROTECTIVE CUSTODY

After making my rounds on SHU, I cross over the courtyard to protective custody (PC). Like all of the other cell galleries at Downstate (except the three dorm units), the cellblock is made up of thirty-six cells on three double-tiered galleries. There are six cells on the upper tiers, six on the lower tiers. One day an inmate tied a sheet around his neck and jumped off the top tier in an attempt to take his life. Fortunately, the sheet he used was too long, and he landed on the lower tier with his heels touching the floor. Some of the people responding were laughing under their breath. It was a sad sight to see: a person crying, with a sheet tied around his neck. It's something one never forgets.

Every six-cell tier has a shower; hopefully the shower is working and has hot water. There are no bars at Downstate—just very thick doors with an opening cut down the side of the door so you can look in the cell and make sure the inmate is not hanging up. There are no cameras on the PC unit.

All doors are opened and locked from a center console in the officers' area called the bubble. The officer in the bubble announces to the inmate in his cell to get ready to be let out of his cell for some activity. "Six cell, get dressed; you got a visitor" or

"Fifteen cell, get ready; you are next in line for the shower" are commonly heard on the unit. As in all galleries at Downstate, cells are routinely randomly searched by correction officers. The inmate is moved to another cell, and the officer goes through the cell with a fine-tooth comb, looking for any contraband or anything that could be used to hurt anyone. The list of which cells are searched comes from the watch commander up front. It is not selected by the gallery officer.

I have personally searched inmate cells to look for a cause for an inmate's bizarre behavior or to check if the inmate has been taking his medications properly. Some inmates who are challenged, both mentally and academically, have slipped through the system, and large amounts of unopened medicine bottles have been found in their cells. The bottles are confiscated, and the inmate is placed on the pill line, where all his medications have to be administered by a nurse on a daily basis. One inmate did "grieve" me (filed a grievance against me), claiming I had no right to his private space by entering his cell when he was not present.

There are a number of ways inmates make it to PC. The first group consists of correction officers or police officers who have broken the law and have been sentenced to do state time. They tend not to be a problem for me. They usually keep to themselves and don't ask for much. The second group consists of inmates who are famous in some way. It may be because of the crime they committed or what they did in the real world. Many of these inmates are placed in PC not because they requested it but because the front office felt it would benefit all parties involved to isolate these inmates from the general population. The term used for this is *administrative segregation*. They could be gang leaders on the street or someone as famous as Dennis Kozlowski, CEO of Tyco, who was convicted of basically using Tyco as his own personal piggy bank. Kozlowski was famous for his six-thousand-dollar shower curtain. Every time I walked past his cell and the shower on the tier, I would think about the fifty-cent shower curtain he now uses. The second-in-command at Tyco, Mark Swartz, was also housed in PC while he was at Downstate.

I remember that both inmates were pleasant, not demanding. Neither of them were problem inmates. They did not cause any problems for me or anyone else on the unit. Placing inmates such as these guys in general population would be an accident waiting to happen. Some other inmate would take a cheap shot at them to make a prison name for himself, just to get his face plastered on the TV or in the outdated newspapers the inmates see lying around.

One day in the incoming draft area, an inmate saw the picture of an inmate sitting next to him on the front page of the newspaper. I am not sure how the newspaper got into the bullpen; it was not a current paper but a few days old. I am guessing that the officers allow inmates something to read while they are waiting to keep them quiet, but I could be wrong. Newspapers are good babysitters. When the inmate recognized this guy and read what he had done to a child to be placed in Downstate, a maximum-security prison, he beat the crap out of him. It was not nice. A big investigation followed. When I first encountered this inmate in the facility emergency room, he was all black-and-blue and bloodied up. I asked him what happened, and he responded that he fell in the shower. He ended up in protective custody until he was quickly transferred to another prison upstate.

What I didn't understand was why this inmate wasn't flagged and separated into a private holding cell when he got to Downstate. Inmates in PC are not locked in twenty-three hours a day as they are in SHU. They have some meals together and rec together on the unit, away from all of the other inmates in the prison. If they need to be taken off the unit for a visit or to go to the hospital or state shop, they are escorted by one officer, not handcuffed—unlike in SHU, where they are handcuffed and escorted by a sergeant and an officer. I understand that they are not handcuffed in case they might have to defend themselves against another inmate. I am not sure if this is true. They act as porters on the unit, cleaning and mopping the floors on the unit.

The men in the next group of inmates in protective custody have committed horrific crimes on the street, mostly to children or women. These inmates would not last long in general population. Other inmates would "take them off the count," jailhouse slang meaning they would be killed. For reasons I still do not understand, the inmates in this group tend to be smart-asses, wise guys, very arrogant and demanding. Occasionally, they get under my skin.

In September of 2012, we had a repeat offender in protective custody. He had a six state-bid number, meaning he had been convicted and sentenced to prison on six different occasions. Knowing this guy as well as I did, I bet he came upstate a number of other times on parole violations, meaning he did not receive new DIN numbers. Recently when I was on rounds on 1F, he demanded that I arrange to have the dentist see him right away for a filling that had just fallen out. When I learned he was leaving on Friday on a conditional release, meaning that he had to answer to a parole officer on the street after being released, I did not let on that I knew. I told him I had gone out of my way to get an appointment for him to be seen first thing Monday morning.

That Friday I passed him, carrying his two sacks of belongings, being escorted by a correction officer down the long tunnel hallway. I stopped the correction officer and told him the inmate had to be returned to his cell because he was not going home. The inmate looked amazed and asked why. I told him, "You have an appointment with the dentist first thing Monday morning. I don't want you released to the street with a missing filling." Again he did not laugh.

One inmate in protective custody was very upset with me because I was not controlling his back pain which he had for more then ten years. I told him I could order physical therapy, which would make a big difference. At first he was gung ho about the thought of having physical therapy while in prison, but after I told him he would be taken out to Green Haven twice a week for about six weeks, he backed down. Green Haven is not the place to be if you are a child molester, he realized.

One Wednesday morning while there were a large number of inmates in the hospital bullpen, an inmate was causing problems with a number of other inmates. He was a Building 4 cadre inmate, specially selected to work at Downstate. Some of the staff referred to the cadre inmates as "civilian inmates" because they seemed to think that they were different or better than the reception inmates or the parole inmates that pass through Downstate. Cadre inmates at Downstate were specially screened medically to make sure that they were able to work. They were selected because they did not have any chronic medical problems that would keep them off their work details. If some medical condition would arise while in cadre, the inmate would be transferred to a facility where his medical needs could be better met. This is no longer true, and Building 4 cadre sick call is getting to be demanding and time-consuming. On this day this cadre inmate thought he was better than the other reception inmates in the bullpen and made it known to them.

Having a fight in the bullpen can be a major problem and needs to be avoided at all costs. The seasoned correction officer on the desk saw what was happening, took the inmate outside of the bullpen, and whispered something in his ear. The inmate returned to the bullpen and did not say another word to any of the other inmates around him.

Later that afternoon after all the inmates had returned to the cellblocks, I asked the CO what he had whispered in that inmate's ear. This was before the time of computers, but the CO knew this inmate from the street and knew he was a child molester. He told the inmate that if he did not shut up, he would let the other inmates back on his gallery know what he was doing time for. Being a child molester is something you don't want anyone in prison to know. You would not last long on the gallery. If you were not taken off the count by another inmate, other inmates would set your cell on fire.

Back in protective custody, an inmate was constantly demanding that I increase his pain medication for his chronic knee pain that he had had for more than seven years. "The pain is unbearable—ten over ten," he cried out to me. "I am unable to walk. If you are unable to control my pain, I need to be sent out to see a specialist," he demanded in front of a group of inmates on the gallery.

Later that morning I received a phone call from the rec officer on 1F, protective custody. He was a seasoned officer. He said, "Drop what you are doing and come right over to the recreation yard in 1F." Looking out the large window to the yard, I watched the inmate who claimed he could not walk playing handball with another inmate. He was quite good at playing handball and was beating his opponent. He had no problem with his knee, maneuvering around the handball court with his crippled leg.

I made it a point that the inmate saw me watching him playing handball. I waved to him and gave him a thumbs-up. I also thanked the correction officer for the heads-up on this inmate. I was always appreciative of the help of the correction staff. I made it a point to enter a long note in the inmate's medical chart.

CHAPTER 21

SICK CALL

After making rounds in FDU (the psychiatric unit), the box (the special housing unit), and PC (protective custody), I walk over to the third level to start my sick call. Remember, any inmate can ask to be seen by a doctor, physician assistant, or nurse practitioner just by dropping a sick-call slip the night before to the correction officer on his unit. At Downstate, slips are not screened by a nurse, nor are the patients triaged by nurses. Nor do nurses do sick call or help in sick call, placing the burden on the MDs, PAs, and NPs to see all of the inmates. This is unlike any other prison in the state, the nation, or any hospital or medical clinic. Just think about the last time you or your family member went to the local emergency room or walk-in clinic. You saw the clerk check your insurance to make sure the hospital or clinic would get paid, then the nurse checked your vital signs, and then you waited forever to see a doctor or PA. I always felt, and let anyone who cared know, that not pre-screening inmates for the doctor or the PA was a waste of valuable, costly resources in the state prison system. Nobody seems to care. Waiting to see an MD or PA at Downstate takes mere minutes, unlike the hours that people wait in the outside world.

On average, anywhere from thirty to fifty inmates sign up for sick call in my building, Building 1.

In the summer of 2013, I visited and took a guided tour of the Fairfax County Jail in Virginia. I was told that at that jail, inmates are charged ten dollars to be seen at sick call, twenty dollars to see the dentist, and five dollars for a prescription. I see inmates complaining about anything from dry skin and dandruff to poorly controlled diabetes or hypertension or inmates who are failing their HIV therapy. Some have cancer, seizure disorders, or other serious medical problems. The inmates complaining of dry skin or dandruff are quick and easy. Shampoos and lotions are not available through medical; inmates need to purchase those items in the commissary. Of course the inmates respond that they don't have any money in the commissary. My response to them is "Next!"—meaning I am ready to see the next patient. I announce it loudly, letting the CO outside my door know that my time with this inmate is finished.

There are a lot of inmates with severe chronic illnesses in Building 1. Many have been moved there to extended classification because they are chronically ill. They take time and patience. I am fortunate to be able to use a number of outside skilled providers and medical clinics when the need arises. My request for specialty consultation is entered on a computer in my office and is reviewed by a private company in Milwauke (this since has changed to a different company in a different state). My request is either approved or disapproved. If it is disapproved it is sent to a higher level of expertise for review. Somewhere in Albany, a bean counter keeps records of how many inmates each medical provider sends out for specialty clinics, how many of this person's consults are approved, and how many are not. It is all kept on someone's computer.

Someone once commented that I refer an unusually large number of inmates to have their hearing checked by an audiologist. I was angry at this remark because this person should already know that all inmates who say that they cannot hear properly during the reception process are moved to Building 1. Then they become my responsibility. I also have to remind that person that we, as a prison in the state of New York, are mandated by a number of lawsuits to evaluate any inmate with questionable hearing loss. I should mention that the man doing the hearing tests, the audiologist, does a great job of determining which inmates are faking their hearing loss and which truly have a hearing problem. We have inmates who were raised by deaf parents and were at a learning disadvantage growing up. A number of programs are available for the deaf inmate, not because the state is kind and generous, but because New York was made to offer these programs after a number of lawsuits. Also a number of deaf inmates are repeat offenders and are known to prison staff from prior bids upstate. A program for people with severe visual impairment is also available.

The trick to doing sick call is to get out to Building 1 early, make your rounds in the special housing areas, and start sick call early. This is done for two important reasons. The first is that you get your prescriptions in to the pharmacy on time so the inmates get their medications that evening and the pharmacist doesn't call you up looking for your scripts late in the morning. The second, also very important, is to keep the waiting area on the third level moving. The waiting room outside my sick-call office holds inmates waiting for their psychiatric medication. The inmates are brought in from other general population buildings and have to wait outside in the courtyard if there is a backup. The area also holds inmates waiting to be tested by counselors for placement purposes; inmates waiting to see a psychiatrist, social worker, or psychologist; and regular sick-call inmates. The area is not large and can be a very busy place with a lot of inmates coming and going.

In some prisons, if an inmate wants to meet up with an old friend from the neighborhood who is in a different building or area, he gets word to him to sign up for sick call on a particular day. Then they meet in the sick-call waiting area and have a regular bullshit session. At Downstate, inmates at sick call are in and out with little or no time to talk to other inmates in the waiting area. The officers do a great job of controlling all the sick-call areas. Getting started at sick call early and getting the inmates in and out before the other groups show up is a great benefit to all, reducing the threat of a fight or an inmate going off on staff.

I am very impressed with how quiet and well run the area outside my door is. The officers are very good at dealing with a very demanding and needy population, some of whom are severely mentally ill and unstable. My hat goes off to them. It must be mentioned that this is all done with respect and dignity for each inmate in the waiting area. Anyone can look at the faces of some of these inmates and see that they have severe mental problems and are trying to deal with or control their demons. I must also say that from time to time an inmate goes off and has to be wrestled to the ground and forcibly removed from the area. The waiting area in Building 1 is highly volatile, but I do feel safe. But, then again, maybe it is my ignorance.

Many times inmates hobble up to the sick-call area, appearing to be in a great deal of pain and having a difficult time walking. They make a grand appearance, and the waiting room becomes quiet as other inmates watch. After the person's name is called, he slowly makes his way to the exam room. After a brief encounter with me and finding out that he is not going to get any OxyContin or oxycodone, the inmate becomes very angry, belligerent, and demanding. I then usually shout out "Next!" to signal to the officer that the inmate's time with me is up and I am ready for the next inmate. The great part of this encounter is that the inmate jumps out of his chair, yelling at me all the way to the exit, without any difficulty walking. Jokingly I will say to the officer, "Tell me that I am not good; a man comes into my office unable to walk, and in a matter of minutes, he jumps up from the chair and runs out of the area, yelling for joy."

It is a common fact that prescription-drug addiction is a serious problem in this country. I recently had the displeasure of having a colonoscopy done. When the anesthesiologist interviewed me the morning of the procedure, he asked why I was having a colonos- copy done; was I experiencing any bowel difficulties, or was it just a routine screening? I told the doctor that I was there just for the propofol (Diprivan), the drug used to put you to sleep during the procedure. He laughed and said, "You are here for the Jackson Juice." Propofol is the drug that Michael Jackson used to fall asleep and is believed to have contributed to his death. I had never heard it called "Jackson Juice." In August 2013, one state, Missouri, was granted permission to use propofol to execute convicted felons who were sentenced to death.

Just the other day, a busy Monday morning at sick call, I was rushing to see all my patients. I did not pick up on the fact that an inmate was upset, angry, and anxious. I did not take the time to look at his face or look him in the eye. I was just interested in getting my sick call done and my prescriptions into the pharmacy. The seasoned correction officer working in the area picked right up on it. This officer had recently switched his bid (job assign- ment) from the psychiatric unit to the sick-call area in Building 1. If you remember, that is the area where all the mentally ill inmates come down to line up for their psychiatric medication. The officer spotted that the inmate was having some sort of difficulty, and he was able to defuse what could have turned out to be an ugly situ- ation. The inmate was not particularly mad at me, but as it turns out, he had been refusing his psychiatric medication and was start- ing to unravel.

The officer was able to calm the inmate down and talk him through his difficulties, something a new jack or an officer who was held over from the night shift working an extra eight hours would not have recognized or been able to do. I was very impressed by this correction officer and how he handled the inmate. Looking through the inmate's chart, I saw that he was a level-one psychiatric classification, which means he was the most severely mentally ill and was prone to violent outbursts.

Before I was responsible for Building 1 patients, I was assigned to Building 3 patients. This had to be more than twenty years ago. It was a lot easier; inmates were not as sick and were less demanding, and HIV had not yet become a major problem. I was able to finish my sick call early and get back to the square, the central processing area, and get a head start on admission physicals.

On a recent Mother's Day, I was sitting in Saint Mary's in Fishkill, listening to Monsignor's homily. He said something that reminded me of the awful toll that drug addiction can take on a person. His words reminded me of a correction officer who worked with me on the third level in Building 3, about twenty-five or thirty yearsago. He was a pleasant person, an older man, with older children who were almost, if not already, on their own. During the brief time while I was organizing my charts, before the count cleared and before inmates were available to be called down for sick call, we would talk. I should say we would bullshit about the weekend, sports, or anything else that might come up. He was always upbeat, did not bad-mouth anyone, and remained positive about the job and life in general. I was always happy to see him.

Before sick call one day, this officer surprised me by telling me he was going to be a father again. I was surprised because I knew his children were older, and I could not picture him starting over again with a new baby. He did seem genuinely happy about the situation. It made me feel somewhat guilty about my feelings. I quickly responded to him with the question "Your wife is pregnant?" He laughed and said no, not at all. He explained to me that a couple of church elders in the church he attended had approached him and asked if he and his wife would be interested in adopting a new-born baby. I believe that he was a Pentecostal, but I am not certain. He said his first response to the group of women was "of course," with no doubt in his heart or mind. He told me that the women had told him and his wife that the mother was a single parent in the parish who had had a long battle with drugs. The mother was looking to give the baby up to a couple who could raise the child properly.

The officer first mentioned this to me on a Monday after his usual church service on Sunday. I was somewhat stunned, but because of the happiness I saw on his face, I was also happy for him. The following week after Sunday at his church, the officer, even happier, spoke about his upcoming adoption. But I began to have my doubts—not for him, because he was solid in his desire to adopt this child. The doubts were in my mind and in my heart, not his. Not once did I hear or see any doubt in this person.

That Monday I learned from him that he and his wife had been informed that because of the mother's drug addiction, she had failed to have prenatal care. Being in the medical profession, I knew firsthand the importance of proper prenatal care. To the officer it seemed not to matter one bit. I felt that he was being blind to the situation, and I told him how I felt. At this point I began to worry. When he was told that the mother had not had any prenatal care, the elders first asked if he was still interested in the adoption. "Of course," he said.

The child was born in a local hospital, via a normal vaginal delivery. The officer and his wife were present. As it turned out, the boy acquired a herpetic infection from the mother during delivery and was not allowed to go home with the new parents. The officer was informed that the infection could be life-threatening, or it could leave the child retarded, blind, and/or deaf. My friend reported to me that he and his wife were taken down the hall by a nurse away from the child and informed that the boy might be very sick and in need of daily care for the rest of his life. The nurse suggested that the child be placed in a long-term care facility because the burden placed upon the adoptive parents would be crippling to their marriage and their other children. He reported to me that she was clear and attempted to dissuade the couple from going forward with the adoption.

He looked me in the eye and said, "Who will take care of this child if not me?" Again he said, "Who will take care of my son, if not me?"

I cried. As I reread this, I cried again. It did turn out that the child was bedridden, needing constant care. The child was blind and retarded and needed to be fed and turned on a regular basis. I lost contact with the officer for a number of weeks after he took the baby home. I guess he took a short medical leave from work to take care of his new son. When I did meet up with him, he was as happy as I was when I brought my two sons home after they were born. There was still no doubt in his mind about his decision. I learned later that his wife left her job to provide round-the-clock care for the child. The new family later moved, to Florida I think. All was not well with the boy, and it was not easy, but they were happy together as a family.

To return to the topic of doing regular sick call, I would like to discuss the importance of proper training. As I said earlier in this book, the physician assistant program at Long Island University taught me well. One thing that was drilled into our heads, something I still use on a daily basis after graduating more than thirty years ago, is the importance of doing a proper history before the physical examination. You learn that to take a proper history, you must cover two important items each time you see a new patient: the chief complaint and what is called the history of the present illness. If you stick to this format as a medical provider, you will never go wrong. For the first thing, the chief complaint, you ask the patient what is bothering him or her, and most importantly, how long he or she has had this problem or pain. When a new patient sits down in your chair, you always ask what is the matter, and most importantly, you must—I repeat—you must ask how long has he or she has had the problem.

I've had countless inmates come into my office complaining of severe pain: either headache, back pain, or numerous other complaints. After they tell me what hurts, they usually tell me what will cure them. "I have this pain, and I need oxycodone to relieve it" is a phrase that I hear repeated frequently, on a daily basis. Many times they say they need an MRI or CT scan to find out what has been troubling them for years. When I ask them how long they have had the problem, many will say for the past many years or since the early 2000s. Then I ask them what their doctor on the street did for them. Suddenly their eyes open a little bit wider. "I never saw a doctor on the street," they respond.

"The pain has been this bad for years, and you never went to see a doctor?" I ask. At times they say their doctor gave them oxycodone, which always helped. "Did you tell your doctor that you were also using cocaine or heroin when he was prescribing oxycodone?" I ask. Then I reach for the phone and ask the inmate the name and street address of his family doctor so I can call information and then call the inmate's doctor for a telephone consultation. Of course I request that the inmate sign a HIPAA form allowing me to talk with his primary care provider. (HIPAA is an acronym that stands for the Health Insurance Portability and Accountability Act, a US law designed to provide privacy standards to protect patients' medical records and other health information provided to health plans, doctors, hospitals, and other health-care providers.)

Of course they can never remember the doctor's or clinic's name. I get angry and say, "You have been going to this doctor for years, and you cannot remember his name or address? If some doctor on the street was supplying me with oxycodone on a regular basis, I would never forget who he was or where his office was. I would send him a Christmas card."

As I was writing this, another angry inmate came to my office demanding Percocet for his chronic back pain. He said he had a herniated lumbar disc as a result of a motor-vehicle accident nine years ago and had been on Percocet for years. I ask him when and where his MRI was done that resulted in the diagnosis of a herniated disc. He said, "Capital Imaging in Latham, New York," and that he had it done nine months prior to seeing me. I made sure that I had the right location and date of the MRI and wrote it down in his chart. I then surprised the inmate by reaching for the phone and calling information for the phone number to Capital Imaging. He then began to squirm in his chair.

I called Capital Imaging, informed the person at Capital Imaging that the patient was in the room with me and what his date of birth was. She clearly replied that he had not been a patient there for the past ten years. I hung up the phone, told the inmate to have a nice day, and proceeded to write my lengthy note in his chart. Of course I first fingered my way through his chart, looking for his drug-abuse history.

A very close friend works in a busy emergency department (ED) in a large teaching hospital that has a number of prisons in its catchment area. He told me that in the ED there is a term for inmates demanding highly potent pain medications or treatment, as soon as possible, for conditions that the inmate has had for many years: "acute incarceratitis." These are the patients who say, "I want it done now, right away, before I get released back on the street."

After hearing the inmate's chief complaint about the medical problem he is looking for a resolution to, I review the history of the present illness with the inmate. My next questions are "What happened, how did it happen, and when did it happen?"

Two of the many responses I often get from the inmates are variations on these answers: "I've been having this pain since the police beat me" or "Since a motor-vehicle accident on the street that I am going to sue for." The inmates get angry with me (and I with them), expecting me to resolve an issue that went on for years or to bolster their alleged pending ligation. On more than one occasion, the front office has questioned my response to an inmate's grievance. In a short tone, I always ask the person how much time, money, and effort I should spend in a reception facility on a medical problem that has existed for more than five years and for which the inmate did nothing prior to coming to prison. I could lock up the reception process at Downstate trying to resolve chronic medical conditions of new inmates. Ordering X-rays, sending inmates out for physical therapy, or sending inmates out for MRIs or CT scans would bankrupt the system. I always finish by asking the front-office person what they would like me to do.

Another swallower, an inmate who swallows foreign objects, spent five weeks at a local hospital at a cost to the taxpayers of over $1 million. He would swallow just about anything. While in the outside hospital, he swallowed the entire length of the IV tubing. During his outside hospital stay, he told the CO he needed to use the toilet. While in the bathroom he took the toilet-tank cover off and began to swallow the screws and various parts inside of the tank. When he came back to Downstate, I suggested that his spoon be attached to the wall with a chain. If he swallowed the spoon, the correction officers could pull him away from the wall by the ankles to get the spoon out of his stomach. The psych department was not amused at my suggestion. I don't think I am a favorite with some in the psych department.

After my paperwork and computer work are done early in the morning, I grab my charts, sometimes as many as fifty, and head out to the sick-call area in Building 1.

One day, in the middle of sick call, the deputy superintendent called me. This was highly unusual. An inmate whom I had seen about a half hour earlier had gone back to the cellblock and called his lawyer, complaining about the care he received from me in the previous hour. His lawyer called the deputy superintendent, the acting superintendent at the time, about the care that his client received. The deputy superintendent was not angry or accusatory, but he was interested in what I had done.

I reviewed the inmate's chart and noted that he had signed up for sick call ten times in the previous twenty-two days. Not including weekends, he had asked to be seen at sick call about three times a week. Many times he did not show up for sick call because he was at the law library. His complaints were many and varied. I thought I had done a good job addressing all of his needs; I guess I was just not doing what he wanted fast enough. I doubt that when this convict was on the street he would see his physician ten times in the previous six months. As it turns out, the inmate was a lawyer himself, or should I say that he had been a lawyer but was disbarred after a felony conviction. I think it was a case of "I want it, and I want now." This belief that a patient must receive the treatment he or she wants immediately is a misconception, not only in the prison system but in the general public. This attitude is bankrupting the health-care system.

The first sick call on the day after Christmas in early 2012, more than 160 inmates signed up at Downstate Correctional Facility, requesting to be seen by a physician assistant, medical doctor, or nurse practitioner. That is 160 inmates for the entire facility. This is greater than 10 percent of the inmate population at Downstate. The inmates are not prescreened or triaged by a nurse beforehand. All an inmate has to do is drop a sick-call slip, and he will be seen by an MD, PA, or NP.

Around this time in early 2012, an inmate got very angry with me because I would not refer him to the orthopedic clinic to get his shoulder repaired. He reported that it had been frequently dislocating for years and was now demanding that I have it fixed. Another inmate who had had a colostomy for the past three years became very angry and loud because it would not be reversed to normal before he went home in one hundred days. When I questioned the inmates as to why they did not have these procedures done on the street, they became angrier with me. I asked them if they came back to prison just to have their non-acute, chronic medical conditions corrected. Some inmates treat prison sort of a like a health spa, or they act as if they are medical tourists, flying to foreign counties to have medical procedures done at low cost to them.

This week alone, an inmate wrote to the front office complaining about my attitude because I would not give him Klonopin (long-acting Valium) for his questionable seizure disorder. The inmate was on his sixth state bid, meaning he had been convicted and sent to prison on six different occasions, not including his parole violations. Five of his six convictions were for *criminal sale of a controlled substance.* I asked the inmate if I had the word *asshole* written on my forehead. When I contacted his doctor on the street to ask if he was giving the inmate Klonopin, his doctor laughed.

I make it a point to get a medical-release form signed before contacting outside providers. I hate to have to defend my actions after thirty-five years of dealing with inmates. I would feel much better if the front office would just say that the practitioner is skilled, well trained, and experienced in dealing with the demanding clients in the prison. Many of the people I work alongside with also work in the community outside the walls of the prison.

I have seen many sick-call slips submitted by many different inmates requesting, sometimes demanding, eyeglasses, dentures, hearing aids, and special-order boots. Dental sick-call slips are even more amusing: "I just got to state prison and need my teeth cleaned," they say, or, "How do I get braces for my teeth?" or even, "Do they whiten teeth at this facility?"

Fortunately, the dental department keeps a great records system, and inmates are allowed only one pair of dentures every four years. The inmates are only allowed to see the eye doctor every two years. The state is obligated, however, to give inmates new hearing aids every time they come back into state service without them; this is because of lawsuits filed in the past. Every day inmates demand shampoo, dry-skin lotion, vitamins, supplements, extra pillows, extra mattresses, Timberland boots (yes, at one time inmates were given special-order Timberland boots!). It never ceases to amaze me.

One thing that I very seldom hear is that the food is bad. There are few complaints about the quality of the food or the amount. Once in a while, an inmate will say that he does not eat liver, and he gets upset at me when I tell him not to eat the liver. Inmates receive about 3,400 calories a day, which many people feel is more than enough. In general, the state is doing a wonderful job of feeding its incarcerated. The food tastes and looks better than the food that I ate at college in Brooklyn. Early on in my career in corrections, PAs ate state-inmate food and had to report on a special form how it was presented and how it tasted.

There is a bill pending in the New York State Assembly, having already passed the New York State Senate that would require that inmates be charged seven dollars for each sick-call visit. From what I understand, New York State is one of very few states, if not the only state, that gives the inmates free, unlimited access to health care, with no copay. At Downstate, inmates have unlimited access to a PA, NP, or MD without being prescreened by a nurse. Try to see an MD on the street and see how many obstacles you will encounter, even with the best insurance. I have learned that the bill to charge inmates for medical care is piggybacked onto another bill that would extend the retirement age of New York State judges from age seventy to age eighty. The two bills have a good chance of passing.

I hope to have this book finished before the bill comes up in the assembly in the New Year. If this bill is passed, my sick call will drop from forty or fifty inmates a day to single digits. This is just in my building, one of four buildings that has sick call four times a week. The bill never passed.

What also annoys me to no end is when an inmate, already on large doses of muscles relaxers and pain medication, comes to me and asks for additional medication because he has just had a tooth extracted. I check these inmates' vital signs, and my first question to them is how much pain are they in? Of course their response is always ten out of ten. I ask them why the dentist did not give them any additional pain medication, and they respond that the dentist told them to see me at sick call for additional pain medication. I confront them with the fact that they do not appear to be in any discomfort, their pulse is very low for someone who is in severe pain, and their blood pressure does not indicate that they are in severe pain either. I ask them why the current pain medication that they are on for chronic back pain is not relieving their mouth pain. They seem to think that with each procedure they have done, I would ratchet up the pain medication. I finish by asking the inmate if his history of cocaine abuse, long history of opiate addiction, or prescription-drug abuse has anything to do with his request for more and more pain medication. Every week in the media, articles are written about the prescription-drug abuse epidemic in this country. The narcotic pain medication abuse on the street is out of control and is spilling into the state prison system. Or is the reverse true?

Often inmates claim they are unable to fall asleep in the evening. I respond that if any other person spent the whole day sleeping, they would not be able to fall asleep in the evening either. The evenings are loud in the box, with inmates shouting across to other inmates into the wee hours of the morning. The next day they sleep the whole day away. I think the professional term for this is an *inverted sleep pattern*.

If I am able to get to sick call early and see everybody, take care of my outside medical-consult referrals (inmates who need care that we are unable to provide in-house), and get my prescriptions in to the pharmacy and they are legible, I show up in the square for an afternoon of new-inmate reception physical examinations. The square is the center core building at Downstate where much, but not all, of the processing is done for the medical, psych, and dental departments.

One thing that bugs the shit out of me is when I walk into the exam room and the inmate greets me with a written list of things he wants me to list in his chart and the medical problems he thinks he will get addressed while in prison. We call that a "laundry list" of medical demands. One day I caught a new nurse telling a group of reception inmates to tell the doctor all your medical needs when you see him. I asked her if she was nuts. I told her that we do not care about problems that the inmate has had for decades and that he now thinks will be rectified while in prison. "This ain't no health spa," I told her.

"While I am in prison, I want to be tested for sleep apnea"; "I want my shoulder fixed"; I need a colonoscopy" are demands that are commonly voiced by the new inmates. Most if not all chronic problems are addressed when inmates are at their permanent facility. The problem is that many inmates are doing a short bid, spending less than two years in prison (called a "skid bid"), and do not follow up on their complaints.

Recently, after completing my quick physical on an inmate, he told me that he was "heat sensitive" and needed to be housed in an air-conditioned dorm. Because of his asthma, the inmate claimed he could not breathe when it got hot. I was angry and told him that it was because of his heavy smoking that he could not breathe when it got hot. He got louder and more demanding, claiming that he did not smoke. I got angrier and asked him if the brown stains on his fingertips came from wiping his butt without toilet paper or from smoking unfiltered cigarettes. Then I told him that he would be fast-tracked to Dannemora, where the heat is not a problem. When he left my exam room, I could hear him asking the correction officer where Dannemora was. The officer replied that when he got to Dannemora, he would be able to look out his cell window and see Canada. This was in April, and I heard the correction officer add that in Dannemora there was still snow on the ground.

There is a very funny joke about Dannemora I cannot resist sharing. It concerns a woman who was awakened by the sound of her husband crying in the kitchen. She ran down the stairs to find him sitting at the kitchen table, holding his head and bawling. She asked why he was crying. He asked, "Do you remember twenty years ago when your father caught us having sex in my car? He said that if I didn't marry you, I would be doing twenty years in Dannemora."

She responded, "I remember that night."

"Well," he said, "I would have been getting out today."

I have had inmates demand to have tattoos removed, scars removed, braces for crooked teeth, ACL repairs on knees that were injured years ago, and hernia repairs that were not done when the inmate was in custody ten years ago. Inmates commonly demand special boots and better-quality sneakers. "I don't eat pork or bologna" is a common complaint as well.

Recently a correction officer had his nose broken by a deranged inmate. The officer could not find an ear, nose, and throat doctor who would see him because it was a workers' compensation case. Yet, if an inmate had his nose broken in an altercation, we would have no difficulty in finding a specialist to see the inmate.

I had an inmate in protective custody recently who had passed through Downstate many times. He had many DIN numbers, which means he had many convictions. He was always a pain in the ass about something, demanding this and demanding that. He would remind me that that is what I am paid for. One day on the PC unit, the correction officer told me this inmate was leaving to go back to the street. I ran up the stairs in the unit and caught him packing his bags. In all seriousness, I told him not to pack up but to leave everything the way it was. He became very concerned, thinking that he was not going home the next morning. He came to the door at once and asked why. I told him that there was a very good chance that he would be back again soon, so there was no sense in moving his belongings. Carrying his bags back and forth would be a lot of work. Sure as shit, about two weeks later, I came face-to-face with this guy in the same cell, on a parole violation. "Didn't I tell you not to pack your things the last time you were here?" I reminded him. Jokingly he told me to go fuck myself. In all actuality the inmate was not a bad guy at all. He just could not control his desire to steal buses and subway trains. I must mention that when he drove off with the buses and subway trains, they were full of people. He would show up in a transit-company or bus-company uniform and jump in the driver's seat when the driver got out to use the restroom. I am not making this up. There is a movie about this guy. The COs in the bubble were listening on the overhead system and laughed when I came down the stairs from the gallery.

I have the pleasure of working with a great staff of PAs, MDs, and NPs. They are all knowledgeable and approachable and always do the right thing when it comes to treating inmates. A PA whom I have worked with for years also works in the community in hospital emergency rooms. He is very skilled at what he does and does a better job in the ER than some of the doctors I have known. Not only would I trust my life to him in a medical emergency, but I would also trust him with the life of any family member.

One afternoon when it was near time to leave, a correction officer was in our triage room, what we call the facility emergency room. He was in his fifties, appeared diaphoretic, sweating profusely, and complained of flu-like symptoms. His vital signs were slightly elevated. He wanted to leave work and go home to bed.

He was not seeking treatment, just a note for his supervisor. The PA, who had years of experience working in the emergency room, came into the room and told me to have the nurse run an EKG strip. Because the correction officer had a history of having a stent placed in his coronary artery, the PA told me that we always had to remember that he might be having another blockage. In this situation, he said, the patient should always get an EKG, no matter how vague the complaints are, how busy the nurses are, or how much the patient resists. Sure as shit, the EKG was grossly abnormal with S-T wave changes, indicating that the patient was having another heart attack. He was transferred to a local hospital by an advanced cardiac life-support ambulance. I learned later that the gentleman did well thanks to the quick diagnosis and treatment.

One morning late in my career, I was getting my charts ready for sick call when the draft nurse looked up at me from her desk with a smile. She said, "I got one you never heard of. A new inmate came into the facility draft area. He was arrested for burglary. It gets better." She laughed. "The home that he burglarized had a nanny cam, a hidden camera in the ceiling of the living room. After taking what he wanted from the apartment, he stopped to have sex with the owner's golden retriever. This was all caught on camera." I was told he got more time for having sex with the dog than he did for the burglary.

Someone jokingly said that the inmate must have had a thing for blondes. There is never a dull day at Downstate Reception Center.

CHAPTER 22
GENDER IDENTITY DISORDERS

I was recently stopped by a corrections lieutenant who was puzzling over a new corrections form of some type. Under "sex," the initials *M/F/GD* appeared. He did not know what *GD* meant. "I know *M* for male and *F* for female, but I cannot figure out *GD*," he said. I told him it meant "gender disorder."

Gender disorders are psychiatric conditions. In the third edition of the *Diagnostic and Statistical Manual of Mental Disorders* (DSM-3), this condition was referred to as *gender identity disorder* and defined to mean a condition in which a person feels discomfort and inappropriateness about his or her anatomic sex. In the more recent DSM-5, the disorder was reclassified to *gender dysphoria*, meaning distress or discomfort with one's sex or gender. In the *New England Journal of Medicine* in 2011, Louis Gooren, MD, referred to it as "a significant incongruence between gender identity and physical phenotype." In the past, the disorder has been referred to as transsexualism or as being a transvestite.

Gender identity disorders are not as common in the prison system as one might think, but the inmates with this disorder whom we meet are memorable and tend to stand out from the other inmates in the system. Some of these inmates seem to want to stand out from the crowd. Using burned matchsticks for makeup and wearing their state-issue clothing in a certain provocative way, they attract attention with their manner of walking and talking.

Last summer there was a transgender inmate who demanded that I schedule him to have the silicone implants removed from his cheeks. I told him that because the silicone had been implanted more than two years ago, it would not be removed while he was in the reception process at Downstate. He needed to wait until he was placed at his permanent facility upstate. He got bent out of shape and in an angry voice told me that it needed to be done right away. He was concerned because the silicone he had used in his face was purchased or obtained in some way from the Home Depot. He admitted that one of his friends had taken store-quality silicone caulking, cut small slits in his cheeks, and injected the silicone into his face. The inmate thought that he would get some kind of cancer from the silicone that had been injected into his cheeks and wanted it removed as soon as possible.

I had never heard of such a thing and had no idea what to do. I knew that if I entered a consult for plastic surgery for the purpose of removing the silicone, it would probably be pended or denied. I told the inmate to sign up for regular sick call and to discuss it with the PA who was covering that particular building. The following week one of my colleagues stopped me in the hall and said, "You will never believe this. Some inmate had his friend inject store-bought silicone caulk into his cheeks to make him look more like a woman." The PA also did not know what to do with this inmate. I suggested that the regional medical director be contacted and consulted on what to do.

In chapter 9, I mentioned encountering a transgender inmate at Green Haven during my early rounds on the protective custody unit. He was standing bare-ass naked in his cell, waiting for me to come down the hall on my rounds. Not only was he proud of his erection, but he was also very proud of his very large breasts (referred to as "breasteses"—plural for *breast*—by many in the prison system). It was difficult not to show my shock and amazement at seeing this person's body, a reaction I think he was waiting for. I ignored him, walking to the end of the tier. On my way back up the tier, he angrily said, "People in New York pay fifty dollars to see my naked body with my big penis and breasts, especially a stiff penis." I did not say a word but finished my rounds.

I had very few inmates with gender dysphoria who requested to have their bodies surgically altered, or I should say, a very small number requested a sex-change operation while they were in the state prison system. New York State Department of Corrections policy is that you leave the prison system the way you came into it. We, the practitioners, are not allowed to start an inmate on female hormones or to change the hormones that they are taking when they enter the New York State Department of Corrections. This policy has caused some difficulties with transgender inmates.

On an August day during a busy sick call, an inmate came in asking for female hormones. Out of the clear blue sky, this inmate requested two specific drugs, with specific doses that were not common. I was caught off guard because nowhere in this inmate's history or screening at Downstate or Rikers Island had he indicated that he was transgender and on medication. When I began to question him as to where and when he had begun to take female hormones, his history did not add up. I told him that because he was not on female hormones when he came into Downstate, I was unable to start or restart them.

It was not until after he left my office that I remembered another transgender patient who had requested the exact same medication and the exact same dose. I looked up his location, and sure enough, he was in a cell across from the inmate I had just seen. I still am not sure why he came to sick call seeking these particular drugs. During my first encounter with the inmate requesting female hormones, his voice was very soft and feminine. When the inmate came back to sick call two days later, in a deep, masculine voice he demanded lotion for dry skin and shampoo. When I told him that he had to purchase shampoo and body lotion in the commissary, his voice became louder, more demanding, and more masculine.

For years, transgender inmates came to the state prison system only taking one female hormone: Premarin (conjugated estrogen), which is used by women to reduce hot flashes and night sweats, to prevent bone loss, and to ease vaginal symptoms during menopause. After a while, many transgender inmates came up from Rikers Island also taking Provera (medroxyprogesterone acetate), a drug used by doctors to treat women with abnormal menstruation or irregular vaginal bleeding. A female physician assistant whom I have worked with for more than thirty years and who had worked at Bedford Hills Correctional Facility for Women told me often that she wondered why a male would be placed on Provera when he did not have a uterus.

A drug called spironolactone is being used more frequently to treat transgender male patients, patients transitioning from male to female. Spironolactone is a potassium-sparing diuretic used to treat patients with edema and hypertension. Spironolactone has antiandrogen properties and directly inhibits testosterone secretion. Testosterone and drugs that increase testosterone in nontransgender men are monitored much more closely than drugs that suppress testosterone in the transgender population. Gynecomastia is a condition in which breasts in males become enlarged. It is high on the list of adverse drug reactions of spironlactone, and it appears to be a desired side effect that transgender patients seek. Spironolactone is also noted to control facial hair in women. My only difficulty with spironolactone is the many interactions with other drugs and many other side effects of this drug. I am uncomfortable with prescribing a drug only to get its side effect such as enlarged breasts. However, I was told recently by Albany that if a transgender inmate comes into the state system on spironolactone I am required to continue it.

In recent years, estrogen given by injection has been seen more frequently in transgender patients. Giving an injection of estradiol valerate or testosterone cypionate every week or every two weeks is becoming more common among new-intake inmates at Downstate.

Many wonder how and if the transgender population is treated differently from the regular inmates. Are they coddled or given things out of the ordinary to keep them quiet? Sometimes they are. For instance, on one of my busiest mornings, when I got to the box (special housing unit), the officer called me into the bubble and told me to call the pharmacist right away. The pharmacist informed me that the front office wanted me to stop what I was doing and bring a jar of moisturizing cream to a transgender inmate in the SHU in cell 19. I was hustling to get my rounds done quickly so I could start my heavy sick call and get my prescriptions in on time. I told the pharmacist, "You got to be shitting me. I don't have time for nonsense right now." The pharmacist's response was that she wished she was joking, but it was true.

When I got back to my sick-call office, I faxed a copy of the directive regarding the use of moisturizing creams from the deputy commissioner, who also happened to be a physician and the chief medical officer for the department, to the pharmacy to forward to my boss. The document had been sent to me by the superintendent many years ago. The memo was clear and concise on when to order moisturizing creams for inmates. The memo did not differentiate between regular inmates and transgender inmates.

What upset me was that I think the front office thought I was being biased against or arbitrary toward the transgender population. I pride myself on treating everyone as I would expect to be treated. I had examined the inmate days prior when he was in a strip cell, with no clothing on, for psychiatric or emotional reasons. This was the inmate's choice not to wear clothing. He was totally naked; he had a smock but refused to wear it. Back in the observation cell, he demanded that I give him moisturizer cream. I think he enjoyed the reactions of new people on the unit seeing him with very large breasts and no clothing on. He wanted to show off his body to the officers who were watching him 24-7. He had no conditions that warranted the use of topical moisturizing creams, and I clearly and neatly documented that in his medical record, knowing that someone would be looking over my shoulder and second-guessing my decision.

When an inmate claims he needs topical moisturizing cream, I make it a point to check his skin. Inmates with severe HIV disease or diabetes receive moistening creams. I do dispense topical moisturizing creams when I examine the inmate and deem it necessary. I don't just hand the stuff out because an inmate demands it or has a temper tantrum. If you give an inmate a jar of skin cream, he goes back and tells his friends, and the next sick call you have two inmates demanding skin cream. They go back to the gallery and tell their friends, and then you have four, and it goes on and on. Sick call would be a free-for-all.

I cannot understand why the front office does not understand this. I am angry that the front office thought I was being arbitrary or that I did not like the transgender population. These are all God's children, and we will be judged on how we treat them. Not only did he not need a topical moisturizing cream, but the inmate also had a deprivation order while in special housing, so he was not to be let out of his cell. When he was being moved out of his cell days earlier, he had slipped out of his handcuffs and refused to give the handcuffs back to the correction officer. The cell door was locked with him inside waving the handcuffs at the officer. He was not allowed out of his cell for rec or for showers. His crime on the street was assault.

This inmate exhibited signs of histrionic personality disorder, or HPD. His behavior frequently consisted of patterns of excessive emotions and attention seeking, which was seen in the provocative way he dressed and walked when others were watching, a sort of exhibitionist behavior. His behavior and emotions were exaggerated to the point of being theatrical. The staff mostly ignored this behavior.

Months prior to this incident, two other box inmates were able to slip their hands out of the handcuffs. One inmate, about six foot two inches tall, beat the snot out of another inmate after freeing his hands. When he was finished beating on this inmate, he turned to the correction officer and did not resist being handcuffed again.

This brings up another reason that I do not routinely provide inmates with moisturizing lotions. When inmates escaped from Elmira Correctional Facility a few years ago, they used A+D ointment that was provided to them by the medical department. From what I understand, they greased themselves up so they could squeeze through a very tight area. Back in the days at Sing Sing, inmates would put creams and ointments on their wrists so correction officers could not grab them by the wrists to cuff them during an altercation. The front office should know this. It is not wise to give out moisturizing creams or grease to an inmate, especially in the box, just to shut him up because he is having a hissy fit. Every day I get many requests, or I should say demands, for moisturizing creams, shampoos, vitamins, vegan diets, special shoes, special sneakers, and sunglasses. I tell the inmates that I am not Walgreens or CVS. I refer them to the commissary, where they can purchase these items.

Juxtaposed with this transgender inmate who was labor intensive and very verbally abusive, there was an inmate who regularly passed through Downstate's special housing unit on his way to court in New York City. He had been convicted of murder and kidnapping. His first parole date was 2083. As is said in corrections, the grandfather of his parole officer has not been born yet. This inmate would be transported down to court in NYC by the emergency service unit (ESU) from Rikers Island.

The ESU would drive up from Rikers Island very early in the morning to pick the inmate up and transport him in a van that had a custom-made strong metal box in the back. The inmate would frequently complain to me about the uncomfortable ride in the box in the back of the van. At the end of the day, the ESU unit would drive the guy back to Downstate. I guess that Rikers did not want to keep him overnight because he was a problem child and a magnet for altercations involving him, staff, and other inmates.

Although this inmate was never verbally abusive to me, he was very demanding and wrote well. His handwriting and spelling were much better than mine, and I was somewhat jealous. Knowing his crime and his sentence, I found this guy a very intimidating convict. I would get the heads-up from the correction officers, sergeants, and lieutenants that he would be passing through Downstate days before he got there. He demanded just about everything in writing the day he arrived at Downstate. His demands included special diets: "I don't eat this, and I don't eat that." He wanted a cane because he claimed he could not walk. He demanded that I admit him into the infirmary because of the long walk to the draft area from the special housing unit.

On almost all my encounters with this inmate, he requested in a loud voice to be placed on narcotic pain medication (which he had not been getting at his previous facility). I think he used a loud voice because he knew that he was on camera and was being recorded. He was trying to bait me into saying something that he could use against me. He was playing to the cameras in the special housing unit.

My concern was that he would complain to the front office because I denied him his requests, or I should say his demands. I hate justifying my actions to a nonmedical person. I had made long notes in the inmate's chart that I had observed him on more than one occasion walking up and down many stairs, down the long tunnel to SHU, without any difficulty or signs of pain or discomfort. Because the inmate was handcuffed, he was always helped up and down stairs by a correction officer. I had called his previous sending facility and was told that he did not use a cane while he was there and had no problems going up and down the stairs to his cell on the second floor. I do not like giving out canes, especially to dangerous inmates, because they use them as weapons or to strike out at correction officers or physician assistants who upset them. I make it a point to go through the extra effort to determine the needs versus the wants of the inmate.

The reason I mention this difficult inmate here is best articulated by a correction officer working in the special housing unit. He told me he would rather deal with a lifer like the guy I just mentioned than with a histrionic transgender inmate who was verbally abusive on a daily basis. "You never knew what to expect," the officer said. "At least I know what to expect with a professional convict, and I am able to deal with him."

As I said before, the correction officers who work in the box (SHU) always maintain a very high level of professionalism, even under the most difficult circumstances. I am very impressed with these officers, and I feel somewhat comfortable working in the unit alongside them. I don't think I could maintain my composure or react as they do under very difficult circumstances on a daily basis. God bless them. I am not saying that I have never encountered firsthand, in my thirty-five years in corrections, correction officers who used force a bit excessively. Excessive force does happen, but it is not common.

For the most part, the correction officers I have dealt with in my long career have not only been very professional and restrained in their daily handling of inmates but also a pleasure to work with. It made my life in corrections a lot easier, and maybe that is why I lasted as long as I did. I never minded going to work in the mornings. However, we did have a few bad apples—correction officers who abused inmates. Fortunately they were weeded out early on in their careers.

One morning an RN whose judgment I trust approached me about the dose of a female hormone she was giving to a transgender inmate at the medication window. She said the dose appeared high, and she did not remember ever giving that strength to anyone before. It was not my patient, so I kind of blew her off and told her to speak to the patient's provider. I really did not want to get between a transgender inmate and his hormones. It always turns out to be a hornet's nest of problems. Later that day the pharmacist stopped me in the hall, also questioning the dose. I told her she needed to speak to the facility health-services director, who was a physician. Again, I did not want to open up a can of worms.

After lunch I called the pharmaceutical company that manufactured the medication. Two people I had worked with for years and whose judgment I had learned to trust had made me rethink the dose. The drug company was great about getting back to me and said that using that particular medication at that high of a dose had never been studied in a male-to-female transgender population. It had only been studied at about one-quarter the dose the inmate was receiving. This reminds me of an old story someone told me. An old-timer once asked that if a five-pound sledgehammer would do the job, would a ten-pound sledgehammer do it quicker or better? Does twice the dose of a female hormone make a male feel more like a woman? A more important question is, at what risk?

Reducing the dose back to a level that everybody is more comfortable with, which I did, places me in the crosshairs for complaints from the inmate and those who advocate for the transgender population. I know in the coming weeks the inmate will write to the front office about my cutting the dose of his female hormone in half, to a level more commonly seen in corrections. Was the doctor on the street who was prescribing that dose acting in the role of a physician or as a patient advocate for the transgender population as a whole?

I write about this incident to show my frustration and hopefully to bring this dilemma to light, both to society and to the medical community at large. I personally feel somewhat uncomfortable using drugs to manipulate a person's testosterone and estradiol level. It would be great if the Department of Corrections had a transgender specialist whom I could refer patients to or just have a telephone consultation with. We have a wonderful and useful telephone-consultation service with an HIV specialist in Albany and with a group in White Plains, New York. Answers to the most difficult medical questions regarding HIV can be had by just making a phone call. Likewise, I could reach out to a cardiologist by phone if need be. It would be great if we had the same service for the transgender population.

Of course, Central Office will say that this consultation service already exists. If it does, I don't know about it—nor does my boss. The many consults that I have requested for an endocrinologist to see these patients have been denied. The request denials are saved somewhere in the computer system and would prove my point. The local endocrinologists whom I have spoken with appear to be as uncomfortable as I am with this dilemma of dealing with transgender patients. I must also mention that the Department of Mental Hygiene has been of little help in dealing with these patients.

The most memorable case of a transgender inmate occurred about a decade ago. A transgender inmate who had been in and out of the state prison system for more than two decades turned up at a prison on the far western edge of New York State, allegedly without his penis. This individual was known to many in the prison system because of his frequent visits to the correctional system. He was not a nasty or demanding person, but in some ways, he was not like the other inmates who pass through the system.

A physician who examined this transgender patient in the facility on the far side of the state, near Attica, called Central Office and reported to the powers that be that the inmate had no penis and therefore should not have been housed in a male prison for the previous eleven years. The first mistake made by this MD and by Central Office was to assume that the inmate had been in the system for the entire period. Neither the doctor nor Central Office realized that this inmate, like many others, went in and out of the system and had been examined multiple times by many different practitioners. In addition to his reception physical, he should also have had a routine physical done at some time. I don't think anyone had noted that his penis had gone missing.

When security got wind of this controversy—and they got wind of this quickly—the lieutenant pulled all the strip-search records for the many times the inmate had passed through Downstate. All inmates who come into a state facility and leave a state facility are strip-searched, down to bare ass, with nothing on. They are required to spread their butt cheeks and testicles. Mistake number two: Central Office did not know that inmates were stripped naked every time they were transferred from one prison to another.

The lieutenant interviewed most, if not all, of the correction officers who had done strip searches on this particular inmate, according to careful record keeping. Thank God for good record keeping. When the officers were asked if they remembered the inmate, the common response was how could you forget this guy? Then they were all asked if they remembered seeing if the inmate had a penis. Because of his appearance, they had all made sure he was a he and not a she. In other words, the inmate's penis was present and accounted for. I had examined the inmate in the late 90s, back when the inmate was coming back and forth, in and out of prison. The main issue made by Central Office was that the first examination that I did had not indicated the inmate did not have a penis. We were taught early to make sure all inmates had a penis. It is a major reason physicals are done on reception.

So, almost a decade later, an MD, far off in the western part of New York State, examined the patient again and did not find a penis. He called Central Office, and it was determined that for all these years a female (a male who had his penis removed) had been held in a male prison.

One morning, this questionable female was placed in a state van with two correction officers and was driven far across the state to a female prison in New York. I bet it was an eight-hour drive in one direction. By the time the van arrived at the female prison, it was late in the day. The MD there had stayed late, wanting to see the inmate before going home. When the inmate was escorted to an exam room and pulled down his/her pants, a penis popped out. I later learned that it was a four-inch penis. The MD called Central Office to report that the inmate had a penis. Central Office still did not believe that the inmate had a penis.

Another MD was summoned to drive down from many miles away to see if what the MD the female prison had seen was actually a penis. The MD also confirmed that the inmate had a four-inch penis. I am not making this up! A seasoned nurse who was on duty at the prison laughed at what went on that day. The inmate had to be shackled back up, placed back into the van, and driven back across the state to the male prison from whence he came.

I remember my first encounter with the inmate in question as if it were yesterday. It was a late afternoon, and he was one of the last inmates to be examined. On most days, each physician assistant sees about ten to fifteen inmates. It is a very quick physical exam. Many times it is interrupted when the medical professional is called to the emergency room, needs to sign off on medication orders for nurses, needs to transfer prescriptions to be made out, or has to answer a call from the pharmacy clarifying prescriptions that were submitted earlier in the day.

The physical exam is not the greatest, and not a lot of time is spent on each inmate. I am not happy with the amount of time that is spent on each inmate during the intake physical. Many times you forget to enter important information because of these frequent interruptions. You have to picture a large waiting area with a large number of inmates, and everyone is anxious to get the inmates done and back to their cells before an inmate goes off and creates a problem. If a problem is noted and has to be addressed, the inmate is referred to regular sick call. I don't think Central Office realizes this.

On the day of this exam, the inmate in question refused to pull out his "tuck." His penis was tucked way back into his butt cheeks to make it appear that he did not have a penis. In the transgender world, this is referred to as "a tuck" or "my tuck." Google was not available back then to reference, but it is today, and it does a nice job of explaining what a tuck is.

I bet if you questioned the entire medical staff in Central Office as to what a tuck is, no one would have any idea, to this day. When I insisted the inmate pull his penis out, he began to cry out, and the thirty-six inmates in the waiting room laughed. I did not want any part of this circus and made a note that the inmate would be brought up and examined at a later time. I was not going to forcibly examine the inmate. I saw his penis and was convinced he was in a proper male facility. Having or not having testicles has nothing to do with whether the inmate is placed in a male or female prison; only the presence or absence of a penis has any bearing.

Again, I was sure that when I had first examined him in the late 90s, the inmate had a penis, tucked way back into his buttocks. The following week while making rounds in the prison infirmary, this same inmate was in room A for reasons I can't remember. As the group of MDs and PAs interviewed the inmate, I reminded my boss that this was the inmate who would not let me check whether his testicles were present during a routine exam and that there was still some question that they might not be present. Again the inmate would not allow a proper exam. The facility health-services director (FHSD)—a physician and my boss at that time—happened to be a woman, and she thought that the inmate was a bit shy about showing his genitalia to a group. She said she would come back to his room at a later time to examine him.

Later that morning while I was way down at the other end of the infirmary around the corner, I heard a very loud screech. It sounded like a cat in heat. Officers went running down the hall to see what was going on. The same inmate had begun crying out even before the examination began, before the MD even touched the inmate. I reminded my boss that this was going to be a high-profile case and that she should document clearly in the patient's chart what transpired during the physical exam. I also suggested that the front office be informed, and be kept informed, from the beginning.

I believe that she did record her observations in the patient's record and informed the front office about this inmate. This record was not reviewed a decade later by the MD in western New York, because that information was buried in his old chart somewhere in medical records. I informed the Albany Central Office of this, but it seemed that the staff there was more interested in counseling me and another PA who worked at Downstate at the time about a questionable incident that had occurred more than nine years earlier.

I don't understand why Central Office did not pick up the phone and speak with anyone at Downstate: a phone call would have saved a lengthy van ride back and forth across the state.

I was not too upset with Central Office, I must say. I have seen strange criticisms from Central Office early in my career. Just prior to the TB crisis in the prison system, Central Office criticized us for placing too many inmates in isolation cells for too long in order to make sure they did not have active TB. One particular inmate was moved from our isolation cell and placed in the general population at another facility before being cleared for population by our MD. When the MD at Downstate received the TB culture results, she went looking for the inmate. When my boss determined that the inmate had been moved out of isolation to another prison without her consent, she was livid. I had never seen her so angry. I can remember another PA telling me to stay away from the boss that day that she was very angry.

Central Office also criticized the way we dealt with the administration of tuberculosis prophylaxis medication. We place anyone taking TB prophylaxis medication on a directly observed therapy, or the pill line. As discussed before, this is when the nurse administers each separate dose to each individual inmate multiple times a day, rather than giving him a prescription bottle full of pills. This is how we make sure the inmate is taking his medications properly. We did this at Downstate because we found inmates with full bottles of medication, indicating they were not taking their medication. Central Office said we were wasting valuable nursing time by dispensing each dose separately to each inmate. Central Office was never interested in the whys and the wherefores. Not long after this incident, the New York State Department of Corrections had not only an active TB problem but a problem with resistant TB—that is, TB that is resistant to the common anti-TB medications.

Communication between Central Office and local practitioners was once effective. It seems to have slipped to just one-way communication—top-down, as one might say. There once was an open line of communication between the deputy commissioner/ chief medical officer and local facilities. He was readily available, approachable, and appeared interested in each problem. This guy always returned everyone's phone calls, no matter how busy he was, and he was a very busy man. He exhibited a great deal of compassion and concern for both staff and inmates. This was at a very important time, because of the HIV crisis. He was proactive in training, and if he was unable to answer a particular question, he always got back to you. Often on Friday afternoons, the front office at Downstate would call and say the deputy commissioner was going to stop in late in the afternoon on his way to Westchester from Albany to make rounds in our infirmary. The front office made it a point that someone, a PA or MD, had to be present and make rounds with him, review each sick inmate's treatment plan, and see the inmates.

It was a sad day in corrections in New York State when the deputy commissioner ceased left state service. At that time New York had the third-largest reception processing in the nation. Only California and the federal prison system processed more inmates than New York State did. Our reception-processing budget was staggering. Having good communications with Central Office was and is vital and basic.

The last time we had an inmate with ambiguous genitals at Downstate, the inmate was placed in room J in the prison infirmary until his sexual identity was determined. This was very early on in my career. A special medical doctor who dealt only with these kinds of cases was driven up from New York City at state expense. I met the MD in the front lobby and had to escort him back to the infirmary to both examine and interview the inmate. After spending a lengthy amount of time with the inmate, the MD asked to be escorted back out to his waiting limousine. On the way out, I asked him what his opinion was of the sex of this inmate. He said that he was not sure himself and would contact Central Office to discuss his findings and opinion. This case was much different from the typical one involving a transgender inmate. Here the difficulty was in determining the sexual identity of a person who, since birth, had had an ambiguous sexual identity. This was not a person who was unhappy with the sexual identity he was born with.

CHAPTER 23
THE FUTURE OF CORRECTIONS

With the advent of synthetic marijuana and the havoc it is causing on the street, I have no idea how the Department of Corrections will respond to this ever-growing problem. There is no blood test for it, and drug-sniffing dogs cannot find it. Synthetic cannabis, referred to as a psychoactive designer drug, is known by its early brand names, such as K2 and Spice.

The problem with synthetic cannabis is that it can precipitate psychosis, which can be prolonged in some cases. According to *Wikipedia*, synthetic cannabis has the ability to trigger a chronic, long-term psychotic disorder among vulnerable individuals who might have a family history of mental illness or a predisposition to mental illness. I recently spoke to an MD who works in a very busy ER who told me that the opposite of what you expect occurs with synthetic marijuana. The patient becomes highly agitated and could become violent; he is not the zoned-out patient you would expect to find in people who are on regular cannabis. It is important to mention that synthetic cannabis does not produce positive results for marijuana in drug testing.

As I mentioned before, the prescription pain medication crisis on the street is already spilling over to the inmate population, with inmates demanding Percocet, oxycodone, Dilaudid, and tramadol. There is a large influx of inmates who have been convicted of DWI or driving under the influence of a controlled substance. They take up a lot of prison cells now, placing a greater burden on taxpayers and on the prison system.

Earlier I spoke of an inmate who had a poor outcome from this new type of drug that he tried, synthetic marijuana. His life was changed by his stupid choice to use a so-called recreational drug.

The Department of Corrections needs to stem the number of after-hours trips to outside emergency rooms. In a maximum-security prison, there must be a way to pay physician assistants to be back on call again and to pay them when they come in after hours to see inmates. This would avoid both costly outside medical trips and the possibility of escape. The trend in replacing physician assistants with nurse practitioners also needs to be reevaluated. Nurse practitioners do not suture, and sending inmates out for a few stitches is costing the state a fortune. Nurse practitioners should be trained to suture if they are going to be used in maximum-security prisons.

If Central New York Psychiatric Center is not going to accept severely mentally ill inmates and instead is going to continue to shift the burden of treating severely mentally ill inmates to local state prisons, the care at these local state prisons needs to be upgraded and improved. For example, the state must find a better, more cost-effective way to keep inmates who are on suicide watch from hurting themselves. Having six officers watch six inmates on a gallery the size of a small bathroom is ludicrous. At Downstate there were twelve inmates on suicide watch one particular day. With the large chairs the officers sat on during the watch, there was no room to walk. Downstate was never designed for this purpose.

How will society and corrections deal with inmates with Asperger syndrome or other autistic disorders? With the elderly population growing, how will corrections deal with the ever-increasing number of inmates with Alzheimer's disease? Will corrections just stick these inmates in observation cells for long periods of time?

The state needs to provide programs for inmates in extended classification at Downstate. This means taking inmates, many of whom are academically or psychologically challenged, away from watching television for many hours. They need to do something more productive than watch Jerry Springer shout, "You are the father!" We have gotten to the point that we are warehousing people—or I should say babysitting people—and sticking them in front of a television.

We need to get all the inmates who test positive for hepatitis C or high cholesterol together in a classroom and teach them about these conditions. Showing them a short movie about the transmission of hepatitis C and the effects of either condition on their bodies would be a start. After the movie, a nurse should be available to answer questions the inmates might have. The nurse should make an entry into the inmate's medical chart indicating that the inmate saw the movie and had received patient education. It is very upsetting to me when I hear inmates who have returned to the state system say they were never told they were positive for some treatable disease or a disease that could be transmitted to someone else.

Asthma has become a silent epidemic in New York City. A large number of the inmates we see each morning are there to renew their asthma pumps and medications. Not only do these asthma inhalers cost a fortune, as the pharmacist reminds me frequently, but they also directly affect each person's quality of life on a daily basis. I am angry at women who smoke and upset with young girls who try to imitate their mothers by smoking. Young girls do not smoke because it tastes good; they smoke to be cool and to emulate their mothers. Smoking during and after pregnancy has a direct effect on children developing asthma. Most young boys who are involved in some sort of sports program do not smoke. I hope this trend is passed on to female athletes in high school and junior-high school. Asthma is costing this country a bundle of money.

The addiction to pain medications on the street cannot be carried into the prisons. There are controls in place to limit the types of pain medications inmates get from their medical providers and how often they take them.

I see no end to gun violence and opiate abuse and dependence. These two epidemics are taking the lives of the young in our country. Many die from this scourge or end up in prison.

One thing that will not change in the future is the number of mentally ill people being locked up in state prisons. It is imperative, absolutely necessary, and unavoidable that New York State, as well as all the states in the nation, increase training and services for this ever-growing number of inmates. The ever-growing population of the elderly in the prison system will need to be addressed at some point in the future as well. Will the state's prisons turn out to be the mental hospitals and nursing homes of the future?

In September of my first year at college, I sat in a large auditorium with my fellow freshman classmates. The speaker gave the usual speech that I suspect he gives each September to freshmen. He asked each person in the audience to look to the person on his or her right and then look to the person on his or her left. Then he said that two of us would not be back at college next September. One morning while doing the draft, standing in front of a large group of new inmates, I wanted to say, "Look to the person on your left, and then look to the person on your right. Chances are all three of you will be back here again." We, as a society, need to stop this trend, or it will bankrupt us.

Made in the USA
Columbia, SC
21 September 2021